I Believe in the Historical Jesus

By the same author
CHRISTIAN BELIEFS
ESCHATOLOGY AND THE PARABLES
KEPT BY THE POWER OF GOD
THE WORK OF CHRIST
LUKE: HISTORIAN AND THEOLOGIAN
THE ORIGINS OF NEW TESTAMENT CHRISTOLOGY
THE GOSPEL OF LUKE
(EDITOR) NEW TESTAMENT INTERPRETATION

I Believe in the Historical Jesus

by

I. HOWARD MARSHALL

WILLIAM B. EERDMANS PUBLISHING COMPANY

Reprinted, February 1979

Library of Congress Cataloging in Publication Data
Marshall, I   Howard.
    I believe in the historical Jesus.

    1.   Jesus Christ — Historicity.   I.   Title.
BT303.2.M38   232.9'08   77-2224
ISBN 0-8028-1691-6

Contents

		Page
1	The Rediscovery of Jesus	11
2	A Question of Definition	27
3	Faith and the Supernatural	53
4	Historical Jesus or Christ of Faith?	65
5	Faith and Historical Study	87
6	The Search for the Historical Jesus	109
7	The Nature of the Gospels	143
8	The Form of the Gospel Tradition	164
9	The History of the Gospel Tradition	180
10	The Historical Jesus	214
11	The 'Historic' Jesus	238
	Bibliography	251

Editor's Preface

The question that above all others has dominated New Testament studies during this century is the problem of the historical Jesus. What was he really like? Has the church created a picture of him which is distorted by Christian belief that Jesus is the exalted Lord? It is difficult enough to peel off nearly 2000 years of ecclesiastical wrappings from the person of Jesus; but even if we succeed in that, how can we be sure that the Gospel writers, and those nameless Christians before them from whom they got hold of the stories about Jesus, had not read back into his earthly life convictions they had reached after the resurrection? It is a massive and complex problem, and one to which we may never get a final answer.

The nineteenth century theological writings were littered with 'Lives' of Jesus, attempts to pierce through to what he was really like. They tended to be reductionist works, highly flavoured by what the individual reader believed to be important; they told us more about the author than about Jesus. Schweitzer and Barth between them sounded the death knell of those Liberal 'Lives of Jesus' at the end of the First World War.

But then a new phenomenon appeared. Rudolf Bultmann, himself associated with Barth's recovery of the *kerygma*, combined his strongly Lutheran emphasis on *sola fide* with an almost complete scepticism about the historical Jesus. For one thing, you could never know — how could you get behind the Easter faith (common to all the New Testament writers) to what he was really like? Moreover, what would it matter if you could? We do not worship a dead Jesus, but a living Christ. This apparently evangelical emphasis was combined in Bultmann's work with the most radical (and unwarranted) historical scepticism. He almost took delight in pulling down any putative historical evidence about Jesus lest it should seem to be a prop to the faith which alone saves, and saves only when it is alone. Much of the sceptisism rampant in theological circles in Europe and U.S.A. at present derives basically from the outlook of Rudolf Bultmann.

In 1953 a new development took place. Ernst Käsemann, himself an old pupil of Bultmann's, had the temerity to produce (at a reunion of old Marburg students of all places) a paper on 'The Problem of the Historical Jesus' which strongly criticised Bultmann's excessive scepticism about the historical Jesus. From then on a new quest for the historical Jesus has emerged. Scholars have sought criteria by which to distinguish the authenticity of sayings and actions of Jesus. If, for example, an incident has multiple attestation this counts in its favour; the trouble is, it might well be just as true if mentioned by only one source. If an Aramaic substratum to a saying is evident, this counts in its favour; the trouble is that the Aramaic might have derived from the Aramaic speaking church not from Jesus himself, and moreover a saying whose form is now completely Hellenised might also have come from the lips of Jesus — why should he not have spoken Greek, as many of his compatriots did? The whole situation is, therefore, not only complex but variously treated. This book by Dr. Howard Marshall, himself a distinguished New Testament scholar and author, will have a very wide impact in clarifying these muddied waters.

It will help the *obscurantist Christian* to see the error of his ways. He will realise that it is as impossible to combine all four accounts of Jesus into one harmonious whole as it is to superimpose four photographs of the same person upon one another and expect a clear picture. Dr. Marshall shows all the reverence for Scripture that the fundamentalist believer exhibits, but he is not afraid of facts; he does not fear that truth can hurt faith.

It will help the *sceptical Christian* to see the error of his ways, too. Marshall shows how untenable and indeed self contradictory are the canons of supposed authenticity which a man like Norman Perrin uses in so destructive a manner. He shows how, judged by the canons of historical writing, the New Testament documents are capable of bearing any amount of weight, and are more than secure enough as a base for Christian faith and life.

It will also help the *confused Christian* to clarify his position. He has read a bit of Bultmann; he is studying theology under a professor, perhaps, who is dyed deep in humanist presuppositions. How can he maintain both faith and intellectual integrity? This is a book for him to buy, to study and to refer back to.

We have here a distinguished, timely and helpful book; it brings to readers the urgent faith and the sharp enquiring mind of the author, it shows how these can be integrated in a mature and positive Christian faith. It is a book for which many people will be profoundly grateful.

Michael Green
Christmas 1976.

Foreword

THE PROBLEM OF the historical Jesus is one of the most important themes in New Testament scholarship. The present volume is an attempt to survey modern discussion of the problem, to delineate its most significant aspects, and to attempt a careful appraisal of it. Although I have tried to write for as wide an audience as possible, in accordance with the general aim of the series, I have tried to keep in mind the needs of the student and to tackle the problem as rigorously as possible.

The book falls into two sections. In the first part (chapters 1-5) we look at the general problem of what is meant by the historical Jesus; here we are concerned with the questions that arise in the study of any figure from the past, and more especially with those that arise when the figure in question is the object of religious veneration and worship. In the second part (chapters 6-11) we look at the particular problem of how we can study the historical Jesus and whether we can do so successfully. This book, therefore, is not a historical study of Jesus, setting out what can be known of him; rather it contains the preliminaries to such a study. At a time when some people doubt the possibility of knowing more than a tiny modicum of facts about Jesus, even this preliminary task is of great importance, and it certainly demands a book to itself. It is indeed arguable that there are too many lives of Jesus produced by persons who have not worked out a proper, scientific method for the purpose. If this book manages to lay a firm foundation, it will have accomplished an adequate task.

I am particularly grateful to Michael Green for inviting me to contribute to this series and to both him and Paul Ellingworth for their detailed comments on the manuscript.

HOWARD MARSHALL

CHAPTER 1

The Rediscovery of Jesus

A WRITER IN a secular journal commented recently that so many books about Jesus are appearing at the present time that it would take a full-time reviewer simply to keep track of them without looking at books on other subjects. According to one estimate, the forty years between 1910 and 1950 saw the publication of some 350 lives of Jesus in the English language alone.[1] Since that time the amount of writing about Jesus has swollen to fantastic proportions;[2] even simply to read surveys of books about Jesus would keep a man busy for some time.[3] It is not only the Christians — of every theological hue — who have written about Jesus. A sizable proportion of recent studies have come from the pens of Jews and Communists, each of whom have their own reasons for being interested in Jesus. Nor is the presentation confined to the written word. One has only to think of *Godspell* and *Jesus Christ — Superstar* — to name only the most popular shows — to see how Jesus has invaded the world of light entertainment and attracted enormous attention. There can be no doubt that the life of Jesus is a matter of supreme interest at the present time. Jesus has found his way onto the station bookstall, even though there is a strange reluctance on the part of Western European man to enter his church. (The picture in some other parts of the world is remarkably different.)

But however great the contemporary interest in Jesus, it is far from clear that attempts to write his life story are likely to succeed. At the beginning of the present century Albert

Schweitzer wrote a famous book entitled *The Quest of the Historical Jesus* which was meant to be not only a history of this quest but also its requiem; Schweitzer believed that the quest was impossible, although it must be confessed that he could not resist the temptation to have his own crack at solving the impossible problem. [4]

Rudolf Bultmann is probably the most influential New Testament scholar of the twentieth century; it was from his pen that there came the words: 'I do indeed think that we can now know almost nothing concerning the life and personality of Jesus, since the early Christian sources show no interest in either, are moreover fragmentary and often legendary; and other sources about Jesus do not exist.' [5] It was no doubt because of the influence exerted by this scholar that the life of Jesus received remarkably little attention in Germany for a good quarter of a century. English-speaking scholars, who were either ignorant of the master's *ipse dixit* or chose to dispute its authority, were in general much more sanguine. Nevertheless, one may cite the anecdote regarding Dr W. R. Inge, a former Dean of St Paul's Cathedral; he is supposed to have answered a publisher's request to write a life of Jesus with a terse postcard: 'As there are no materials for a life of Christ, I regret that I cannot comply with your request.' [6]

It is true that there has been some change of outlook among the top brass in New Testament study. German writers are anxious to give the credit for a more optimistic outlook to Bultmann's pupil, Ernst Käsemann, in an essay published in 1953, [7] but many people who read his works may well be highly shocked by the amount of material in the Gospels which even he regards as unhistorical.

And of course it must be admitted that much of the more popular material, to which we referred at the outset, presents pictures of Jesus remarkably different from those which the average reader of these pages picked up in Sunday School. There is much that is frankly imaginative and tendentious. There is much that is based on poor and inadequate historical research. [8] For all we know, the Sunday School portrait may not be much better.

So already at the beginning of our study we are faced by a situation of remarkable confusion. On the one hand, we have distinguished scholars proclaiming the whole attempt to rediscover the historical Jesus to be a forlorn hope; on the other hand, there is a determination on the part of many not to be overawed by such statements but to make an attempt at the allegedly impossible. And when the attempt is made, we are met by a bewildering variety of pictures of Jesus — the traditional Jesus, the almost unknowable Jesus, Jesus the political revolutionary, Jesus the radical, Jesus the fellow-traveller, and many more.

In the face of all this confusion I have the nerve to write a book with the title 'I *believe* in the historical Jesus', while others refer more modestly to 'problems' and 'quests'. Yet is this title any different in content from the confession that most Christians are in the habit of reciting from time to time in public worship: 'I believe in God the Father Almighty ...and in Jesus Christ...Who was...born of the Virgin Mary, Suffered under Pontius Pilate, Was crucified, dead and buried...'? Whatever be the status of the surrounding statements in the Apostles' Creed, the phrase 'under Pontius Pilate' suffices to root the career of Jesus in history and to associate my Christian belief with a historical fact; we are forced to come to terms with the historical Jesus.

To confess belief in Jesus at the start of this book may be reassuring to one group of readers who want to see the confusion cleared away and to be given some basis for their own main-line Christian beliefs. But for that very reason this confession may be like a red rag to another set of readers who fear that they are in for a piece of apologetic, a set of one-sided arguments for a position already reached on other, non-rational grounds. To many people 'apologetic' is a 'dirty' word, and they will not want to read any further. I can only hope that they will give the book a fair trial and examine the case presented in it. It does at least attempt to argue honestly and fairly without misrepresenting different points of view, even if the writer cannot be aware of all his own prejudices.

A very considerable part of the difficulty which surrounds our subject lies in the area of definition. What is meant by 'I believe'? What is the meaning of 'the historical Jesus'? Much of our space will have to deal with these two phrases and their inter-relationship. But before we get down to the trickier problems which they raise, we are going to clear out of the way two preliminary points. Two extreme views regarding 'the historical Jesus' still flourish today, although neither of them can stand up to examination.

DID JESUS REALLY EXIST?

At the very simplest level to believe in a historical person, say the historical Julius Agricola, is to believe, or at least to imply, that the person named actually existed. To be sure, it is doubtful whether we would use the adjective 'historical' in this kind of way with reference to any ordinary person; it seems to be reserved for use with Jesus and one or two other people (like Abraham or Moses) about whose historicity there is some doubt, or about whose names legends have gathered. But in theory it would be possible for a debate to arise whether any personal name that has come to us out of the past refers to somebody who actually existed. The Roman historian, Tacitus, (whose historical existence I shall presuppose) wrote a book purporting to be a life of Julius Agricola (AD 40-93) who attained fame as a Roman military commander responsible for subjugating a considerable part of Britain. [9] It is universally agreed that there was such a person, so that it is possible to trace a good deal of his career by reference to Tacitus' account of his life and also by reference to the work of other contemporary writers and to various contemporary inscriptions and other monuments. To argue that Agricola was not historical, *i.e.* that there was no historical person whose existence gave rise to the literary and archaeological evidence which mentions him, would be the height of folly.

The position is somewhat different with reference to, say, King Arthur, an early English king who finds mention in the history books but is described by modern writers as half-mythical. 'The chief names of this missing period of history,' says G. M. Trevelyan, 'may be those of real or imaginary men.' [10] Nobody doubts that the legends of King Arthur and his knights of the Round Table are fiction; it is open to doubt, however, whether or not there was a real person about whose name these legends clustered. It is a real question whether or not there was a historical Arthur, granted that in this case the stories told about him do *not* relate historical facts.

Now the same Roman historian who writes at some length about Julius Agricola has also a brief reference in another of his works to Jesus: writing about the way in which the blame for the great fire of Rome in AD 64 was fastened upon some 'Christians', he goes on to explain how these people got their name: 'They got their name from Christ, who was executed by sentence of the procurator Pontius Pilate in the reign of Tiberius.' [11] The question arises: is 'Jesus' here the name of a historical character (like Julius Agricola) or is it the name of a fictitious character? Clearly Tacitus himself believed that Jesus was historical enough, and so have nearly all subsequent historians. It could, however, be argued that Tacitus was merely repeating information given to him — he had not consulted the official list of persons put to death by Pontius Pilate — and it could be that he had been misled; it could be that the Christians had called themselves after some fictitious founder of their sect and that they themselves or other people had come to believe falsely that this fictitious founder had really existed. In the same way, the Roman people derived their name from that of Romulus, but the story of Romulus (who is said to have lived in the eighth century BC) cannot be traced back beyond the fourth century BC, and is universally recognised as an aetiological myth, *i.e.* a fictitious story told to explain the origin of some later custom or institution. Probably most educated Romans recognised the legendary character of the story. Could the same be true of the story of Jesus?

There is said to be a Russian encyclopaedia in current use which affirms in a brief entry that Jesus Christ was the mythological founder of Christianity, but it is virtually alone in doing so. [12] The historian will not take its statement very seriously, since (to the best of my knowledge) it offers no evidence for its assertion, and mere assertion cannot stand over against historical enquiry.

But more than mere assertion is involved, for an attempt to show that Jesus never existed has been made in recent years by G. A. Wells, a Professor of German who has ventured into New Testament study and presents a case that the origins of

Christianity can be explained without assuming that Jesus really lived. [13] Earlier presentations of similar views at the turn of the century failed to make any impression on scholarly opinion,[14] and it is certain that this latest presentation of the case will not fare any better. For of course the evidence is not confined to Tacitus; there are the New Testament documents themselves, nearly all of which must be dated in the first century, and behind which there lies a period of transmission of the story of Jesus which can be traced backwards to a date not far from that when Jesus is supposed to have lived. To explain the rise of this tradition without the hypothesis of Jesus is impossible. It is significant that the vast majority of modern writers who are interested in disputing the truth of the Christian religion are content to argue for an unorthodox picture of Jesus rather than to argue that he never existed. The later development of the argument in this book will show how the methods of historical study applied to the Gospels leave us in no doubt that some knowledge of Jesus is possible and that the existence of such knowledge naturally implies that Jesus really existed. [15]

We do not propose, therefore, to spend time at this point in arguing the case that 'Jesus' refers to a historical person, that there was a historical Jesus. We are going to assume that it is possible to say 'I believe in the historical Jesus' in the sense 'I believe that there was a historical person called Jesus'. The more important questions are concerned with what, if anything, can be known about this person.

ARE THE GOSPELS DETAILED BIOGRAPHIES OF JESUS?

If there are some people who display complete scepticism about the historical existence of Jesus, there are also those who believe that we have a fairly large body of absolutely certain historical knowledge about Jesus. We have the four Gospels, and these form part of the Bible which is a book written by men who 'were carried along by the Holy Spirit as they spoke the message that came from God' (2 Pet. 1:21 TEV). If these men were guided by the Spirit, it must surely follow that what they wrote was true and accurate, and that therefore we have an absolutely reliable historical account of Jesus in the Gospels. To say 'I believe in the historical Jesus' is, therefore, to confess one's belief that the Gospels are the work of inspired writers and to accept the historicity of the picture of Jesus contained in them. Two things should be noted about this sort of attitude.

The first is that for such people their acceptance of the historicity of Jesus is a matter of belief. It depends on their acceptance of the Bible as a divinely inspired record rather than upon any kind of historical examination of the evidence. Of course there are differences in attitude at this point. There are some people who are not capable of technical historical study, and it would be unfair to expect them to indulge in it; there are others who have neither the time nor the opportunity to pursue it. In both cases it is natural that such people should be prepared to trust the word of somebody else on the matter. We all do this in daily life with regard to matters on which we ourselves are not experts; for example, I trust the word of the mechanic in the garage who tells me that the cause of bad running in my car was faulty 'timing', and that he has cured the trouble by attending to this esoteric matter deep in the innards of the engine — and I express my trust very tangibly by paying him the appropriate fee for what he claims that he has done (although for all I know he may simply have turned a screw at random somewhere). In the same way, many of us must simply take what the historians say about Jesus and many other persons on trust. And if the historians disagree, as they do at many points, it is not surprising that many people turn to what they consider to be the more sure word of Scripture, preferring to trust the authority of men inspired by God to that of fallible historians.

To take up such an attitude is, of course, not incompatible with an appreciation of the contribution that the historian can make. If, for example, some sceptic assures us that Peter could not have heard a cock crowing after he had betrayed Jesus because the Jewish leaders forbade the rearing of cocks in Jerusalem, we shall not be content to say merely 'There must have been a cock because the Bible tells us that Peter heard one', but we shall gladly summon to our aid the help of historians who can show that the objection is baseless because historical evidence to the contrary exists. [16] And there are many other matters of a like nature. Ultimately, however, this approach bases its belief on the infallible evidence of the Bible itself, and where there is a clash between what the Bible says and what the historians say it will prefer the word of God to the opinions of men.

The second point to note is that this approach leads to a definition of 'the historical Jesus' as 'Jesus as he is described in the Gospels'. For adherents of this school of thought there is a biblical picture of Jesus, based on the teaching of the Gospels as a whole, and this picture corresponds with history, with what actually happened. It is assumed that the various details given in the Gospels can be fitted together to give one single, coherent picture of Jesus without any loose ends. Not only so, but it is often also assumed that we can string together all that we are told about Jesus to produce a reasonably complete story in chronological sequence, describing one after another the various things that he did and said. There are gaps, of course, such as that between his visit to the Temple at the age of twelve (Luke 2:41-52) and his baptism by John at the age of thirty; but, so far as his ministry is concerned, we have an account that is both chronological and reasonably complete. In short, we have an account of the historical Jesus which we can confidently accept as being based on reliable information.

It is no part of our purpose in this book to be destructive of Christian faith, but it is essential that we examine it carefully. When we look more closely at this typical Christian outlook on the question of the historical Jesus, it proves to have a number of concealed difficulties.

This assumption of the reliability of the Gospels at once raises some problems. There are critics who would question the whole idea that the Bible is an authoritative revelation of God, written by men who were moved by the Holy Spirit. The whole question of the inspiration of the Bible raises a veritable battery of arguments against the traditional view on this matter. It is no part of my purpose to discuss this problem here, still less to lead an attack on the doctrine of biblical inspiration. I take my stand with the defenders of that doctrine, but must leave it to others to uphold it rather than be sidetracked on the issue here. [17] For two points arise here which show that an appeal to the reliability of the Gospels based on the doctrine of inspiration cannot solve the problem of the historical Jesus for us.

The first point is that if we are involved in discussion or debate with persons who do not share a belief in the inspiration of the Bible, it is no use our attempting to solve historical problems by appeal to a premise which they do not accept. [18] In such a situation the natural thing to do is to make use of historical argument, and to go as far as we can on the basis of common premises; it is perhaps only when questions of the supernatural and miraculous arise that differences between believers and unbelievers may prevent historical debate. On this basis we can show that there is some historical foundation for Christian teaching.

The second point, which is more fundamental, is that the doctrine of inspiration does not prescribe the nature of the reliability which belongs to inspired documents. While some people have argued that when Jesus told a story beginning, 'A certain man was going down from Jerusalem to Jericho, when robbers attacked him...' (Luke 10:30-37), he was referring to an actual incident, there is nothing in the doctrine of inspiration which requires us to believe that something of the kind actually happened. Jesus' story is generally regarded as a parable, and the lesson taught in a parable does not depend upon the historicity of the story but upon the compulsion produced by the storyteller's art. A verdict that the story is fictional, or at least that it need not be historical, is derived not from any particular doctrine of inspiration but from a consideration of the form and purpose of the story. What the doctrine of inspiration teaches is that the writer was inspired to do what God wanted him to do, and the purpose of his writing is to be learned from a study of the writing itself and not by applying some blanket considerations. So far as the telling of parables is concerned, the recounting of incidents that actually happened is not a necessary part of the process. The point which we have illustrated in this way is of more general application: every part of the Bible must be understood according to its form and purpose, and it cannot be assumed that in every case the writer was attempting to convey historical information, correct in every particular. [19]

We illustrated this point by reference to a sort of story that would be pretty universally agreed to be fictitious. But the point also applies to stories where we might well think that we were reading accounts of what actually happened. Here we must turn to the Gospels to see what is actually happening in them. At the climax of the examination of Jesus by the Jewish council he was cross-examined by the high priest. According to Matthew the high priest said:

'I adjure you by the living God, tell us if you are the Christ, the Son of God.'

Jesus replied, 'You have said so. But I tell you, hereafter you will see the Son of man seated at the right hand of Power, and coming on the clouds of heaven.' (Matt. 26:63f).

If we turn to Mark's account of the same incident we read:

'Are you the Christ, the Son of the Blessed?'

And the reply, 'I am; and you will see the Son of man sitting on the right hand of Power, and coming with the clouds of heaven.' (Mark 14:61f).

Comparison of these two accounts shows that they are both reporting the same dialogue, since the historical setting is the same and the resemblances between the two sets of statements are very considerable. At the same time, it is clear that one or both writers was not giving a word-for-word account of the proceedings, such as we might find in an official shorthand transcript of court proceedings. No doubt the differences in wording are fairly trivial, but the point is that at least one of the writers was not concerned to give a verbatim report of what was said. Evidently the meaning mattered more than the actual words. There are scores of similar examples in the Gospels which demonstrate that if we are looking for a verbatim account of what was actually said we are looking for something that is not necessarily there, since the writers were not concerned to provide it.

In the same way, we cannot always be sure who said particular things. During his last visit to Jerusalem Jesus told a story about some tenants of a vineyard who killed the owner's son when he visited them. The account finishes like this:

(Jesus went on): 'When therefore the owner of the vineyard comes, what will he do to those tenants?'

They said to him, 'He will put those wretches to a miserable death, and let out the vineyard to other tenants who will give him the fruits in their seasons.'

Jesus said to them, 'Have you never read in the Scriptures...?' (Matt. 21:60-62).

Such is Matthew's account, and here is Mark's:

(Jesus went on): 'What will the owner of the vineyard do? He will come and destroy the tenants, and give the vineyard to others. Have you not read this Scripture...?' (Mark 12:9f).

And, finally, to give the complete picture, here is Luke's account:

(Jesus went on): 'What then will the owner of the vineyard do to them? He will come and destroy those tenants, and give the vineyard to others.'

When they heard this, they said, 'God forbid!'

But he looked at them and said, 'What then is this that is written...?' (Luke 20:15-17).

Who said what? All three Gospels agree in ascribing the opening and closing statements to Jesus, but there is no agreement about the middle section. Whatever may have happened historically, at least two of the Gospels have not given a literal account of what happened, and one of them ascribes to Jesus a statement which the third Gospel ascribes to his audience. Plainly we cannot take any one of the accounts and say, 'It happened exactly as it says here'.

Before some of my readers begin to bristle with indignation at having these irrefutable facts pointed out to them, they should remember that what is happening here is only what happens in Sunday School or church every time some Bible story is being recounted. Here is the story of Joseph in prison, as it is told in the Bible:

But the Lord was with Joseph and showed him steadfast love, and gave him favour in the sight of the keeper of the prison. And the keeper of the prison committed to Joseph's care all the prisoners who were in the prison; and whatever was done there, he was the doer of it; the keeper of the prison paid no heed to anything that was in Joseph's care, because the Lord was with him; and whatever he did, the Lord made it prosper.

And here is the same story from a book for children:

Joseph was sad and miserable. He was not important now. He was an ordinary prisoner, but he was not quite the same as all the other men in that prison-house, for God was taking care of him.

When the man in charge of the prison saw Joseph he thought, 'H'm. He's a nice-looking boy.' Another day he thought, 'He doesn't look cruel like some of the men here.' Another day he thought, 'He doesn't say nasty things like some of the men here do.' Another day he thought, 'I think I could trust him.'

So he asked Joseph to do some work for him. God was still looking after Joseph and helped him to do the new work well. Soon...can you guess what happened? Joseph became the most important prisoner in the prison. [20]

Here the writer has imaginatively filled out the story by describing how Joseph's promotion may have taken place. The story gains in interest for a juvenile audience, and the essential meaning is preserved. And this kind of thing goes on all the time in Bible teaching, and we regard it as perfectly legitimate. It would be surprising if the early story-tellers did not exercise the same controlled liberty in telling about Jesus.

All of this may seem trivial in the extreme. It is, however, important. For it shows that the Gospels do not give us the story of Jesus in precise detail. Even if one of the Gospels might be supposed to do so, it would follow that the other Gospels do not, since they differ from it in many details. While the basic meaning is usually quite clear, the difference in detail between different accounts of the same incidents can be quite considerable.

Moreover, the same problems emerge on a larger scale. In Matthew 8 we have records of the following incidents, which are listed with references to the stories of the same incidents in Mark and Luke:

Matt.		Mark	Luke
8:2-4	Healing of a leper	1:40-44	5:12-14
5-13	Healing of centurion's boy	—	7:1-10
14-17	Healing of Peter's mother-in-law	1:29-34	4:38-41
18-22	Call of disciples	—	9:57-60
23-27	Stilling of storm	4:36-41	8:22-25
28-34	Healing of demoniac	5:1-17	8:26-37

No two Gospels have all the incidents in the same order. Those that appear in one chapter in Matthew are scattered through five chapters in Luke, and in the course of these chapters in Luke there appear a number of other incidents which are found elsewhere in Matthew. And this is but one example of a phenomenon that is repeated throughout the Gospels. It may be possible to argue on various grounds for the historical originality of some particular order of the incidents and to explain why the different Evangelists have chosen to differ from it, but this is not the real issue that emerges from this illustration. The real issue is that the Gospels do not profess to give us a chronological account of the ministry of Jesus, nor do they profess to tell us everything in detail just as it happened. Even if one of the four Gospels might be demonstrated to give us such an account, this would simply show that the other three Gospels do not do so. And in fact there is no good reason to suppose that any particular one of the Gospels gives us such a chronological account, recording each detail of the ministry exactly as it happened.

We cannot escape the conclusion that the doctrine of the inspiration of the Bible does not guarantee that everything in the Gospels happened in the exact order in which it is recorded or in precisely the detailed way in which it is told. We cannot take any single Gospel or all the Gospels together and state that the story which they contain is the story of the historical Jesus, telling everything exactly as it happened. To assume that the 'biblical Jesus' or 'the Jesus of the Gospels' is the same thing as 'the historical Jesus' or 'Jesus as he really was' is fundamentally misleading because 'the biblical Jesus' is an abstraction. Even though we believe in the inspiration of the Bible, we must still face up to the question of what historical facts lie behind the Gospels. We cannot assume that everything happened exactly as it is recorded for the single reason that the same events are differently recorded in the several Gospels.

THE TASK AHEAD

We have in effect been looking at two myths in this introductory chapter; two views of the historical Jesus which stand at opposite ends of the spectrum of opinions about him. At the one end is the view that there never was such a person as Jesus; the Gospels are descriptions of a fictitious person. We have no hesitation in declaring that this view of Jesus is false. It is not possible to explain the rise of the Christian church or the writing of the Gospels and the stream of tradition that lies behind them without accepting the fact that the Founder of Christianity actually existed. At the other end of the spectrum is the view that the Gospels give us a picture of the historical Jesus, every detail in the Gospels being recorded just as it happened. This view too must be pronounced false, although it is (as we shall see) much nearer the truth than the first view. It is not possible to fit the Gospel narratives together in such a way that every detail falls into place in a harmonious whole and that each Gospel can be taken to describe everything as it actually happened.

To believe in the historical Jesus obviously implies a rejection of the first of these two extremes; belief and disbelief are incompatible with each another. It might seem that rejection of the other extreme involves disbelief in the historical Jesus, but this is not so because what we have rejected is a non-existent picture of the historical Jesus. What we now have to do is to ask what kind of history lies behind the Gospels. To what extent are they historical documents? Who exactly is the historical Jesus? And what does it mean to believe in this Jesus?

1 From an American bibliography cited by E. Stauffer, *Jesus and his Story*, London, 1960, 8.

2 According to L. Goppelt, more books about Jesus were published in the six years to 1973 than in the previous fifty (cited by J. Piper, 'Was Qumran the Cradle of Christianity? A Critique of Johannes Lehmann's *Jesus Report*', *Studia Biblica et Theologica* 4:2, Oct., 1974, 18-29 (18 n. 2.)

3 See H. Zahrnt, *The Historical Jesus*, London, 1963; J. M. Robinson, *A New Quest of the Historical Jesus*, London, 1959; J. Peter, *Finding the Historical Jesus*, London, 1965; C. F. H. Henry (ed.), *Jesus of Nazareth: Saviour and Lord*, London, 1966; F. G. Downing, *The Church and Jesus*, London, 1968; F. Hahn, W. Lohff and G. Bornkamm, *What can we know about Jesus?* Edinburgh, 1968; C. L. Mitton, *Jesus: the Fact behind the Faith*, London, 1975. Detailed discussions of recent scholarly literature are given by W. G. Kümmel, 'Jesus-Forschung seit 1950', *Theologische Rundschau*, 31, 1965-66, 15-46, 289-315; *ibid.*, 'Ein Jahrzehnt Jesusforschung (1965-1975)', *Theologische Rundschau* 40, 1975, 289-336. E. Grässer ('Motive und Methoden der neueren Jesus-Literatur', *Verkündigung und Forschung* 18, 1973, 3-45) discusses Christian, Jewish and Marxist works, but unfortunately largely ignores the English scene.

4 A. Schweitzer, *The Quest of the Historical Jesus*, London, 1910, third edition with new introduction, 1950.

5 R. Bultmann, *Jesus and the Word*, London, 1934, 8.

6 Cited by F. F. Bruce, *The Spreading Flame*, Exeter, 1958, 33.

7 E. Käsemann, *Essays on New Testament Themes*, London, 1964, 15-47.

8 In this book our attention will be confined to study which can reasonably be regarded as scholarly in approach, and no attempt will be made to deal with ephemeral and merely 'popular' presentations.

9 The work, which is of considerable interest for its own sake, is very conveniently available in a Penguin translation: H. Mattingly, *Tacitus on Britain and Germany*, West Drayton, 1948.

10 G. M. Trevelyan, *History of England*, London, 1945, 33. For the illustration I am indebted to F. Clark, *The Rise of Christianity*, Milton Keynes, 1974, 13f.

11 Tacitus, *Annals* 15:44. Cited (for example) by F. F. Bruce, *Jesus and Christian Origins Outside the New Testament*, London, 1974, 21-23.

12 See F. Clark, *op. cit.*, 12 n.

13 G. A. Wells, *The Jesus of the Early Christians*, London, 1971; *Did Jesus Exist?* London, 1975.

14 See the literature cited by J. Peter, *op. cit.*, 24f.

15 Wells evidently felt that his first volume was not sufficiently convincing and therefore has added many like words to it. In his first book he begins by discussing the Gospel accounts of Jesus, arguing first that the miracles did not happen, second, that the teaching attributed to Jesus has many parallels in Judaism, and third, that even such straightforward narratives as those of the trial and crucifixion of Jesus abound in historical improbabilities. He concludes, 'All this evidence does not exclude the possibility that there was a preacher who was tried and executed and that his career formed the basis

of the existing narratives... The muddle that we find in the Gospels does not in itself point to the conclusion that he never existed' (111). He therefore puts more weight on the claim that Paul knew nothing of the biography of Jesus and the scantiness of reference to the Gospels in other early church writings: 'The Jesus of the earliest records is not the historical figure of the Gospels at all' (184). Pagan sources, such as Tacitus, yield no reliable first-hand evidence. Wells then attempts an alternative explanation of Christian beginnings. He argues that there was a community which held pre-Christian ideas of the Messiah and copied a pre-Christian form of eucharist; the Christian concept of the crucified Messiah arose out of the common ancient idea of the dying god and the belief held by some Jews that the Messiah would suffer. The next step was to regard this figure as historical and to provide him with a detailed biography. Memories of the death of the Teacher of Righteousness in the Qumran sect may have helped this process.

In his more recent book Wells goes over much of the same ground in more detail and with particular reference to criticisms of his earlier work. He capitalises heavily on the work of radical scholars who deny the historicity of much in the Gospels and regards it as grist for his view that Jesus himself never existed. It is doubtful whether the case is any the stronger by the end of the second book.

Despite the wealth of detail with which it is propounded, Wells's view is completely unconvincing. He is quite unable to show how belief in a dying Messiah led to belief in the existence of the historical Jesus. His assumption that the Qumran Teacher of Righteousness was crucified certainly goes beyond the evidence. His view that some Jews expected the Messiah to suffer is at least questionable. The propositions on which he rests his case are far more implausible than the proposition which he seeks to deny. To give a detailed refutation of his arguments in an *ad hominem* manner would be out of place in the present discussion. The book as a whole represents a positive statement of the alternative point of view.

16 W. Brandt denied the historicity of the cockcrow; see to the contrary R. Bultmann, *The History of the Synoptic Tradition*, London, 1968[2], 269 n. 2.

17 See the volume in this series, Leon Morris, *I believe in Revelation*, 1976.

18 It may of course be said in reply that we should not try to discuss historical problems with people who do not believe in the inspiration of the Bible: our first task should be to convince them of the fact of inspiration, and then the historical problems will look after themselves. But this approach must be rejected. Objections to the inspiration of the Bible often rest upon the historical errors which people claim to have found in it; it is surely incumbent upon us to provide some kind of answer to difficulties of this kind.

19 I have developed this point in my essay on 'Historical Criticism' in I. H. Marshall (ed.), *New Testament Interpretation*, Exeter, 1977.

20 J. Wesson, *Story Time Three*, London, 1968, 34.

CHAPTER 2

A Question of Definition

IN OUR INTRODUCTORY chapter we established two ways in which the phrase 'the historical Jesus' could be used. The first was to express the belief that the person called Jesus really existed, as opposed to the possibility that there was no such person. To speak of the 'historical Jesus' is to say 'Jesus is a historical character like Julius Agricola or Henry VIII' and to deny the statement 'Jesus is a fictitious character like King Lear or Dr Who'.

The second way of using the phrase was to express the belief that the account given of Jesus in a particular book corresponds with what actually happened. To speak of the 'historical Jesus' this time is to say: 'The description of Jesus in the Gospels corresponds to what he was actually like.' It is to deny that 'The story of Jesus in the Bible is like the legends of King Arthur'. Arthur existed, but the stories about him are works of imagination. Nevertheless, we saw that we could not simply say that the Bible or, more precisely, the Gospels tell us the story of Jesus exactly as it happened. But whether or not the Gospels do give us such an account of Jesus, we tend to use the phrase 'the historical Jesus' as a means of referring to 'Jesus as he really was', and the question then is whether we can find out what his life really was like.

Before we can try to answer this question, we must observe that it contains a highly slippery phrase. We shall land in considerable confusion if we embark on an enquiry about the historical Jesus if we do not pause to ask ourselves exactly what we are talking about. The slipperiness is obvious from

the fact that we have already used the word 'historical' in two
different ways. We have used it to describe Jesus, and we
have also used it with regard to the Gospels. In the former
case it refers to persons (or events) and indicates that they
really existed (or happened), but in the latter case it indicates
that certain documents contain accounts of people who really
lived or events that really happened. This double use of the
adjective springs from a corresponding ambiguity in the noun
from which it is derived. 'History' can be used to mean 'what
happened in the past' or 'an account of what happened in the
past', and it is perhaps unfortunate that the one word has to
do duty for both of these purposes. It might help towards
clarity if we used 'history' to mean 'what happened' and
'history book' to mean 'an account of what happened', but
this might be merely pedantic.

But the slipperiness of the terms we are using goes much
further than this. In order to clarify them we are going to take
a quick look at what the historian does, and then go through
the various possible meanings of our terms.

THE HISTORIAN'S TASK

How do we get from 'history' = 'what happened in the past'
to 'history' = 'an account of what happened in the past'?
The starting point is a situation in which we have a historian
and a set of past events to which he has no direct access.[1] The
historian lives now, and those events happened long ago.

HISTORIAN

PAST EVENTS

But some things have survived from the past. If the historian
is interested in some ancient city, it may be that some of the
ruins of the city have survived and can be explored. They
may yield stones with inscriptions on them (like modern
gravestones) or even written documents (granted suitable
conditions for their preservation; most ancient writing materials have disintegrated in course of time unless stored in very
dry conditions). There may be accounts of the city and its life

from persons who took part in it or from other writers who were sufficiently near to it in time to get first-hand stories about it. These things are available to the historian, although a lot of what might have survived probably has not survived, and not all that has survived is necessarily known or available (some inscriptions may still be buried in the earth, or may be indecypherable). So we now have something in between the historian and the events

HISTORIAN

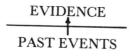

But the historian still has no direct access to the events. He believes that the evidence was 'produced' by the events, in the same way as a corpse is 'produced' by an act of murder. So what the historian has to do is to examine the evidence and reason back from it to what 'produced' it. In effect he has to reverse the process which led from the past events to the evidence by trying to work back from the evidence to what may have caused it. These causes we may call 'historical facts'.

Possibly in a perfect world the evidence would be complete and would permit of only one correct interpretation, so that the facts worked out by the historian would be correct representations of the past events. In general, however, we cannot expect this to happen. The evidence will often be incomplete and it may allow of several interpretations. Consequently the historian's picture of what happened — the historical facts — will not always be a completely reliable picture of the past events. To adopt a piece of jargon which is popular at the moment, we could say that the historian constructs a 'model' of some past event. A model resembles

the real thing, but is not identical with it. A model railway
engine may look just like the real thing, but quite apart from
the difference in scale it will lack various features of the real
engine; nevertheless, for many purposes a model can be as
useful as the real thing, for example in carrying out various
kinds of tests or in determining whether a particular design is
aesthetically pleasing. So too the historian's model of the past
will be an inter-connected set of 'facts' which he hopes will be
an accurate replica of the actual 'events', and in so far as the
postulated 'facts' account satisfactorily for the evidence, they
can be regarded as an accurate reflection of the events which
lie behind the evidence. So we can now complete our scheme

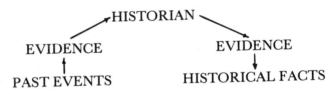

HISTORIAN

EVIDENCE   EVIDENCE

PAST EVENTS   HISTORICAL FACTS

This is a very simple account of what the historian does, and
we must now make the picture somewhat more complex.[2]

HISTORY AND IMAGINATION

When we use the term 'historical' to refer to a book, such as a
Gospel, we mean that it contains an account of what actually
happened, as opposed to accounts of some other kind. Thus a
historical book can certainly be contrasted with a book that is
deliberately concerned to relate a piece of fiction, the sort of
book which may contain in the opening pages a statement to
the effect that 'All the characters in this book are imaginary
and none of the incidents related actually took place'.
Authors sometimes need to safeguard themselves in this way
against the suspicion that they have modelled their characters
on their friends (or their enemies) and have given real
incidents a fictional colouring. In these cases, we cannot
expect to learn any history directly from such a book. It is
true that indirectly we may learn something historical about
the author and his environment from the sort of things that
he writes, but this is another question.

The position is not essentially different when an author tells a fictitious story against a historical background, when, for example, James Bond has adventures at a place called 'Idlewild Airport' in one of Ian Fleming's books. The incident is thoroughly fictitious, but the place itself is quite real — and incidentally the reader who knows that the location has been renamed after the late President John F. Kennedy will be able to draw a historical conclusion about the date before which the book was probably written. A historical setting is utilised, but the story is still basically fiction.

We advance nearer to history in the so-called historical novel, in which some historical incident is recounted by the novelist on the basis of study of historical evidence but with some degree of 'dramatic licence'; the novelist is allowed to manipulate the facts in order to get a 'good' story.[3] From such a book a reader may certainly get an accurate general impression of the mood of a particular period in history, and even get a reliable account of actual events, but he has always to remember that even historical characters may be made to act in ways that do not correspond to what they actually did. But the reader is aware of this situation as he reads and should be prepared to make allowances for it.

The historian can thus be contrasted with the novelist who deliberately writes a work of imagination. But it should be noted that the contrast is not an absolute one, and that the historical novelist may come very close to the historian. Indeed, even the historian needs something of the novelist's imagination if he is to deduce from the incomplete evidence available to him exactly what was happening. It is only as the historian possesses the novelist's feel for how people behave that he may be able to offer scientific guesses on the basis of outward evidence as to what motivated a person to act in a particular way. There are some passages in the Gospels where the scientific historian, closeted in his study, is tempted to say, 'I cannot imagine any real events that can lie behind this strange story recorded in the Gospels; it cannot have happened like that'. In such a situation it is interesting to turn to the work of a skilled novelist or dramatist, such as Dorothy L. Sayers in her series of plays, *The Man Born to be King*, and observe how she is able to construct a plausible train of events which could have given rise to the difficult stories in the Gospels.[4]

Although, then, the edges of the distinction between the historian and the novelist are blurred, we can see that the tasks of the two can be contrasted with each other, and in this way we can differentiate history from fiction.

A further distinction we can make is that between the work of a trained and informed historian and a person who lacks the necessary skill and knowledge. The trained historian knows how to evaluate evidence, separating what is reliable from what is unreliable, and he knows where to find evidence of whose existence the non-expert is unaware. He brings a shrewd knowledge of how people behave to his study of the past so that he is able to get under the skin of his characters and show what makes them tick. He is able to spot the subtle details in the evidence which lead to a more accurate picture of what happened. He is not content with a superficial examination of the evidence, but he cross-examines it minutely so that, as far as possible, he arrives at a reconstruction of the events which will withstand the questioning of a sceptic.

It is obvious that the approach of the historian is different from that of the person who lacks his critical judgment and is not concerned to establish an accurate picture in detail or would be unable to do so even if he tried. Not only so, but historians differ from one another. There is a great variation in the technical ability of those who attempt to recreate what happened in the past. Moreover, sheer accident may deprive one man of the resources to produce a definitive study of a particular period in history. Until recently, scholars working on the character of the Essene sect had to depend on a comparatively meagre set of reports on this esoteric group by a few ancient writers. It is only since the discovery of the Dead Sea Scrolls that it has been possible to enlarge our knowledge of this sect — always assuming with the majority of scholars that the group who produced the Dead Sea Scrolls were related to the Essenes, if not actually to be identified with an Essene group. Before the discovery of the Scrolls it was easy for historians to produce erroneous or fanciful pictures of the Essenes. It is a measure of the stature of the English New Testament scholar Joseph B. Lightfoot that his

essay on the Essenes published a century ago has been essentially confirmed by the recent discoveries, while the writings of
other historians have been superseded. [5] Happy is the man who
possesses both the historical talent of a Lightfoot and also the
opportunity to use the relevant source materials.

The relevance of all this to the pursuit of the historical
Jesus can easily be seen. In effect, we have been suggesting
that 'the historical Jesus' can mean 'Jesus, as seen by a
competent historian', in contrast to the inaccurate or imaginative picture that might be produced by a lesser historian, an
unskilled story-teller, or even a novelist. There is a difference
between, let us say, the picture of David Livingstone in a
critical biography and the picture given in a popular series of
brief lives of famous men. In the same way, there will be a
difference between a critical study of the life of Jesus and a
popular, devotional life by a writer with no particular claims
to be a historian; the latter may tell us more about the ideals
of the writer than the real character of Jesus.

But the same point arises in a more pressing form when we
go back to the Gospels and ask whether the Evangelists
thought that they were writing fiction or history or something
in between. How did they conceive their rôles? Are the
Gospels more like historical novels or history books? How far
did the Evangelists possess both the historical competence
and the necessary source materials to write accurate history?
And if the Gospels do not offer us a narrative measuring up to
the standards of critical historical study, how can we use their
contents to find out what Jesus was really like? At the
moment we must be content simply to raise these questions;
later on we must attempt to come to grips with them. [6]

THE NEED FOR EVIDENCE

It is not difficult to think of people who really existed and are
thus 'historical', but about whom we know next to nothing.
In Romans 16:14 Paul sends greetings to a number of people
(Asyncritus, Phlegon, Hermes, Patrobas and Hermas) about
whom we know nothing beyond their names and the fact that
they were Christians whom Paul knew. [7] Yet there is no
reason whatever to doubt the historicity of these people since

their names occur in what is undoubtedly a genuine piece of correspondence by Paul, and it is quite out of the question that he introduced fictitious names into it. The characters are historical enough, in the sense that they really existed, but we possess next to no historical information about any of them. The reason for our ignorance is simply lack of evidence; little more than their names has been handed down to us. We cannot write a description of 'the historical Asyncritus' or 'the historical Phlegon' simply because we do not have the necessary data to enable us to do so; they remain shadowy unknown figures. How much does one need to know about a person in order to speak about 'the historical X'? Here the word 'historical' has taken on a slightly different nuance. It now implies not merely that a certain person existed, but also that we have a certain amount of detailed information about him.

When R. Bultmann and other scholars claim that we can know next to nothing about the historical Jesus, they are in effect saying that although Jesus really lived he is hardly a historical figure in the sense of a person who can be known by the historian or by the historian's readers. For Bultmann, we can know next to nothing about the personality and career of Jesus, indeed little more than a handful of his sayings have come down to us; in that sense there is for him no 'historical Jesus'. The point is a valid one. _If_ the evidence is as meagre as Bultmann claims, then there is no 'historical Jesus' in the sense of a person who can be known by later generations of men. Clearly our task is to see whether this is so.

There is a further aspect to this problem. In an English court of law a jury is required to deliver a verdict of 'guilty' or 'not guilty' on the person who is standing in the dock. The scales of justice are tilted in favour of the accused man in that the jury are entitled to bring in a verdict of 'guilty' only if in their opinion the evidence positively shows that the person committed the crime in question; if there is any doubt in their minds, if the evidence merely suggests that the man is guilty, then they are bound to acquit him. No doubt there are criminals who are acquitted in the courts simply because the available evidence is insufficient to prove beyond all peradventure that they were guilty. The Scottish legal system acknowledges this fact more clearly by allowing a third verdict to be returned by the jury, namely 'not proven'. It has been said that what this means is 'Not guilty — but don't do it again!' The evidence has been insufficient to prove guilt, although the jury strongly suspect that the accused man is in fact guilty and they are not persuaded that they are justified in unambiguously declaring him innocent.

The point of this illustration is that it raises the question, how much evidence does a historian need in order to state that a particular event is historical? Does he need to prove beyond all doubt that a particular event took place or is it sufficient for him to establish a strong likelihood? Some historians would certainly take the line that an event is not 'historical' unless it can be proved to have taken place; in each and every case positive proof is required. If, for example, there is a report that a person uttered some particular statement, it is not enough to show merely that he *may* have said it; one must produce positive evidence that he actually *did* say it. The historian has a moral obligation to offer proof for his statements.

Some New Testament scholars appear to use the word 'historical' in this sense. They will say that a story in the Gospels is historical only if there is some kind of positive proof that it describes what really happened. The number of 'historical facts' about Jesus may then become quite small. There are lots of things that he may have done and said; there are not so many which he can be proved to have done or said.

Here, then, we have yet another nuance of the word 'historical'. In effect it draws a distinction between the many things which Jesus actually said and did but of which the historian is either ignorant or incapable of offering proof, and the smaller number of things which he can be proved to have said or done. No doubt Jesus had meals with his friends in the house of Simon in Capernaum on various occasions, but the menus remain unknown to the historian, and their contents cannot be reckoned as historical facts. But all the evidence goes to show that Jesus died while Pontius Pilate was the ruler of Judaea, and this can be regarded as a historical fact.

All this raises the question as to what constitutes historical proof, and whether *anything* can be proved by historians. A little reflection will suggest that historical statements are attended by various degrees of probability, and that the lines between 'certainly historical', 'probably historical' and 'possibly historical' are hard to draw. A mathematician working out the consequences of a set of postulates may be able to produce a set of certain propositions; we would be surprised to find the word 'probably' in the conclusion of a theorem in geometry or the solution of an equation (although mathematicians do have to be content with 'approximately' on many occasions). [8] But the historian is compelled to use 'probably' and 'possibly' very often. There are a minority of historical facts, especially with regard to the ancient world, which are so firmly established that the historian can say 'certainly', and be confident that no chance new discovery by archaeologists and no fresh reading of existing evidence will shatter his conclusions. Time and again, however, history is a matter of probabilities, and the historian must be prepared to admit the relative probability of many of his statements.

In any case, it is impossible for the historian to assess minutely the truth of every statement which he makes. If he had to do so, he would never say anything. He has, for instance, to assume that a witness who is normally truthful will also be truthful on this particular occasion under investigation. He has to build on the statements of other historians without being able to test them for himself. Otherwise, he would be subject to an infinite regress in seeking reliable evidence, and would finish up even by doubting his own truthfulness! There must be limits to doubt. Even so, the historian has a moral duty as a historian to strive for truth and accuracy and not to be content with anything less.

Some historians take the view that every piece of evidence must be regarded with scepticism until it can be proved to be true. It is the historian's duty, we are told, to accept nothing without proof, and in the particular case of the Gospels this means that the inauthenticity of every saying ascribed to Jesus must be assumed until the contrary can be proved. We shall examine the particular reasons for this sceptical stance at a later stage. It is sufficient to observe at this stage that the most rigorous demands of historical science hardly justify such an extreme position.

THE BIAS OF THE HISTORIAN

We have seen that the aim of the historian is to ascertain precisely what can be proved to have taken place during a particular period in time, and that one of the factors which may render this difficult is the possible lack of evidence or the unreliability of what is available. There is another factor which makes the task of the historian difficult, and this lies in himself. Here we are thinking not so much of the variations in technical expertise between different historians, to which we have already devoted some attention, but rather of the fact that each individual student of the past inevitably sees it from his own point of view and as a result gains a different picture of it from another observer. A well-known example of this from British history was pointed out by H. Butterfield in *The Whig Interpretation of History*. [9] Here he showed how a certain school of historians were impressed by certain factors in history which were congenial to their own point of view and ideals — the idea of progress; the result was that they tended to see only the evidence from the past which supported their own interpretation of the past as a smooth progression towards the excellences of their own time, and they were blind to evidence which pointed in a different direction. They were not incompetent researchers, nor was the evidence not available. It was simply that their own outlook prevented them from seeing the evidence in its own light and assessing its significance accordingly. In the contemporary world it is well known how the Nazis tried to rewrite history in accordance with their own presuppositions. On a lighter level perhaps is the remarkable difference of which a schoolboy is conscious when he comes to read a history of, say, France written by a Frenchman after knowing only what is said casually about France in a history of England by an Englishman. A war can appear quite different to the two sides involved in it. Similarly, in the standard history of modern England by A. J. P. Taylor the attention is concentrated on politics. [10] The names in the index are largely those of politicians. Critics have pointed out the comparative lack of attention to advances in science and technology and to the social factors which governed and characterised the life of ordinary people. What guides a historian to choose what he will describe in his book? [11]

These considerations are clearly relevant to the study of Jesus. So far as the modern historian is concerned, it is very hard for him not to see Jesus through twentieth-century eyes, to concentrate on those elements which are congenial to a modern outlook and to play down the importance of other elements which may be equally important. The process is dramatically illustrated by the various schools of art which portray Jesus and his followers in medieval Italian costumes and settings or in Dutch Renaissance styles or the like. The child from an equatorial country who painted Jesus with a black skin was only doing the same thing; it never occurred to her that Jesus was other than her own colour. On a more serious level it has been observed that liberal Christians in the early twentieth-century tended to portray Jesus as an early liberal Christian, and it is no accident that Rudolf Bultmann, himself much influenced by existentialist philosophy, should produce a summary of the teaching of Jesus which is remarkably like his own theological views. Claude Montefiore, a liberal Jew, made Jesus into a liberal Jew. Orthodox Christians make him into an orthodox Christian. And so we might go on. Each historian is influenced by his own outlook and by the outlook of the age in which he lives.

But will not the same thing apply to the earliest historians of Jesus? The Gospel writers themselves surely saw Jesus from a particular point of view, and it is arguable that they portrayed Jesus in their own likeness as the first Christian. They certainly passed over a lot of facts about Jesus which did not interest them. May it not be the case that they omitted details which might radically alter our understanding of Jesus? Suppose that some Pharisaic opponent of Jesus had written his life: what would that be like compared with a Christian composition? Is it not the case that our sources themselves are the product of bias, and that we are precluded from any real access to the historical Jesus? Here we begin to approach one of the central issues in our subject, which will need to be developed at greater length in the pages that follow.

It would seem that what is wanted is a set of facts rather than an interpretation by a historian. This ideal was expressed in a phrase, used in a different context by the historian von Ranke, who spoke of merely describing things 'as they actually happened'. [12] This sounds a fine ideal until we begin to look at it more closely, and then three things become apparent.

Seeing the whole picture

The first of them is that 'as it actually happened' is something that must be determined by some particular spectator, and a spectator can only see things from one point of view. Suppose that we could get a report from an eye-witness of the Battle of Tours which was fought in AD 733 by Charles Martel, leader of the Franks, against the invading Saracens. Such a person would be able to describe the outward course of the battle to us; if he had himself been a soldier in one of the armies, he could give us a first-hand account of what it felt like to be in the battle and convey to us something about the morale of the troops, their attitude to the leaders, and so on. Here, we might say, is real history; here is what actually happened. Yet such an account would be unsatisfactory from the point of view of the modern historian. Standing so close in time to the actual event, our eye-witness would not be able to tell us that the battle was one of the most significant in European history in that it ended once and for all the threat caused by the Muslims to Christian Europe, significant too in that it established the claims of the Franks to a leading place in the affairs of Europe, significant further for the innovation in military tactics to be seen in increased reliance on cavalry. None of this could be seen by our eye-witness; it is only against the perspective of succeeding events that the place of this battle in history can be seen. Nor would our imaginary eye-witness be able to tell us about the thoughts that filled the mind of Charles Martel during the battle, although a historian might well be interested to know not simply what was going on at the scene of battle but also how this was related to the plans and purposes of the leader; on a knowledge of how the leader planned the battle depends a verdict as to whether he stumbled on the secret of victory simply by accident or as the result of careful military thinking.

It is apparent from this one, fairly simple, example that there is no one standpoint from which a person can claim to have seen the battle 'as it actually happened'. An eye-witness would be perplexed by the historian's account of the battle; there would be so much contained in it that he neither saw nor could see. The simple concept of 'as it actually happened' turns out to be not so simple after all. Indeed, the eye-witness may turn out to be quite misleading and unhelpful if he was only able to see a tiny part of what was going on and was unable to grasp the larger significance.

The necessity of interpretation

This leads on to the second point. The historian is not interested simply in a catalogue of events. A complete list of all that happened at the battle may well form his raw material, and in fact he could wish for nothing better than a complete package of information. But his task is not simply to gather such information. He has to interpret it. Part of his interpretation will consist in selecting what is significant and discarding what is irrelevant, like a detective confronted by a mass of statements in which various people claim to have seen a wanted man everywhere from Exeter to Newcastle; most of the statements can be set aside as of no further value for the investigation in hand, but the mark of the good detective is to single out the statement that is important and which may lead to an arrest. The other part of the task consists in interpreting the evidence by showing the connections between different parts of it, analysing individual parts to elucidate their message, and combining the whole into a coherent picture of what he believes to have happened. A set of unrelated facts is simply a set of unrelated facts; history begins only when facts are interpreted and related to one another. A later historian's interpretation may well give a better account of 'what actually happened' than the diary of a participant. Sir Winston Churchill's detailed account of *The Second World War* is the story of what happened by a leading participant. As such it has tremendous value as a source for the facts, or rather, some of the facts, and it also has tremendous value as an actual history of what happened, since it is not simply a set of extracts from the writer's diary and the various official papers produced at the time, but it also contains the author's analysis of what was happening, what were the important breakthroughs and what might have been done otherwise in the light of experience. At the same time it could be argued that the author sees things from his own standpoint, and is unable to allow for his own lack of vision at certain points. It has been said of Churchill that while he was an excellent over-all administrator for a war-machine, whenever he attempted to take control of actual tactics in a limited sphere, things went wrong. It may be that when writing things up afterwards Churchill was conscious of this and tried to make allowances for it. But it is certain that it needs another person, detached from the events in a way that Churchill could never be, to use Churchill's memoirs and a host of other pieces of information in order to construct a better picture, an interpretation which will be closer to the ideal of 'what actually happened'.

The personal factor

We have glided over almost unconsciously into our third consideration. If a history book must contain the element of interpretation, it is inevitable that it be the interpretation of a particular historian (or group of historians). And at once we reach the point which has been mentioned earlier, namely that the historian cannot free himself from holding a particular viewpoint. There is necessarily a 'personal' element in his outlook, whether that personal element be due to his own character or to the effect of the environment which has moulded his way of looking at things. It seems impossible, for example, for a politician belonging to one of the major parties to give an objective assessment of the policies of another party; the temptation to show that 'our policy is better than theirs' creeps into every political speech or interview, and one suspects that it creeps into every political history. No doubt the politician cannot give any more objective an account of his own party's policies, but this merely proves the point further, that it is virtually impossible to get rid of the personal factor.

These three points show that the concept of 'what actually happened' is a much more complicated one than we may have imagined. At first sight it seemed to be the answer to our problems when confronted by the opposing views of historians; in reality it turns out to be a much more intricate affair.

This does not mean that it is valueless or meaningless. On a vast number of historical facts virtually all historians would be in agreement with one another; it is most often in the area of interpretation that differences arise, but the borderline between fact and interpretation is a fluid one. In many cases, therefore, the attempt to discover what actually happened is proper and can be fruitful, and von Ranke's phrase stands for ever as a warning to historians to refrain from all inaccuracy, and to be led by the evidence rather than by their own ideas, even if this means giving up a cherished interpretation. Recently I was involved in some discussion regarding the views of the group known as Jehovah's Witnesses. One important point in their theology is concerned with dating various events prophesied in the Bible, and it becomes necessary to work out the number of years that separate these events from the fall of Jerusalem. The Witnesses tell us that the fall of Jerusalem took place in 607 BC, and calculate their dates accordingly. [13] Their interpretation rests on this chronological fact. But it is an established fact of ancient history that the fall of Jerusalem took place in 587/586 BC, a fact determined on the basis of ancient evidence by scholars with no particular axe to grind theologically. I would be rash enough to affirm that there is *no* support in the evidence for dating the fall of Jerusalem to the year accepted by the Witnesses. But if so, it follows that their interpretation based on the evidence is at fault and that they ought to revise it. This is certainly what an honest historian would do. He is governed by the spirit of von Ranke's dictum, and if he finds that something he has recorded is not 'as it actually happened', then he will immediately correct it and rethink his position.

'HISTORICAL' AND 'HISTORIC'

When Mrs Billy-Jean King won the Women's Singles tennis championship at Wimbledon in the summer of 1975 and thereby set up a record for the number of times that one person has won this coveted award, her concluding match could be described by sportswriters as 'historic'. This word is used to describe certain events which possess a greater significance than other events which also took place in history. Whatever has happened in history can be called 'historical'; only a minority of events can be called 'historic'. Future historians of tennis who have cause to describe what happened at Wimbledon in 1975 will presumably find room to mention Mrs King's battle for the title, but there will be many other contestants who took part that summer who will not qualify for mention.

On another famous occasion a boy at Rugby School in England once took up the ball in his hands and ran with it during a game of football. In the context of the rules of Association Football at that time (and ever since) the significance of his action was simply that it was a breaking of the rules of the game which do not permit handling of the ball. But the action set up a train of events and led to the creation of a new game in which the use of the hands as well as the feet was permitted. In the history of sport the birth of Rugby Football was a historic event.

These two examples may help us to see once again the distinction between an event and its significance, and between events which have no especial significance and those which do. A 'historic' event is one which stands out from other events because of its significance. A 'historical' event is simply one that happened — admittedly with all the qualifications indicated earlier.

The difficulty that arises is that while we have the two adjectives 'historical' and 'historic' to express these two different ideas, we only have the one noun 'history' to cover both. Here the German language has an advantage over our own, in that it possesses two nouns, *Historie* and *Geschichte*, along with the corresponding adjectives *historisch* and *geschichtlich*. The former noun refers to what actually happened; to say that something is *'historisch'* is to say that it really took place. The latter noun is used to describe events which have significance. To say that something is *'geschichtlich'* is to say that it forms a significant part of history. It follows that when the word 'history' is being used in the sense of 'history book' the Germans use *Geschichte*. When they are discussing the question of whether Jesus really existed and did what he is alleged to have done, they talk about the question of the *'historischer Jesus'*. [14]

This difference between two senses of 'history' can lead to difficulties. One is that the determination of significance and the selection of what is 'historic' rests upon the verdict of the historian. It means that a particular event may not be 'complete' at the time of its happening; one has to take into account its subsequent effect or lack of effect before one can pronounce on its 'historic' significance. Other lads playing football have committed various fouls down the years, but to the best of my knowledge none of them has had the significance of introducing a new version of the game; the players have simply been told not to do it again. Only in the light of the subsequent development of Rugby Football has one particular foul come to have historic significance. And that significance can be differently evaluated. An enthusiast for 'rugger' will claim that what happened on the playing field at Rugby led to a notable development in the evolution of ball games, but a dyed-in-the-wool 'soccer' fan may be tempted to regard the same event as the source of a woefully degenerate manner of playing. A good deal of beauty lies in the eye of the beholder.

But if the beauty lies in the eye of the beholder, it may not matter too much whether the original event actually happened. Martin Luther probably did *not* say, 'Here I stand, I cannot do otherwise', at the Diet of Worms when he was called upon to recant his position. So say the modern historians, although Roland Bainton allows that the words, though not recorded on the spot, may be genuine. [15] But whether genuine or not, the saying attributed to Luther fitly sums up his position and the stance taken by his followers; here is the spirit of the Reformation. The saying may not be *historisch*, if the historians are to be believed, but it is nevertheless *geschichtlich* in that it expresses the significance of what was happening and shows how subsequent Protestants regarded Luther. An event which did not happen can still exercise great influence over the minds of subsequent generations.

THE HISTORIAN AND THE PAST

Throughout the discussion we have been speaking as though the historian comes to his study of the past with his own particular historical expertise and with his own personal and environmental background. He sees what happened through his own eyes, and his account of what happened will be coloured accordingly. One has only to read a life of Jesus by a Jew and compare it with one by a Christian to see that quite different estimates of the significance of Jesus will emerge. There will be agreement on many of the basic facts, although some will be disputed. There may be wildly differing views of what makes Jesus 'historic'.

What is perhaps not so obvious is that the historian himself may be altered by his encounter with his subject. This has certainly happened with historians who have studied the life of Jesus. A contemporary example is that of E. V. Rieu, a Classical scholar who undertook a translation of the Gospels for a well known series. It is reported that his son commented on hearing of the venture: 'It will be very interesting to see what Father makes of the Gospels; it'll be still more interesting to see what the Gospels make of Father'. [16] In fact the task led Rieu to see Jesus in a new way, and in his preface he wrote:

Of what I have learnt from these documents in the course of my long task, I will say nothing now. Only this, that they bear the seal of the Son of Man and God, they are the Magna Charta of the human spirit. Were we to devote to their comprehension a little of the selfless enthusiasm that is now expended on the riddle of our physical surroundings, we should cease to say that Christianity is coming to an end — we might even feel that it had only just begun. [17]

A person's self-understanding may thus be altered by contact with history, and as a result his understanding of history may be altered. A process of this kind obviously involves a to and fro between the historian and the subject he is investigating and thus involves a process that we may call 'dialectical' in the sense that a continuous dialogue is taking place in which the historian's understanding of the past and the past's effect on the historian are continually changing.

This aspect of the study of history has attracted greater attention in recent years. It has been seen that the historian's interest is not confined to the outward shape of events but must reach to an understanding of the human motives and attitudes which lie behind the events. And the historian cannot enter into a real contact with the past in this way without laying himself open to the possibility of a real encounter with the past which may radically alter his own self-understanding. If the word 'dialectical' expresses the to and fro of this process, the word 'existential' expresses the personal significance of the process for the historian.

This however, means that the study of history ceases to be entirely objective and takes on a subjective quality to some extent. If the interpreter cannot stand aloof from his subject but must become personally involved in it so that his own standards of reference become a matter for discussion and reformulation, the quest for objectivity becomes all the more difficult. The goal of the historian is by no means a simple one.

THE MEANING OF 'HISTORICAL'

Our purpose in this chapter has been the double one of discussing what exactly is involved in historical study and also of laying bare the various nuances of meaning which may lie in the words 'history', 'historical' and 'historic'. It may be useful to try to sum up the various different meanings of these two key words at this point.

'History'

First, we have seen that 'history' can refer to what has

actually happened in the past, as when we talk of 'events in history'. It is the area to be studied by a historian.

'History', however, can also mean a record of historical facts established by a historian's research, as in such a book title as *A History of England*. Closely similar to this use of 'history' to refer to the results of historical study is the use of the word to refer to the activity involved: 'He is studying history' means that he is engaged in studying past events by means of the available evidence and in the light of existing historical accounts.

'Historical'

Second, there is the word 'historical' which has developed a complex set of shades of meaning.

1. It can be used to refer to the names or descriptions of persons or events to indicate that they actually existed or happened. To say that the Battle of Hastings is historical is to say there was an event corresponding to this name.

2. The word 'historical' can be used in much the same way as in 1. to refer to events which actually happened, whether or not the historian can actually describe them. Granted that the Battle of Hastings actually happened, the precise details of what happened may not be known to the historian for lack of evidence, although no historian doubts that there were detailed happenings during the battle.

3. 'Historical' can also be applied to narratives to signify that they refer (or are believed to refer) to events which actually happened; they contain historical facts which reflect historical events. This is the familiar distinction between 'history' and 'fiction'.

4. There are, however, various nuances in use 3. Sometimes (as we saw in chapter 1) the word 'historical' may be used to imply that the narrative in question is fully accurate in every particular. We have already suggested that this is an impossible ideal in principle.

5. Or the word may imply relative accuracy as when we talk of a 'historical novel' in comparison with a purely imaginary story.

6. Or again the word may be used of a narrative by a

trained historian which achieves a high degree of accuracy in contrast to a narrative by an unskilled or tendentious historian which contains errors.

7.   Closely allied to use 6 is the use of the word to refer to facts which may be regarded as established beyond all reasonable doubt, as compared with other facts which have varying degrees of probability.

8.   Some people would reserve the term 'historical' for accounts which are thought to present the 'bare facts' without any interpretation coloured by an individual historian's bias or idiosyncrasy of outlook.

9.   But most people recognise both that the element of interpretation cannot be excluded, and also that a mere chronicle of facts which the historian has not tried to relate to one another is not really 'history'. Hence it is more usual to speak of an interpreted set of facts as a 'historical' account in contrast to a mere chronicle or annal which is more the raw material for the historian. A 'historical' account must express the significance and inter-connection of events.

'Historic'

Third, there is the word 'historic'. This is used of facts which are regarded as significant in comparison with other facts. We have seen that so little may be known about a particular person that although he may be 'historical', *i.e.* he really lived, he has no 'historic' significance (1). But among facts of which we have some real knowledge it is clear that some have greater significance than others in the light of the historical process as a whole, and these are said to be 'historic' (2). Finally, we noted that some facts are sometimes claimed to be 'historic' (3), even though it is doubtful whether they are 'historical'; an apocryphal story may sum up the significance of a historical character better than a true story.

This catalogue of the uses of words is no doubt incomplete, but it is sufficiently long to make us acutely aware that the answers to many questions regarding the historical Jesus may well begin, 'It all depends what you mean by "historical"'. Did Jesus really live (1)? What were the real events in his life (2)? In what sense are the Gospels historical (3)? Are they true in every particular (4)? Are they like historical novels (5), or were they the work of trained historians (6)? What facts about Jesus are historically certain (7)? What was Jesus really like as seen by an unbiased observer (8)? What is the 'correct' interpretation of his life (9)?

And, using the word 'historic', we may also ask: do we know enough about Jesus for him to be a significant figure (1)? Can he really be allotted a place in 'history' as a significant, influential figure (2)? Would the story of Jesus still be significant, even if the historicity of some parts of it was open to doubt (3)?

THE POSSIBILITY OF HISTORICAL STUDY

Now that we have gained some idea of what 'historical' means, it is possible for us to ask whether we can find out anything about the historical Jesus. In the course of our discussion we gave a brief outline of historical method, and then proceeded to fill it out in various ways. We have seen that the task of the historian is to determine and understand what has happened in the past. Since he has no direct contact with the past, he has to make use of the various kinds of evidence by means of which past events have left traces of themselves for the historian. He has to interpret their significance and work back from them to the facts which underlie them. In doing so he has to use his skills and talents for decyphering the evidence and to draw up a creative hypothesis which will account for the formation of the evidence. He has to think 'historically', in the sense that he has to be able to work out what human processes of thinking and action are the most probable inferences from the evidence.

This task is obviously not an easy one. There is the fact that evidence is irregularly distributed. Some areas of history have left copious evidence behind them, while others have left little or none. We can draw up a relatively full account of the period of Jewish history between the reign of David and the exile because a fair amount of written evidence has survived in the Old Testament and elsewhere; but for the period from Ezra and Nehemiah down to about 200 BC we know next to nothing of the Jewish state under Persian and Greek rule simply because scarcely any evidence has survived. Again, there is the difficulty of interpreting the evidence. The wording on an inscription may have been damaged, or it may not be possible to rely on an early writer (even an early historian) who trusted to gossip and his imagination. Even eye-witnesses can be inaccurate and partial.

There are also all the personal factors which may prejudice the historian's accuracy. He may not have sufficient command of the necessary skills, he may be ignorant of vital evidence, he may allow bias to darken his judgment.

Despite these difficulties history, including ancient history, is a flourishing science, and it has considerable achievements to its credit. Although the process may be an intricate one, and although historians may go on arguing about the philosophy and methodology of history, the fact is that historical study is carried on successfully. While the historian must often deal with probabilities, this does not mean that historical knowledge is impossible. The task of the historian is no different in principle from that of other searchers after knowledge, and there is a well-founded body of historical knowledge.

These points have been made with reference to history in general and to ancient history in particular. The problem of the historical Jesus is a part of the general problem of studying ancient history, and it must be studied basically by the same methods. The point which can now be made is that to a considerable extent the quest for the historical Jesus is amenable to the same methods of study and faces the same difficulties as any other historical study of the same period. There are particular aspects of the life of Jesus, such as the stories of his miraculous powers, which raise their own special problems, but basically the problems of writing the story of Jesus are the same kind of problems as those in history generally. But there is nothing about the nature of historical study as such which forbids the possibility of gaining reliable knowledge about Jesus or implies that the historical Jesus is necessarily a figure shrouded in uncertainty. There is no reason in principle why historical study should lead a reader who has accepted the biblical story as 'Gospel truth' to confess in desperation, 'They have taken away my Lord'. On the contrary, historical science can supply a sound basis for assessing the historical worth of the Gospels, and there is no reason to suppose that this verdict will necessarily be a negative one.

It is now possible to chart the course of our enquiry more precisely. First, we must examine the particular problem of the application of historical study to Jesus in order to see whether investigation of this particular figure contains any special difficulties of its own (chs. 3-5). Second, we must examine the sources to see whether they are of such a character as to give us reliable knowledge about Jesus, and we must discuss the appropriate methods for dealing with them (chs. 6-9). Finally, we can determine what sort of picture of Jesus emerges from such study (chs. 8-10) and what its significance is (ch. 11).

NOTES

1   It will be helpful throughout this chapter to think of examples of the general statements made in the text. Reference to events in the ancient world will provide useful analogies to the events in the life of Jesus.

2   On the nature of historical method see J. Peter, *Finding the Historical Jesus*, ch. 2; R. G. Collingwood, *The Idea of History*, Oxford, 1946; M. Bloch, *The Historian's Craft*, Manchester, 1954; Van A. Hervey, *The Historian and the Believer*, London, 1966.

3   Thus R. L. Stevenson, in the 'Dedication' of *Kidnapped*: 'If you ever read this tale, you will likely ask yourself more questions than I should care to answer: as for instance how the Appin murder has come to fall in the year 1751, how the Torren rocks have crept so near to Earraid, or why the printed trial is silent as to all that touches David Balfour.'

4   In a similar manner, the preacher may have something to contribute to the study of the Gospels. See W. Lillie, 'The Preacher and the Critic', *Scottish Journal of Theology* 6, 1953, 181-188; for the same writer's own positive estimate of the Gospel narrative, see W. Lillie, *Jesus — then and now*, London, 1964.

5   J. B. Lightfoot, *Saint Paul's Epistles to the Colossians and to Philemon*, London, 1886[8], 347-417.

6   For discussion of these questions with particular reference to the Gospel of Luke see I. H. Marshall, *Luke: Historian and Theologian*, Exeter, 1970, chs. 2 and 3.

7   There is even some dispute as to whether Romans 16 was sent with the rest of the letter to Rome, so that we cannot know for sure that these people lived in Rome — although this remains the more probable view.

8   And of course probability has a proper place in statistics and other branches of mathematics.

9   H. Butterfield, *The Whig Interpretation of History*, London, 1931.

10 A. J. P. Taylor, *English History 1914-1945*, Oxford, 1965.

11 It is only fair to cite from Taylor's preface: 'When I had dealt with these subjects (*sc.* the two great wars and mass unemployment), and with the politics which sprang from them, there was not much room left. Some omissions are excused only by ignorance. There were, for instance, advances in science of the greatest importance: beneficent as with vitamins, potentially catastrophic as with nuclear explosions. I do not understand the internal-combustion engine, let alone the atomic bomb, and any discussion of scientific subjects was beyond me. Nor could I have made much sense of modern philosophy. At any rate, I chose the subjects which seemed most urgent, most interesting, and with which I was most competent to deal.' (*ibid.*, vi).

12 Over against attempts to stand in judgment over the past or to draw lessons for the future, von Ranke stated as the function of history: '*Er will bloss zeigen, wie es eigentlich gewesen*' (L. von Ranke, *Geschichten der romanischen und germanischen Völker von 1494 bis 1514*, in *Sämmtliche Werke*, Leipzig, 1874, vol. 33, vii. The preface, from which the citation is taken, was not included in the English translation, *History of the Latin and Teutonic Nations (1494-1514)*, 1909). I have included the citation and reference in full, since they are often hard to find in the secondary literature.

13 Cited from *Things in which it is Impossible for God to Lie*, by D. and M. Phypers, 'Witnessing to Jehovah's Witnesses', *Christian Graduate*, Dec., 1970, 101-103.

14 '*Historie* means the study of past events with a view to discovering in an objective, detached manner what actually happened. *Geschichte* on the other hand means the study of past events in such a way that the discovery of what happened calls for decision on our part. Corresponding to these words and the distinction between them are the two adjectives, *historisch* and *geschichtlich*, the former referring to what can be established in an objective way by the generally accepted methods of historiographical science, and the latter to what, occurring in the past, has an existential significance in the present' (J. Peter, *Finding the Historical Jesus*, 174). Note that the author comments in a footnote that 'this distinction is not germane to the words as they are commonly used, but has been adopted for purposes of technical discussion'.

15 R. Bainton, *Here I Stand. A Life of Martin Luther*, Nashville, 1955, 144.

16 E. H. Robertson, *The New Translations of the Bible*, London, 1959, 121.

17 E. V. Rieu, *The Four Gospels*, Harmondsworth, 1952, xxxiif.

CHAPTER 3

Faith and the Supernatural

IN THE PRECEDING chapter we examined the task of the historian and saw some of the problems that surround the historicity of any past event. The problems that we discussed there inevitably arise when we turn our attention to Jesus, but there are other problems which are peculiar to the historicity of Jesus or of any similar person who occupies a place in religious devotion. It is time now to come to grips with these.

JESUS THROUGH CHRISTIAN EYES

The first of the problems which confront us is a special case of one of the problems which we discussed earlier. We saw that the attitude of a historian to his subject is often coloured by his own outlook. He records the things that are of particular interest to him and can overlook or play down the significance of things that are of no interest to him or which would qualify or even contradict the picture that he wants to present. Bias can easily affect his attitude. This can certainly be true of political history. But it can also be the case with religious history. And if it applies to modern historians, it can also apply to ancient historians. For our knowledge of Jesus we depend for all practical purposes on the writings of Christians.[1] The Gospels were written by men who believed that Jesus was Messiah and Lord. They applied to him terms which indicated that they regarded him as the supreme representative of God and hence as the one who possessed the key to human destiny. They were committed men who gave to Jesus religious veneration. This can be taken as historical fact, denied by nobody. But what are the implications as regards the historicity of what they wrote? If they wrote as committed men, does this not call in question the impartiality with which they wrote their Gospels? And if they were dependent on other Christians for their information, will not the same consideration apply to these intermediaries? The history of the historical study of Jesus shows that few modern historians have been able to avoid recreating Jesus in their own image: is it not all the more likely that the same thing would happen in the early days? How can we be sure that the whole story has not been coloured by the pious imagination of the earliest Christians who saw the story of Jesus in the light of the religious position which they ascribed to him after his death? Thus it can be argued that when Peter is said to confess to Jesus, 'You are the Christ' (Mark 8:29), this really represents what the early Christians thought about Jesus *after* his death and that they credited Peter with coming to this belief earlier than was in fact the case. [2] Similarly, when Jesus is said to make claims for himself during his lifetime, such as 'I am the way, the truth and the life' (John 14:6), these could be statements put on his lips by later Christians in the light of what they believed him to be after his death; if he held such a position now after his death, then surely (they argued) he must have been conscious of this before his death and said so. [3]

If the Evangelists had been scientific historians, disinterested recorders of what happened, then there is some chance that they might have avoided displaying such bias. But this is not what they were. They were writers of Gospels, works intended to convert the outsider and strengthen the believer. They were not writing history but religious propaganda. It is, therefore, unlikely (so it can be argued) that they paid particular attention to the requirements of careful historical writing. Did they for example check their sources to see if they were reliable? Did they cross-examine the people who told them about Jesus? Or did they simply believe whatever they were told which was edifying and interesting? How can we know whether they made any effort to tell the story to any degree of accuracy?

The effect of these considerations has led many scholars to seek for the 'historical' Jesus in the sense of 'the uninterpreted Jesus' (*cf.* no. 8. in our list of definitions of 'historical' above). Let us, they say, get away from the dogmatic picture painted by credulous early Christians and their modern successors, and let us get back to Jesus as he really was. Implicit in this demand in its more extreme form is the assumption that the 'real' Jesus will be somehow free from the 'religious' elements found in the typical Christian picture of him. The real Jesus will be an ordinary human being, and it will be possible to explain the rise of religious faith in him in terms of ordinary psychological and sociological processes — in the same way as a non-Buddhist might give a 'rationalist' account of how the figure of Buddha was transformed over the years from being a simple religious teacher to become a more than human figure. It is safe to say that a good deal of nineteenth century searching for 'the historical Jesus' was built on this assumption, namely that the original 'event' was an ordinary human life, and that it should therefore be possible by careful probing of the records to uncover this ordinary life as a historical fact. And it is still the case that the search for the historical Jesus often carries this built-in assumption. The result is that the term 'historical' is used in a specialised sense which may trap the unwary. It does not mean simply 'Jesus as he really was' but rather 'Jesus as the ordinary man that he must have been'.

NATURAL OR SUPERNATURAL

The problem which we have just been considering is accentuated when we take another aspect of the biblical picture of Jesus into account. In the Gospels Jesus is presented as a person who possessed various powers that for want of a better term must be called 'supernatural'. This, at least, was how they appeared to the men who wrote the story, and even the Jews admitted the same. Information about Jesus from Jewish sources is admittedly scanty, and what there is can be suspected of being influenced by bias as much as is the case with the Christian accounts — only from the other side. But it is significant that despite the polemical character of the

Jewish reports and the clear desire to play down Christian claims about Jesus, there is no denial of the supernatural elements: Jesus is said to have acted like a sorcerer and led the people astray by his magic.[4] For both Jews and Christians the Jesus described in the Gospels performs various acts that do not correspond with normal human ability. He cures people without the usual therapeutic aids and in an instant. He lives in a world where exorcism of demons is a necessary art and shows that he has graduated in it. Lots of people in the ancient world were believed to have prophetic powers: they could see into the future (with greater or lesser success) and they had powers of clairvoyance. Jesus too showed an insight into what people were thinking that went beyond ordinary intuition. To the Gospel writers he was clearly different from other people, and they certainly believed that he had unusual powers given by God. They were perhaps not unique powers, for in some measure similar claims were made for other men of God, but they were supernatural. It is not too much to say that he was regarded as a divine being.

Now the very term 'supernatural' implies that what is described by it is not 'natural'. Men do not normally behave in this kind of way. When the ordinary man today speaks of something as a miracle he does not usually think of something that is beyond human powers or due to the act of a divine being. Many people would deny outright that supernatural acts of the kind ascribed to Jesus can take place. [5] If so, we may say that the ascription of supernatural acts to Jesus is a special case of the theme dealt with in the preceding section. It is a case of regarding Jesus as more than an ordinary man, and the historical Jesus must (again that 'must'!) have been an ordinary man with ordinary powers. The description of Jesus in the Gospels surely does not correspond to historical reality. And therefore the task of the historian is to prise away the layers of Christian embellishment that have overlaid the picture of the 'real' Jesus and show that he was, after all, an ordinary man who did nothing miraculous. The 'historical Jesus' has often been taken to mean 'the non-supernatural Jesus', a Jesus stripped of all the legends that ascribed to him the power to heal the sick, to turn water into wine, and to walk upon the surface of the sea.

But why should the historian assume that 'the historical Jesus' must have been this kind of person? The Christian believer may be tempted to say in reply: 'You are merely assuming that Jesus could not have done things out of the ordinary. Something more than assumption is required. Give me your reasons.' The request is fair enough, and there are reasons that can be offered in response to it.

First of all, it can be pointed out that similar stories of unusual powers have been told about all kinds of respected figures in antiquity. The Jews had stories about some of their rabbis which attributed to them powers of healing similar to those attributed to Jesus. [6] The Roman Emperor Vespasian who reigned after Nero was credited with the ability to heal. One can produce an impressive list of miracle stories from the age and environment of Jesus and the early church.[7] Now granted the existence of these stories, the critic can pose two awkward questions. First of all, he will ask the person who believes that Jesus did miracles whether he also believes that these other stories about other great men in the first century are also true. Did Rabbi Hanina ben Dosi, for example, perform the wonders attributed to him? Why should we accept one set of stories and not another? After all, (it may be claimed) the historical evidence for both kinds of stories, those about Jesus and those about other people, seems to be of the same value. Why do Christians accept only the stories about Jesus and his immediate followers? (It should be observed in passing that nobody is likely to believe both the stories about Jesus and his followers and the stories about other wonder-workers). The second awkward question which can be asked in relation to these stories of Jewish and pagan wonder-workers is: if such stories were being told about other great men, would not Christians face an overwhelming temptation to tell similar stories about Jesus to show that he was at least on their level, if not actually superior to them? If Christians believed that Jesus was 'the greatest', would they not have to present him in such a way that he would clearly be greater than other miracle-workers, men who were believed to be in especially close touch with the gods? According to the Gospels, Jesus himself admitted the existence of Jews who were able to cast out demons (Matt. 12:27);

Christians pushing the claims of Jesus could say no less about him. Hence it can be argued that it was almost inevitable that such stories would be told about Jesus whether they were true or not.

Second, the modern historian lives in a world in which miracles and supernatural events do not take place. He believes that all events in this world have causes which are also part of this world, and that a natural explanation can be found for each and every event. The whole of history is one gigantic network of natural causes and natural effects, and there is no need to postulate any sort of outside, supernatural influence in order to account for an unusual event. The historian has no need to invoke the idea of God in order to make history 'work', any more than Laplace had any need of the hypothesis of God in order to understand the nature of the physical universe. In short, in writing modern history the historian finds no need to leave room for the supernatural. Everything can be explained in terms of natural causes.

But if this is true of the modern world, it is surely also true of the ancient world. There is no reason to suppose that the world of history ever behaved any differently from the way in which it behaves now. There is continuity between the past and the present. There is an analogy between the present and the past, so that the historian can take it for granted that things worked on the same principle of cause and effect in the first century as in the twentieth. And, therefore, when confronted by accounts of supernatural occurrences in the first century, the historian will say to himself, 'There must be a natural explanation'. When he hears of a wonder cure performed by some famous man, he will examine the possibilities of an ordinary explanation. It may be, for example, that the man would have recovered anyhow by natural processes of healing and that the miracle-worker got the credit for doing what was taking place already. Or the story may have been exaggerated. Or the cure may have been a psychological one, in which the miracle-worker functioned as a primitive psychiatrist or faith-healer; what looked miraculous was in fact quite normal. Or again, the whole story may be simply a legend told to enhance the reputation of the miracle-worker. With a set of such explanations in his bag, the historian is capable of resolving most of the puzzles of this kind. A natural explanation can normally be found.

In general, the historian will prefer such an explanation in any case because of a simple argument which was formulated by David Hume. [8] The essence of the argument is that while it is not uncommon for witnesses to be mistaken, it is uncommon for miracles to take place. Hence the historicity of a miracle cannot be accepted except on the most reliable and unequivocal evidence. We demand different grades of evidence for different purposes; where a miracle is in question, the evidence must pass the strictest tests, since witnesses can be so easily mistaken. Hume himself believed that in every case it was more probable that the witnesses were wrong than that a miracle had actually taken place. Measured by this standard, many of the miracles attributed to Jesus could be said to have little claim to historicity, since the evidence for them is meagre and its reliability is suspect.

But suppose that miracles did take place. Even so, many historians — the great majority in fact — would say that miracles fall outside their orbit as historians. For to accept the miraculous as a possibility in history is to admit an irrational element which cannot be included under the ordinary laws of history. [9] The laws of cause and effect break down, and the historian is left powerless to deal with a situation in which anything can happen. Even if the historical Jesus performed miracles, the historian cannot deal with these; he cannot say in his history, 'Jesus performed miracles', because this is not a 'historical statement' in the same sense as 'Many of his followers believed that Jesus performed miracles' — a statement which tells us what certain people believed.

The result is that the historian believes himself justified in writing a 'history' of Jesus in which the miraculous and supernatural do not appear in historical statements. The 'historical Jesus' — Jesus as he appears to the historian — is an ordinary man. To some historians he is that and no more. To others, however, the possibility is open that he was more than an ordinary man — but this possibility lies beyond the reach of historical study as such. It is a matter of 'faith'.

THE CHRIST OF FAITH

We have proceeded thus far without much consideration of the place of faith in relation to Jesus, and it is now time to take up this topic in order to see what place has traditionally been occupied by faith in relation to Jesus. We are still in the area of definition, trying to see what is meant by the historical Jesus, and contrasting this phrase with others which may shed light on its meaning.

In this connection a distinction is often made between 'the Jesus of history' and 'the Christ of faith', but this distinction is in itself not a very helpful one, since the phrase 'the Christ of faith' is almost as ambiguous as 'the Jesus of history' or 'the historical Jesus'. If, however, we can list the various possible meanings of the phrase, this will shed some light on our enterprise. [10]

If a visitor were to join a company of Christians meeting in the town of Corinth sometime in the first century, he would find that one of their distinctive marks was to make the confession 'Jesus is Lord' (1 Cor. 12:3). Paul, their founder and teacher, expressed the same thought when he commented that although there were many 'gods' and 'lords' in the surrounding pagan world as the objects of men's religious devotion, yet for Christians 'there is one God, the Father, from whom are all things and for whom we exist, and one Lord, Jesus Christ, through whom are all things and through whom we exist' (1 Cor. 8:6). It is clear that in Corinth 'Lord' was a term of religious veneration, used to describe pagan deities, and that the first Christians used this term to describe Jesus, placing him alongside God the Father as the creator and sustainer of the universe. This linking of the two figures was, of course, possible because Christians believed that Jesus was the Son of God, and they were able to place the Father and the Son alongside each other in this way without feeling that they were compromising the traditional Jewish belief that there is only one God. Jesus Christ was thus the name of a divine figure who was the object of Christian belief. Further examination of Christian teaching would show that they believed that Jesus Christ was 'seated' in heaven beside God

(Rom. 8:34) and yet also somehow present 'in spirit' with Christians when they met together for worship (1 Cor. 5:4). Thus their belief was directed towards a spiritual being, present and contemporary, heavenly and yet omnipresent. Such a figure is not 'historical' in the sense of being a figure of the past living in this world. He is 'beyond history' in the same way as God is 'beyond history'. This figure in whom Christians believe can be termed 'the Christ of faith'. It is clear that he is known not by means of historical study but by some other means, such as spiritual revelation; fortunately we do not need to look into this area more closely for our present purpose.

But of course this contemporary figure is Jesus Christ. The message which Paul had preached in Corinth had as its centre the belief that 'Christ died for our sins..., that he was buried, that he was raised on the third day...and that he appeared...' (1 Cor. 15:3-5). It was the historical figure Jesus who, having died, came alive in a new way and entered into the heavenly sphere so as to become the contemporary Christ. 'God has made him both Lord and Christ, this Jesus whom you crucified', is the claim made by Peter to the Jews (Acts 2:36).

The result is that the Jesus of history and the Christ of faith are one and the same person, or rather the same person at two stages in his career. It is precisely this identity and continuity that forms the centre of the problem. Consider the resurrection of Jesus. The confession of faith is that by this act God exalted Jesus as Lord and Christ. The 'Christ of faith' has a 'beginning', and this beginning is God's act in raising Jesus from the dead. But this exaltation is not a historical act, in the sense that it took place in the world of space and time as something that could be observed in the same way as the death of Jesus could be observed. Is, then, the resurrection a historical event? It is certainly historical (*i.e.* it really happened) that certain followers of Jesus believed that he had come to life after having died and that they had seen him. But did he in fact come to life, and did they in fact see him? Is the 'event' which forms the bridge between the 'Jesus of history' and the 'Christ of faith' a historical event or not? Whatever be the historical evidence for the resurrection, is it because of their belief in the present 'Christ of faith' that Christians interpret the evidence concerning what happened immediately after the death of Jesus in a particular way, by affirming that Jesus came alive again, and that this coming to life was an act of God the Father in which he exalted Jesus as Lord and Christ?

What is emerging at this point is that once Christians start to talk about the 'Christ of faith' and to identify the present object of their belief with the past figure of the historical Jesus, then inevitably the historical Jesus begins to be seen in the light of faith. This is most conspicuous in the case of the resurrection; Christians now believe that the end of the earthly life of Jesus included an element which goes beyond ordinary historical happenings and which has to be interpreted in a manner that lies beyond ordinary human historical explanation. But the point may not be too easy to grasp in the case of this particular event, since here we are concerned with an event whose status as a historical event is certainly open to question — since a historian is not making a fool of himself if he tries to argue that Jesus did not rise from the dead.

Consider, therefore, a different event. It is historical fact that Jesus died. No historian, who allows that Jesus really existed, doubts that Jesus died. The historical 'fact' is as certain as anything can be. But the New Testament writers tell us that 'Christ died for our sins' or that 'the Son of God loved me and gave himself for me' (Gal. 2:20). Plainly this is an interpretation of the fact which cannot be read straight off it, but which represents a Christian insight into what the death of One who was exalted as Lord and Christ must signify. This goes beyond an interpretation on the level of ordinary history. On *that* level we might well interpret the death of Jesus as that of a martyr for a cause, or as that of an innocent sufferer who experienced a tragic miscarriage of justice; we might even see in it the ultimate expression of the conviction of a man who believed that he was called to oppose the Jewish establishment for its failure to proclaim a true religion. We might even go so far as to see here the willingness of Jesus to seal his teaching about love for all men with his death. But that is a far cry from making Paul's claim that the Son of God loved *him* and died for *his* sins. Here is interpretation indeed. The acts of the historical Jesus are now seen *sub specie aeternitatis*. The element of interpretation by faith enters into the ordinary historical facts of the life and death of Jesus.

We started this section by distinguishing the 'Christ of faith' as the present object of Christian belief from 'the Jesus of history' as the historical man, who can be investigated by historical methods. But now we have seen that there is a second sense of 'the Christ of faith' in which the historical figure is also seen in the light of faith and his acts are given an interpretation that goes beyond the level of ordinary human interpretation. If we leave aside the resurrection for the moment, we have the possibility that ordinary human actions, entirely possible on the level of normal human history, can be given a theological significance. Thus there is no reason in principle why Jesus should not have demonstrated love to unfortunate people through acts of kindness and care. The historical evidence that he did in fact behave in this way is perfectly good, just as it is in the case of his death. It is, therefore, perfectly possible for the Christian believer to affirm that in these acts the love of God for needy mankind was being concretely shown, and even to go further and affirm that in Jesus God was somehow present to show his love to the world. This is the verdict of faith, and it raises no great problems about the historicity of the events which are being interpreted in this way.

But there are those other stories reported in the Gospels, of which the chief is the resurrection, stories which not only involve a theological interpretation but which also involve events unlike ordinary historical events. There are the miracles, and there are the statements made by Jesus which imply a more-than-ordinary knowledge and insight into the mind of God. The accounts of such incidents are, as we saw, suspect to the historian. But if the believer is justified in giving a theological explanation of 'historically possible' facts, is he also justified in claiming the historicity of 'historically impossible' facts such as the resurrection and the miracles? If history as a science cannot affirm the historicity of the resurrection, can faith affirm its historicity? In short, there is a sense in which 'the Christ of faith' expands to include 'the historical Jesus', miracles and all. Is this feasible? Can faith affirm the historicity of facts which to the historian are either impossible or at least uncertain? Does 'faith' provide an alternative means of access to the historical Jesus than that provided by historical study?

Clearly this question of the place of faith in relation to the historical Jesus must be examined with some care before we can find ourselves in a position to examine the actual problem of applying historical study to Jesus. Our next two chapters, therefore, will take up this matter, looking first of all at the question of the Christ of faith, and then at the relation of faith to historical study.

NOTES

1 Other materials are conveniently assembled in F. F. Bruce, *Jesus and Christian Origins outside the New Testament*, London, 1974.
2 'It is just as possible that belief in the messiahship of Jesus arose with and out of belief in his resurrection. The scene of *Peter's* Confession (Mark 8:27-30) is no counter-evidence — on the contrary! For it is an Easter-story projected backward into Jesus' lifetime, just like the story of the Transfiguration (Mark 9:2-8). (R. Bultmann, *Theology of the New Testament*, London, 1952, I, 26.)
3 Although there is a growing tendency to recognise that the teaching attributed to Jesus in John ultimately rests on historical tradition, the present form of it is generally recognised to be due to the Evangelist.
4 F. F. Bruce, *op. cit.*, 56.
5 E. and M. -L. Keller, *Miracles in Dispute*, London, 1969.
6 G. Vermes, *Jesus the Jew*, London, 1973, ch. 3.
7 R. Bultmann, *The History of the Synoptic Tradition*, London, 1968 [2], 218-244.
8 D. Hume, *Enquiry concerning Human Understanding*, Oxford, 1961, Sect. 10; *cf.* R. Wollheim, *Hume on Religion*, London, 1963.
9 G. E. Ladd, *Jesus and the Kingdom*, London, 1966, 188 n. 53.
10 Since 'Jesus' was the *name* of the historical figure and 'Christ' (*i.e.* Messiah) was the *title* assigned to him by his followers, it has become accepted practice to speak of the historical *Jesus* and the *Christ* of faith, although, of course, Jesus, Christ and Jesus Christ are all found as names for both the historical figure and the object of Christian faith in ordinary Christian usage.

CHAPTER 4

Historical Jesus
or Christ of Faith?

So FAR OUR aim has been to pose problems rather than to solve them, and it is now time to retrace our steps by taking up these problems and discussing some possible solutions to them. We have, unfortunately, not finished with the posing of problems, but at this point we ought to establish some basis for further advance before we again complicate the issue by taking note of these additional difficulties.

The title of this book is *I believe in the historical Jesus*. Various implications might be drawn out of that statement. Perhaps the most important of these is the suggestion that I know the historical Jesus by faith rather than by means of historical science. But another possible implication demands scrutiny first of all.

ONLY THE HISTORICAL JESUS?

Does the affirmation, 'I believe in the historical Jesus', imply a rejection of the corresponding statement, 'I believe in the Christ of faith'? Or does it imply at least a displacement of the latter statement to a secondary or subordinate position? Is it enough to believe in the historical Jesus and to ignore the Christ of faith? This is not a new question, and the classical statement of the issues involved with reference to contemporary discussion of it is now nearly thirty years old, but has lost none of its relevance. The opening pages of D. M. Baillie's study of christology and atonement, entitled *God was in Christ*, are devoted to this topic.[1] Here the author examines in turn the views of scholars who declared their exclusive allegiance either to the earthly Jesus or to the Christ of faith, and argued that both groups were attempting to separate things that should be inseparable. Baillie's point still stands, and scholars who have subsequently attempted to operate with the dichotomy can profitably be referred to Baillie's discussion. In what follows we are considerably indebted to his study.

In the first place, then, there are those who would argue that the historical Jesus is enough, and that we can dispense with the Christ of faith. Those who talk in these terms are rejecting the notion of faith in the present Christ; and usually this means that they also reject any supernatural elements in the earthly life of Jesus. For such people the importance of Jesus is as a teacher of eternal truths and as the supreme example of how men ought to live. The concept of Jesus as a present Saviour and spiritual presence is either denied or retreats into a position of comparative insignificance.

In its classical form this attitude was typical of theological liberalism in the earlier part of the century. It produced the kind of picture of Jesus which we find in T. R. Glover's popular book, *The Jesus of History*, although it should be emphasised that Glover himself did not repudiate the Christ of faith. [2] The book presented a Jesus who was a religious genius, opening up the way for men to God and showing them how they might serve him aright. This approach played down the supernatural elements in the Gospel presentation of Jesus, and it also attached little importance to the idea of faith-union with Christ or the hope of the future advent of the Son of man. Many people, it is true, did not go out of their way to deny these elements in the Christian faith. Indeed, they subscribed to the great creeds of the church which testified to them, but these elements were scarcely part of their working creed, in the same way as it could be said that many people today subscribe to what the creed says about the Holy Spirit, but the Holy Spirit is not exactly a living and vital feature of their Christian experience as they understand it. Their faith was faith in God, and it was Jesus who was the great revealer of God and his love through his teaching and example. The attitude still continues. It finds its most pronounced expression in Unitarianism, the brand of Christianity which believes in the reality of God, but denies the divinity of Jesus. The historical Jesus for this outlook is a human Jesus.

A more radical type of attitude can be found today as the successor of such liberalism. The characteristic of this outlook is the denial of the reality of God the Father as a personal being with some kind of metaphysical status. There is no God in this sense. But the word 'god' can be used to describe that to which men attach supreme value and to which they accord the highest status. In *this* sense Jesus can be 'god'; his life is the perfect life, and his teaching is of such quality that men may attach supreme significance to him and give to him (or rather to his memory) a veneration that might be called religious. 'I believe that there is no God and that Jesus is his Son', is a sarcastic summary of this outlook. Here again it will be obvious that when Jesus died, the story ended. For the denial of belief in God carries with it denial of the resurrection and denial of the existence of that heavenly sphere in which a risen Jesus might continue to exist as the eternal Lord and Christ. There are various forms of 'Death of God' theology current in the contemporary world; the form which claims that there is no God, as distinct from those forms which claim that our 'image' of God is lifeless, must necessarily embrace this kind of view of Jesus. [3] And theologies which lay much stress on the significance of the manhood of Jesus may tend towards a similar type of attitude in practice, even if their proponents do not go to the length of categorically denying the existence of God.

The definition of 'Christian'

Before we ask whether this type of approach is satisfactory, a point of definition should be made. We shall consider in a moment whether or not this is a possible understanding of Jesus. It is certainly 'possible' in the sense that some people do hold it. But it should not be described as a possible 'Christian' understanding, since this is not what the term 'Christian' implies. As historically used, 'Christian' refers to the kind of belief enshrined in the Apostles' and Nicene

Creeds which speak of Jesus as the Son of God. Those creeds may be wrong in what they say; the beliefs stated in them may be false and untenable, but the creeds define what is meant by *Christian* belief, and it causes nothing but confusion when people who deny that Jesus is the Son of God claim the title of 'Christian' for themselves and their views. Whatever they are, they are not Christians.

Of course they may justify their use of the description by claiming that what they believe is 'really' what the creeds are saying when stripped of their mythological form of expression. They are attempting to give us a 'persuasive redefinition' of 'Christian', by showing that views which until now were not regarded as Christian can be regarded as Christian in a broad sense of the term. It is, however, not easy to see how the teaching of the creeds can be understood in so attenuated a sense. In the interests of clarity, therefore, it should be noted that the attitude which we are discussing is not in the proper sense 'Christian'. [4]

The place of Christ in New Testament Christianity

This leads to our second point, which is a criticism of the attitude in question. Its basic failure is that it can in no way be said to reflect the growth and structure of New Testament Christianity. The historical phenomenon with which we are dealing is not just the life of Jesus but also the movement which was triggered off by his life. The earliest written records of the Christian movement are contained in the Epistles in the New Testament, especially those of Paul. There is no reason to doubt their historical value as testimonies to what the early Christians believed. Their evidence shows that for the first Christians the decisive factor in their consciousness was the death and resurrection of Jesus with his consequent exaltation as Lord and Christ and the hope of his parousia or advent in glory at the end of the world. They were conscious of the presence of his Spirit with them. There is remarkably little about his earthly life, his moral example and his teaching in these writings. It was evidently possible for early Christians to go a long way without reference to Jesus as a man. This fact demands some explanation. [5] It cannot just be put on one side and dismissed as unimportant. Some explanation is needed as to why the life of Jesus led to this kind of belief about him. Why did the first Christians concentrate their attention so much on the Christ of faith and ignore the Jesus of history? If the vital thing in Christianity is the historical Jesus as example and teacher, why did the early church not see it that way?

Various counter-arguments may be brought against this point. Thus, first, it may be observed that there were in fact some early Christians who did adopt an attitude of this kind. For some Jewish Christians, known as Ebionites, Jesus was little more than a wise teacher who gave true insight into the Old Testament law. May it not be that this group preserved the truth about Jesus, while the rest of Christendom went astray? [6] But the claims of this group of people to represent authentic Christianity are more than feeble. They were certainly not the earliest group of followers of Jesus, and their views entirely fail to do justice to the teaching of Jesus himself.

Second, it might be noted that the principal witness to the early Christianity which we have been describing was Paul. But was not he the great corruptor of the Gospel? Did he not transform the simple message of Jesus into a complicated theology and hide the teacher of Galilee behind a mass of dogma? There have not been lacking scholars who have put up the choice 'Jesus or Paul?' and chosen the former, castigating Paul for transmuting the moral teaching of Jesus into an unattractive metaphysic. But the charge will not stand. [7] One of the most important insights of modern Pauline study is its realisation that at point after point Paul was not the great innovator who recreated Christianity in his own image; his indebtedness to his Christian predecessors was deep and far-reaching, and there was no essential point at which he was out on a limb compared with his predecessors. He himself referred to his agreement with Peter on the fundamental issues of the faith. If the charge of innovator is to be laid against anybody, it will have to be laid against the very earliest Christians. Which leads to the crucial question: what turned the earliest Christians into innovators?

But before taking up that point, there is the third

counter-argument to be considered. It can be urged that we
have left the Gospels themselves out of consideration. Do not
the Gospels testify to a Christianity which was centred on the
historical Jesus? Do they not preserve memories of his life and
teaching which were remembered by people for whom the
earthly Jesus was a person of supreme importance? Were
these memories not preserved by people who thought that it
was vital to re-tell the teaching of Jesus, to continue his
ministry, and to bring his challenge afresh to succeeding
generations? [8]

Of course this point is true and valid. But it does not prove
that the persons who preserved the story of Jesus were
interested only in his earthly life. For the thing that makes
the Gospels so difficult to use as historical sources for the
earthly life of Jesus is the simple fact that they were written
after his death and resurrection by people who believed that
God had exalted Jesus as Lord and Christ and hence believed
that the person who had been exalted in this way could not
have lived an ordinary human life. The Gospels were written
in the light of Easter, and the picture which they give of Jesus
is a picture written from the perspective of those who believed
that Jesus was more than a good man and a wise teacher. At
no stage in the transmission of the material contained in the
Gospels can we find evidence for the existence of people who
thought that they were merely preserving the memory of an
ordinary man who was nothing more than a gifted prophet
and a martyr for his beliefs.

So the innovators can be traced back to the earliest days of
the Christian church. And the thing that made them
innovators, if such they were, was their belief that God had
raised Jesus from the dead so that he was now the exalted
Lord. This tended to overshadow everything else. Early
Christianity was dominated by the resurrection of Jesus and
hence by the risen Lord.

Was Jesus merely human?

Our third point is that the way for this was prepared by the
historical Jesus. Here we must to some extent anticipate the
conclusions to which we shall come in a later chapter, a

procedure which may be unsatisfactory for people who like a straight argument in which each link of the chain is joined directly to the preceding one, but which is unfortunately necessary in view of the complex, inter-connected nature of the subject. When we come to look at the evidence regarding the historical life of Jesus we shall find that there are elements in it which raise the question of Jesus' relation to God. Various features indicate that he cannot be understood on a merely human level. This is true even if we allow that the presentation of Jesus in the Gospels has been coloured by the early church's belief in the resurrection. But when all allowance has been made for Christian accretions to the historical facts, it still remains true in our opinion that the remaining historical facts point to a phenomenon that cannot be accounted for in purely human terms. For the moment, however, we cannot insist on this point: it remains to be proved in the light of further investigation.

The Christian view of God and history

Fourth, Baillie built a major part of his case on the Christian ideas of God and history. He insisted that the Christian concept of God demands that we frame a christo-logy, *i.e.* a doctrine of who Jesus is in relation to God. For the Christian understanding of God, according to Baillie, is of a God who reveals himself and acts in history. The God whom Jesus spoke of is a God who seeks out and saves man. But if Jesus is merely a teacher *about* God then the message is false. The concept of a God who seeks and saves demands expression in the incarnation, in God coming among men in some tangible way, otherwise God remains remote and unknowable. Similarly, the Christian understanding of his-tory as a whole is that it finds its centre in the coming of Jesus. This event is the climax of history, the fulfilment of prophecy and the basis of hope for the future. It rescues history from being a cyclical process, in which the same things continually go on happening, and makes it into a process with a goal. But to accept the Christian view of history is to assert that Jesus is more than a mere man who 'discovered' the truth about God; it is to assert that God acted in Jesus in a decisive way for all mankind, and to assert this is to express the conviction that Jesus is related to God in a unique way.[9]

Let us be clear what Baillie is doing with this rather subtle argument. He is saying, in effect, that some people may think it possible to combine a traditional belief in God with the belief that the 'Jesus of history' is 'sufficient'. But in fact when these two beliefs are analysed it becomes apparent that they are incompatible. The traditional Christian view of God is incompatible with the view that 'the Christ of faith' is a figure that can be dispensed with. You cannot have the Father without also having the Son (1 John 2:23). As a Christian viewpoint, this way of thinking is inconsistent.

It is possible, however, to sidestep the force of Baillie's argument. It was directed against people who believed in a God who acts in history, and he himself used the term *Heilsgeschichte* or 'salvation history' in this connection. [10] This phrase refers to the quality of certain historical events as events in which God is believed to be active in judgment and salvation. On this view the Bible is regarded as the record of such events in which God reveals himself to men, and the events are understood as 'sacred history' either in their own light or in the light of the interpretation given to them in the Bible itself. God is then understood as a God who acts in history and speaks through prophets in order that men may understand the significance of his acts.

But this is not the only understanding of the Bible and of God which is current today. It is opposed by the outlook of an existentialist theology according to which the function of the Bible is to bring man to self-awareness and thus to save him by setting him free from himself. No act of God is needed to save men in the sense that some historical event (such as the cross) is a means of setting him free from sin. But when the Christian message about the cross comes to men, it enables man to see himself, to acknowledge the poverty of his existence, and to lay himself open to the future with its possibility of genuine existence. Such a message is almost completely independent of history, and needs no historical proof or historical backing. On this view the traditional concept of God is a mythological survival from the past; when demythologised and restated in modern terms, it conveys the existentialist message. Even Jesus himself is scarcely necessary, although the fact of Jesus as the One through whom man comes to self-awareness is strenuously defended. [11]

It could be said that the fundamental issue in modern theology is between the view which believes in a living God, active in history, [12] and that which asserts, in one way or another, that God is 'dead'. What is clear is that biblical religion is centred on historical acts which are regarded as acts of divine revelation and interpreted as such. These acts and their significance are indissolubly joined together, so that it represents a complete misunderstanding of the Bible when attempts are made to reinterpret it as a testimony to a non-historical form of revelation.

It is not our task in this book to argue for the truth of biblical religion or the traditional idea of the living God. That must be left to other occasions and writers. Our concern is with the place of the historical Jesus in Christian belief. The argument of this section has been intended to show that 'the historical Jesus' is inadequate as the basis of Christianity without 'the Christ of faith'. The concept of Jesus as a religious teacher and moral example is insufficient by itself to account for biblical Christianity. Biblical Christianity is centred on the risen Christ and on the consequent understanding of the earthly Jesus as the incarnate Son of God.

ONLY THE CHRIST OF FAITH?

But now we must look at the alternative. In view of the emphasis that we have been placing on the Christ of faith, it might be felt that he alone is sufficient for the Christian believer. Those, however, who accept Charles Simeon's dictum that the truth lies at both extremes [13] will be prepared for a presentation of the view that we need *both* the Christ of faith *and* the historical Jesus; they know the answer already. But the answer makes better sense when the question is properly understood; and therefore we must first try to see why some people adopt the position that the Christ of faith is enough. At least two varieties of this position must be examined.

Dispensing with the historical Jesus

In the first place, it is possible to have a religion which is concerned almost exclusively with the risen Lord. Some members of the early church were clearly in danger of this attitude. If we only had the Epistles to go on — and for a time the only written documents that some parts of the early church possessed were the Epistles — then we might well conclude that it is possible to manage perfectly well without the Gospels and the Figure whom they describe. Conscious of the presence of the risen Lord and his Spirit, and looking forward to the future advent of the Lord, the early church could well believe that here it had a sufficient basis for its faith. And there were people in the early church who believed precisely this. Their particular brand of Christianity came to full flower in the second century, but already in the first century we can see the beginnings of the trends which led in this direction. A variety of groups, collectively known as Gnostic sects, held a view of Christianity in which the historical Jesus was a dispensable figure. It is true that he appeared in their teaching, but it is equally clear that he could be omitted without great loss or replaced by somebody else. For the Gnostics mankind was in the grip of evil, demonic forces which had created the world and endeavoured to keep it separate from God; men were kept in ignorance that they could have a spiritual destiny. But it was possible for men to come to know of their spiritual destiny, and such knowledge enabled them to cast off their ignorance and thus be 'saved'. This knowledge was brought by a redeemer figure who (in some Gnostic systems) had come down to earth from heaven and then ascended above. But no particular significance was attached to his sojourn on earth. He did not become incarnate in the Christian sense, and he did not die on the cross — and if he had, it would not have mattered. The important thing was that he brought to men knowledge of their real nature and thus set them free from the shackles of ignorance.

It is a curious fact that in the modern world this kind of attitude is shared by groups of Christians who may seem at first sight to be poles apart from each other. The evangelical wing of Christianity has a strong temptation to concentrate its attention on the crucified and risen Lord Jesus and to ignore his earthly life. To be sure, this never happens completely, and it certainly never happens consciously: evangelical Christians would be swift to denounce as heretical any suggestions that the historical Jesus was unimportant. But the fact remains that there is a temptation to ignore the religion of the Gospels and to concentrate on the Epistles. The evangelical Christian can become so interested in dogma and doctrine that he has little interest in history. Of course he accepts the history (a point to which we shall return below), but he is not very interested in it as history.

The position of R. Bultmann

When D. M. Baillie was discussing this issue, however, the theological party which he had in mind was that of the so-called dialectical or neo-orthodox theologians, Emil Brunner and the early Karl Barth, who felt that the historical Jesus, i.e. Jesus as the object of historical science, had little or no place in theology. But the most radical expression of this attitude is to be found in Rudolf Bultmann whose position has some resemblance to that of the second century Gnostics. [14] For Bultmann (as we noted at the outset of our study) it is not possible to know (and therefore believe in) the historical Jesus because it is not possible to find reliable historical evidence about him. In his magisterial survey of the *Theology of the New Testament* Bultmann does not discuss the teaching of Jesus as a *part* of New Testament theology but as a *presupposition* of it. The little that we can know is not part of the theological message of the New Testament. [15] Bultmann has often been accused of making a virtue of necessity by his neglect of the historical Jesus in his theological study. He himself has carefully denied that this is his motivation, at least in reference to the personality of Jesus. Whether or not we believe him — and I find it hard to believe that his historical scepticism has not influenced his theological judgment at this point — we must listen to his defence of his position. [16] For Bultmann what 'saves' us is the 'preaching'

found in the New Testament, the message which acts as a
revelation of God and of myself, bringing me to see my failure
to live life as it should be lived and setting me free to do
precisely this. If the truth of this message depended on the
establishment of historical facts, for example, if the truth of
the message depended on historical proof that Jesus physical-
ly rose from the dead, then my faith would be dependent on
what the historians have to tell me. It would cease to be faith
and would be based on historical knowledge. But historical
knowledge is a very precarious thing; it is dangerous to pin
one's faith on a historical fact which may perhaps be shown
to be false tomorrow. Perhaps tomorrow the bones of Jesus
might be discovered in a grave in Jerusalem, just as the bones
of another victim of crucifixion from first century Palestine
have in fact been discovered by archaeologists. Religious faith
must not be dependent on the vagaries of historical discovery.
And for Bultmann the Christian message is free from such
vagaries for it is not dependent upon historical research.

This does not mean that Bultmann is uninterested in Jesus.
While he insists that historical study is not the way to come
into contact with Jesus, since it can tell us next to nothing
about him, he does insist strongly on the fact that Jesus
existed and died. He is not a believer, however, in the
physical resurrection of Jesus; for him Jesus rose 'into the
preaching', in the sense that his influence now makes itself
felt through the Christian message; the resurrection serves as
a means of explaining the significance of the death of Jesus.
Nor is Bultmann uninterested in the teaching of Jesus and
the accounts of Jesus given in the Gospels. He himself wrote a
book about Jesus, or rather about the teaching of Jesus as it is
presented in the Gospels; in it Jesus appears as the preacher
of the kind of existential decision that according to Bultmann
is typical of the message of the New Testament generally. For
Bultmann the Gospels are important because they give us the
church's understanding of the significance of Jesus; whether
this significance is based on history is irrelevant, and it is
illegitimate to seek to verify the Gospels on the church's
message historically. We have access to Jesus only through
the New Testament preaching, and there is no alternative
means of access by historical research. There cannot be two

routes to Jesus, only one. The only one accessible to us is via the New Testament message which presents to us the Christ of faith as the figure who is the means of salvation, and historical study cannot add to or take away from this figure.

Bultmann's position is a self-consistent one, and it has considerable attraction, precisely because it releases Christian faith from being dependent upon the vagaries of historical research. Moreover, it does not remove Jesus from Christianity, as might be thought at first sight. What Bultmann is denying is that we can obtain access to Jesus by means of historical study. He is not denying that we can have access to him by means of the message contained in the New Testament. At this stage he is taking up a point made by Martin Kähler at the end of the last century when he insisted that we can know only the biblical Christ; the historical Jesus is hidden from us. [17] We can certainly know the saving message of Jesus in the preaching of the early church, and we can see what impact he made upon the early church, even if this impact cannot be explored historically with any certain results.

The need to relate the Christ of faith to the historical Jesus

But we need to ask some searching questions about this estimate of the place of the historical Jesus in Christian faith. [18] It is clear that Bultmann regards a Jesus whose character and teaching have been discovered by historical research as irrelevant to Christian faith. But his understanding of the Christ of faith also differs from that of traditional Christianity. This is because he does not pay proper regard to the historical Jesus. For Bultmann, Jesus is 'alive' in the message of the church and not in any kind of transcendent or metaphysical sense; and the cross saves men not as any kind of objective act by God but as the means of revealing man's plight to him and the possibility of authentic existence. It is obvious that this is not the usual understanding of the cross and resurrection, and that Bultmann's view of the 'Christ of faith' is consequently unusual. For Bultmann there is no such thing as the spiritual presence of Christ with the believer, and the Holy Spirit is merely a name for 'the new possibility

of genuine, human life' rather than a real, spiritual power. [19]
One may well ask whether Bultmann has really preserved the
Christ of faith in his theological system. Certainly he has not
preserved the traditional understanding of the risen Lord.
The question is whether the traditional view or Bultmann's
view is right.

So we ask Bultmann, 'Why should we believe the Christian
message?' — naturally in Bultmann's version of it. How do
we know that it is true? Is there any proof of it? And the
answer which we receive is that there is no way of knowing.
There is no historical proof of it. [20] All that we can do is
accept it or reject it. But this is profoundly unsatisfactory. For
we now have no way of telling whether the Christian message
is to be regarded as true while the Buddhist or humanist
messages are false: how do we discriminate between the one
and the others? To this question Bultmann, so far as I can see,
has no answer. Here is grist for the mill of those who tell us
that it does not matter what you believe, for all religions (and
non-religions?) lead to the same destination.

But this will not do at all. For in effect what has happened
is that Jesus has ceased to be a unique figure, or perhaps even
a necessary figure. I am aware that Bultmann would probably deny this implication of his position, but I do not see how
he can logically do so.

What has happened? On the view that we are discussing,
certain essential elements in Christian experience have in
effect been declared illusory; no proof can be offered for the
'truth' of Christianity; and the uniqueness of Jesus has
disappeared. In reaching this position Bultmann would claim
that he was representing the 'real' message of the New
Testament in a 'demythologised' form. He has transmuted
what is expressed in the New Testament in mythological
forms, no longer acceptable to modern man, into a new form
which makes sense to modern man. Translation into the
categories of Heidegger's philosophy releases the New Testament message from its mythological, time-bound form, and
allows it to speak with new power to modern man. But here
too there are difficulties.

First, it is very doubtful whether this modern form of the
message is any more appealing to modern man than the old

form. The apostles of Bultmannite Christianity cannot be said to have been more successful at evangelism than their more traditional counterparts. This must be said with a sense of real sorrow, for it has often been argued that Bultmann's basic aim is to remove the obstacles in the way of modern man's acceptance of the Gospel.

Second, and more important, Bultmann has to admit that the various New Testament writers grasped the point of the Gospel with varying degrees of insight, and some of them misunderstood it fairly seriously. Paul got it right, and John came close behind him, but the others tended to get it wrong in part or as a whole, and the later writers especially fossilised the traditions which they inherited instead of dealing creatively with them in their new situations. The result is that the essential kerygma is clouded over and misunderstood in the later books of the New Testament, and Bultmann's Gospel is found in its pristine purity only in Paul and John — although even John did not get it quite right. One may, however, ask with considerable justification whether an understanding of the Christian message which rests only on a small part of the New Testament evidence can be regarded as a correct interpretation of the evidence. A view which in effect jettisons half the evidence before it can make any headway is surely in danger of sinking. Needless to say, Bultmann and his colleagues have their answer to this criticism. They insist that the New Testament is not a collection of books each proclaiming the same message. It is a mixture of different types of approach, and once we have found out what is central and correct, then we can use this criterion to criticise and reject whatever is not in accord with it. But it is surely more than passing strange that the second generation of Christians so thoroughly misunderstood the Christian message that we have had to wait until the twentieth century to be called back to the true version of the faith. One may well wonder whether this new version of the Gospel is not rather a perversion of it.

Third, if Bultmann's view of the Gospel carries the implication that the latest writers in the New Testament misunderstood their predecessors, we may equally well wonder whether it is not Bultmann himself who has in fact misunderstood them. Is Bultmann's view of Paul and John true or false? And in fact, despite the light which he has shed on some aspects of their thought, Bultmann's understanding of Paul and John is open to serious criticism. For example, he thinks that the structure of Paul's theology is determined by the concepts of 'man prior to faith' and 'man under faith'; that is to say, for Bultmann Paul's theology is basically about man, and all that Paul says can be listed under one or other of these categories. But it has been rightly pointed out by subsequent writers that Paul's theology is not about man but about God and Jesus Christ, and that its structure is determined by the central significance of Jesus Christ. [21] If Bultmann has so misunderstood Paul as to think that he is writing about man when his thoughts are really centred on Jesus Christ, then we must wonder whether he is a very reliable guide.

These considerations, which are not exhaustive, may suffice to indicate that Bultmann's understanding of the New Testament is exposed to grave criticism and hence that his understanding of the place of Jesus is faulty. For the New Testament writers the historical fact of Jesus was decisive. Their religion was built on what God had done through Jesus. It was not the message in itself that saved men, but the fact to which the message bore witness. An understanding of Christianity which fails to appreciate this fact is a misinterpretation of Christianity. The historical fact of Jesus is essential to the Gospel. However much the writers of the Epistles may centre their attention on the risen Christ, they insist that it is the crucified Jesus who is the risen Christ. If there had been no crucified Jesus, there would have been no risen Christ. It is as simple as that.

The need for knowledge of the historical Jesus

But, granted this fact, we are still not out of the wood. For it was claimed that even though Jesus was a historical person who really existed, we cannot find out about him by means of historical study. Our only access to him is by means of the message preached in the New Testament, and it is illegitimate to try to confirm the message by means of historical study. Whether or not historical study of Jesus is possible, we ought not to attempt it in the hope of confirming the message, for that would be to base our faith on the shifting sand of what the historians may tell us.

There are two points concealed within this argument. The first of them is that we should not be interested in finding out about the historical Jesus. It was against this argument that D. M. Baillie stressed that we are in effect saying that the incarnation was unnecessary if the incarnate Son of God was not a vehicle of revelation. [22] It becomes incomprehensible why Jesus lived and worked and taught at all if the sole thing that mattered was his death and resurrection and if the sole thing that is to be proclaimed is the risen Christ. If we were to accept the position of Bultmann, the New Testament should say nothing about the historical Jesus. But it is full of references to him. Of course it is true that there is little information about his ministry in the Epistles, but the fact of the incarnation is undeniably present and important, even if the details of the earthly life of Jesus are largely absent. What are the Gospels doing in the New Testament if the historical Jesus is unimportant? Before the Gospels were written, Christians handed down the stories of Jesus: why did they do so if they were of so little importance for faith? If Christians believed that God was revealed in Jesus, then some knowledge of Jesus is indispensable; otherwise there is no revelation. Moreover, says Baillie, if we want to say that it was Jesus who was the Son of God and not some other human figure, we must know something about Jesus in order to be able to make the identification. We cannot say that the arbitrarily chosen figure of Jesus is the Son of God; we must have some reason for saying so. [23] We are bound to be interested in the historical Jesus if we believe in the incarnation, for we are bound to ask what justification there is for believing that the incarnation took place in Jesus. Why do we believe this about Jesus and not about somebody else, such as one of the modern gurus?

This question leads us to Bultmann's second point, which is that we must be content with the Jesus presented in the kerygma. If we ask why we should accept Jesus as the revealer of God, the answer is that this is the identification made in the kerygma, and that we cannot go beyond this. All that we can do is to accept the kerygma and prove that it is true in the situation of existential commitment. To a certain extent this is good evangelical advice. If a person is hovering on the brink of faith and wondering whether Jesus can save him from his sins, the evangelical preacher will appeal to him to make the experiment of trusting Jesus and seeing whether it works; only in the act of commitment can he prove the truth of the Gospel. On the level of ordinary life too a man cannot know for sure whether the girl of his choice loves him and is prepared to marry him unless he is prepared to take the plunge by asking her and declaring his own love.

But there is a significant difference between these situations and that proposed by Bultmann. The ardent lover has some reason to believe that the girl will respond positively to his proposal; she has already consented to go out with him, and a harmony has developed between them to which the proposal and its acceptance form an almost inevitable natural climax. The sinner seeking for forgiveness has been assured from the Gospels that Jesus did receive sinners and that as the risen Saviour he still receives them. It is not a jump in the dark. It is a commitment based on reasonable knowledge. It is not clutching at a straw, but laying hold on a firm hope. Faith starts from knowledge, even if it reaches beyond it, and its character as faith is not destroyed by its association with knowledge.

In the New Testament itself the demand for faith is also based on the supplying of information about Jesus. The kerygma contains reference to the historical Jesus. This has been recently demonstrated yet again in an important book by Graham N. Stanton, *Jesus of Nazareth in New Testament Preaching*, in which the author shows that in the preaching of the early church the historical Jesus occupied an important place; and that this is true not just of the later period but of the earlier period also. It is often alleged that the kerygma was given historical backing only at a late stage; Stanton is concerned to dispute this allegation and show that it is erroneous. [24]

What this means is that in New Testament times the Christian preachers gave their audiences historical information as part of their teaching and instruction. It was for this purpose that the Gospels were written, namely to preach the gospel on the basis of what purports to be historical information about Jesus. The message contained historical facts as a basis for faith. Anybody who doubts this can be referred to the prologue to the Gospel of Luke which sets out clearly the author's purpose in writing (Luke 1:1-4). But the same is true of the other Gospels, even if they do not state the point with equal explicitness. It is no less true of Paul who based the authority of his own preaching on his own personal experience of being called by the risen Jesus and also on the fact that his message was the same as that of the earliest Christians — a message that centred on the historical facts of Jesus' death, burial and resurrection, and of his appearances to reliable witnesses (1 Cor. 15:1-5). In other words, the message contained the sort of historical backing which would make sense to first-century audiences.

Why, then, should it be thought odd to offer to twentieth-century audiences the historical backing that they need in order to know whether they should commit themselves in faith to the Jesus who is the subject of Christian preaching? Modern people want to know if Jesus really existed. They want to know if he was the kind of person that the Gospels make him out to be. They want to know if he died and rose from the dead. They want to know whether his general manner of life supports the claims made on his behalf by Christians. And they are entitled to receive answers to these questions. [25]

Of course it is possible to believe in Jesus without having answers to these questions. Many people naïvely believe the message without having any proof offered to them. One does not need to know how electric current works in order to make use of it. But other people demand evidence before they will commit themselves. It is true that John's Gospel refers to the happy position of those who can believe in the risen Jesus without having seen him in the way that the first disciples did (John 20:29). This has sometimes been taken to mean that people ought to believe in the risen Jesus without evidence of any kind; but of course this is not the point. The contrast is between those who were the first believers, privileged to see the risen Jesus with their own eyes, and the later generations who have to believe on the evidence of those first witnesses and with the confirmation provided by their own spiritual experience; Jesus is emphasising that the latter group are no less privileged than the first group, and have not missed out on anything essential. But the latter group do have the evidence of the first group to confirm their own spiritual experience, and to demonstrate that their experience is an experience of Jesus and not of somebody or something else. And this question of identity and continuity remains important for the modern believer. Like the early church he has to ask what connection there is between his experience and that of the first Christians. He has to investigate the 'historical early church' as well as the 'historical Jesus'.

It appears, then, that we cannot do without the historical Jesus if we are to believe in the Christ of faith. And this necessity is twofold. On the one hand, the Christ of faith is related to the Jesus of history; the experience of the risen Lord has its historical root in the fact of Jesus. On the other hand, this historical root must be open to historical investigation, so that the believer may have both grounds for his faith and confirmation of his faith. The person who has Christian faith is a believer in the historical Jesus as the one who is now alive as the risen Lord. The person who believes simply in the supreme worth of the historical Jesus as a mere man is not a Christian believer, and his attitude fails to do justice to the transcendent elements in the New Testament picture of Jesus.

NOTES

1   D. M. Baillie, *God was in Christ: An Essay on Incarnation and Atonement*, London, 1948.
2   T. R. Glover, *The Jesus of History*, London, 1917.
3   T. W. Ogletree, *The 'Death of God' Controversy*, London, 1966.
4   Perhaps such people should call themselves 'Neo-Christians' or the like, but unfortunately most 'neo-' movements quickly become old hat.
5   One possible explanation is that such people knew nothing about the earthly life of Jesus. This view creates more difficulties than it solves. See I. H. Marshall, *Luke: Historian and Theologian*, Exeter, 1970, 48.
6   H.-J. Schoeps, *Jewish Christianity*, London, 1969.
7   For a survey of recent thinking on this subject see J. W. Fraser, *Jesus and Paul*, Abingdon, 1974.
8   H. E. Tödt, *The Son of Man in the Synoptic Tradition*, London, 1965, ch. 5.

9   D. M. Baillie, *op. cit.*, 63-79.

10   *Ibid.*, 74.

11   The existentialist understanding of biblical thought is particularly
     associated with R. Bultmann, although he himself would not go so far
     in this direction as some of those who have drawn inspiration from
     him. Thus it has been claimed that to be consistent Bultmann ought
     to demythologise the idea of God and get rid of it (S. M. Ogden, *Christ
     without Myth*, London, 1961), but he himself has refused to take this
     step. Similarly, Bultmann holds fast to the *fact* of Jesus, although he
     insists that we can know little about him by historical means. Others,
     however, (see n. 3 above for surveys of this school of thought) would
     attempt to dispense with God.

12   For the interpretation of biblical thought in terms of 'salvation
     history' see especially O. Cullmann, *Salvation in History*, London, 1967;
     cf. Christ and Time, London, 1951.

13   'The truth is not in the middle, and not in one extreme, but in both
     extremes.' Cited by H. C. G. Moule, *Charles Simeon*, London, 1948
     (originally 1892).

14   G. L. Borchert, 'Is Bultmann's Theology a New Gnosticism?' *The
     Evangelical Quarterly*, 36, 1964, 222-228; W. Rordorf, 'The Theology of
     Rudolf Bultmann and Second-Century Gnosis', *New Testament Studies*
     13, 1966-67, 351-362.

15   R. Bultmann, *Theology of the New Testament*, I, 3: '*The message of Jesus* is
     a presupposition for the theology of the New Testament rather than a
     part of that theology itself'.

16   Bultmann's 'last word' is contained in his essay, 'The Primitive
     Christian Kerygma and the Historical Jesus', in C. E. Braaten and R.
     A. Harrisville, *The Historical Jesus and the Kerygmatic Christ*, New York,
     1964, 15-42. Bultmann's thought is to be found scattered in a number
     of works, including *Essays, Philosophical and Theological*, London, 1954;
     Existence and Faith, London, 1961; *Jesus Christ and Mythology*. London,
     1960. The best guide to his thought, written from a sympathetic
     standpoint, is W. Schmithals, *An Introduction to the Theology of Rudolf
     Bultmann*, London, 1968.

17   M. Kähler, *The So-called Historical Jesus and the Historic Biblical Christ*,
     Philadelphia, 1964; the German original, *Der sogennante historische Jesus
     and der geschichtliche biblische Christus*, was published in 1896. It must be
     observed, however, that there has been a shift in terminology between
     Kähler and Bultmann. For Kähler, the 'historical Jesus' was a
     phantom created by rationalist scholars, while the 'biblical Christ' was
     the person who actually lived. For Bultmann, however, it is the former
     who actually lived. See D. Cairns, *A Gospel without Myth?* London,
     1960, 148; G. E. Ladd, 'The Search for Perspective', *Interpretation* 25,
     1971, 41-62.

18   See P. Althaus, *The So-called Kerygma and the Historical Jesus*, Edinburgh,
     1959.

19   R. Bultmann, *Theology of the New Testament*, I, 336.

20   'Thus it turns out in the end that Jesus as the Revealer of God *reveals*

nothing but that he is the Revealer. And that amounts to saying that it is he for whom the world is waiting, he who brings in his own person that for which all the longing of man yearns... But how is he that and how does he bring it? In no other way than that he says that he is it and says that he brings it — he, a man with his human word, which, without legitimation, demands faith.' (R. Bultmann, *Theology of the New Testament*, II, 66). Although this is a characterisation of the message of John's Gospel, it represents Bultmann's own position.

21   H. Conzelmann, *An Outline of the Theology of the New Testament*, London, 1969, 159f.

22   D. M. Baillie, *op. cit.*, 50.

23   *Ibid.*, 52.

24   G. N. Stanton, *Jesus of Nazareth in New Testament Preaching*, Cambridge, 1974.

25   The kind of proof demanded by modern readers will no doubt be different from that demanded by first-century readers and provided by the Evangelists. Our task is to see whether the Gospels contain the ingredients for a fresh presentation of the historical facts of the ministry of Jesus in a way that will appear cogent to the modern reader.

CHAPTER 5

Faith and Historical Study

WE BEGAN THIS book by listing some of the difficulties that
arise when we use the phrase 'the historical Jesus', and that
consequently surround any attempt to say something about
this mysterious person. We saw that considerable, though by
no means insurmountable, difficulties surround the task of
knowing anything for sure about the past (ch. 2) and that
these difficulties are increased when the figure in question is
possibly a unique one (ch. 3). We then explored the possibility of side-stepping these difficulties by leaving aside the
historical Jesus and basing religious faith on the risen Lord,
the Christ of faith, or upon the 'Christian message' through
which his religious significance may be communicated to us.
But we found that this simple solution would not work; belief
in the risen Lord inevitably pushes us towards the question of
the relation of the risen Lord to the historical figure, Jesus of
Nazareth (ch. 4).

We have now reached the point where we must look more
closely, but still in general terms, at the question of our
relationship to Jesus. Let us remind ourselves again that the
'text' which we are elucidating is 'I believe in the historical
Jesus'. So far we have not taken that word 'believe' very
seriously; it is time to bring it more fully into the discussion.

THE MEANING OF 'BELIEVE'

Our problem is that the word 'believe' can be used in various
ways. [1] First, it can be used with reference to statements
whose truth is uncertain. I say, 'I believe that John is forty

years old' in a situation where I cannot claim certain knowledge; and in such contexts the use of 'believe' is a way of expressing a certain degree of doubt. When I say, 'I know that John is forty years old', I am attaching a quality of certainty to the statement. I am implying that John himself has told me his age (and that I have no reasonable grounds for thinking that he is mistaken, or that he deliberately told a lie, or that I misheard what he said), or that I have seen his birth certificate, or that I have some other evidence which in normal circumstances can be regarded as putting the point beyond *reasonable* dispute. Doubt is perhaps not altogether excluded — my informant might have been mistaken, or the birth certificate might have been forged — but the evidence is what would normally be considered adequate. If, however, I say that I *believe* that John is forty years old, I am allowing for the possibility of mistake. I am perhaps remembering what somebody else told me, and allowing for the possibility that I have not remembered the figure accurately or that the informant was misinformed. I am admitting that the statement could be challenged, and that I would be prepared to change my opinion in the light of better evidence.

When, however, I say, 'I believe that God exists', I am doing something slightly different. Here the function of 'believe' is not so much to express doubt as to express conviction. I am expressing a sentiment on which I am willing to stake my life, although it may not be susceptible of strict proof. [2] I am taking up a position, perhaps because I consider the evidence to be adequate for me to believe it, while I recognise that it will not necessarily convince everybody else. In this sense, 'believe' suggests that the believer has grounds for his conviction other than the usual type of historical or scientific evidence.

A further use of 'believe' is with reference to persons or things in which a person puts his trust and to which he commits himself. So 'I believe in the Liberal Party' is to be taken as meaning that I believe that this political party is trustworthy and that I am prepared to give it my support by voting and working for it. In the same way 'I believe in God' *includes* the statement 'I believe that God exists' but also includes the idea of commitment to God. This is an important distinction because a person who declares that he believes that God exists is not necessarily committing himself to a way of life based on positive acceptance of this belief. Religious commitment is different from religious knowledge, but depends upon religious knowledge. [3]

The distinction between these two types of belief, which we may label as 'belief that' and 'belief in', is obvious enough once it has been stated. Difficulties arise, first, because, 'belief in' implies 'belief that', and second, because the grammatical form of a statement is not necessarily a reliable guide to its logical form. When I say 'I believe that the Liberal Party has the answer to the country's problems', I am at the same time expressing a belief *in* that Party. A person who says 'I believe in God' may be implying no more than his belief that God exists. But he may be expressing his trust in God to comfort and help him in a time of grief or difficulty. So Paul comforted his fellow-travellers in a storm at sea by declaring, 'Take heart, men, for I have faith in God that it will be exactly as I have been told' (Acts 27:25). [4]

DOES HISTORY REST ON FAITH?

We now come back to the historical Jesus. From what has just been said it is clear that the statement, 'I believe in the historical Jesus', can convey a number of different ideas. It could mean, 'I trust in Jesus'. A typical form of service for persons becoming members of the church of Jesus Christ includes the question: 'Do you truly repent of your sins, and believe in the Lord Jesus Christ as your Saviour?' When the candidate replies, 'I do', he obviously means more than that he simply believes in the existence of Jesus and the fact that he is portrayed in the Bible as a saviour; he means that he puts his trust in Jesus to act as a saviour to him, and that he declares his allegiance to Jesus. We are not concerned with this kind of belief at this point in our enquiry. We are dealing with the prior question whether there was a historical Jesus who can be regarded as a saviour. To say, 'I believe in the historical Jesus', is therefore to say, 'I believe that Jesus existed and that he said and did such-and-such'.

But why do we use 'believe' rather than 'know' in this statement? One reason is that we are expressing a conviction and taking up a position. There are people who do not believe in Jesus in this way, and we are declaring a stance over against them. Where other people may scoff at the policies of, say, the Liberal Party, the person who says that he believes in the Liberal Party is affirming his conviction that its policies are right and good for the nation. We use 'I believe' to express a conviction in matters that are disputed, and very often in matters (like politics and religion) where we have strong feelings on the subject.

Another reason, however, may be that we are not certain about the truth of the statement which we are making. We know that other people disagree with us, and therefore we have in all honesty to recognise the fact that we may be wrong. We may be fairly sure that time will show that the policies of the Liberal Party were justified, but we have to admit that it may not turn out like that; we could be wrong, and so we let our expression of conviction be coloured by a certain degree of caution.

It is also possible, however, that we are implying that our conviction lies beyond strict proof by experiment or reason. We use the statement, 'I know', in situations where we think that *any* rational person having full access to the relevant information will come to the same conclusion as ourselves.

In practice we use 'I know' in situations where such certainty is not absolutely attainable. It is doubtful whether we can make statements of absolute certainty outside the spheres of mathematics and logic where we are dealing with the working out of the logical consequences of given propositions. As soon as we emerge into the world of real events, we find that we can make only statements of high probability or statements which are imprecise. And this is true even in the area of scientific theory. A scientific theory is 'true' only until it is disproved, and progress in science depends on the continuous sifting of theories and their replacement by better ones. This point is worth emphasising, because people often contrast the certainties of science with the uncertainties of history. It needs to be remembered that absolute knowledge is hard to obtain in any sphere. Nevertheless, we can use the phrase 'I know' to refer to statements whose truth is as near to certainty as makes no difference; within our existing frame of reference we can rightly speak of 'knowing'. And the characteristic of 'knowing' is that it is a common possession; 'knowledge' is knowledge for everybody.

But there are areas where it is inappropriate to speak of knowledge. We have taken political theory as an obvious example. Here the range of relevant evidence is so great and the difficulty in assessing its significance so vast that equally competent workers can come to differing conclusions from the same evidence. In such situations a man can only express a conviction based on study of the evidence — and must have the grace to admit that he may be wrong. There is an element in such study that goes, as it were, beyond reason. It is inappropriate to speak of 'knowledge' in such a context. Similar considerations will apply in philosophy and metaphysics, and also in the study of history, which is our present interest.

Our problem is complicated by the fact that the borderline between 'knowledge' and 'belief' is a fluid and imprecise one. In any subject there is a mixture of items of information, some of which are matters of knowledge and others of which are matters of belief. Many of these items may be capable of passing from one category to another. Fresh evidence may make some matter of belief into a matter of knowledge or may suggest that some piece of knowledge is not as well-founded as it was thought to be.

This situation applies in science as much as in other less precise areas of knowledge. It used to be thought that science contained a body of knowledge, built up by means of reasoning on the basis of evidence and offering certain conclusions. Nowadays it is recognised that things are not so simple. The scientist does not assemble a body of evidence and then erect a theory on the basis of it, which can be confirmed by further experiment. Rather he postulates a theory, often as a result of some imaginative insight, and then proceeds to see whether it can be refined into something more precise; and this process of falsifying existing hypotheses and replacing them by better ones goes on continually. There is no final knowledge in science. Even so respectable a theory as Newton's laws of gravitation proved inadequate to explain all the phenomena and had to be replaced by Einstein's theory of relativity. And Einstein's theory itself is not the last word on the subject. [5]

The historian, therefore, need not feel ashamed if he has to qualify many of his statements with a 'probably' or an 'as far as we can tell'. He is not really in a different situation from the physicist, although the latter is able to claim a much higher degree of certainty for his statements.

Consequently, when a person says 'I believe in the historical Jesus', he may not be expressing any greater uncertainty than a historian who says that he believes in the historical Julius Caesar. In the last analysis all historical knowledge is a matter of belief — belief in the validity of historical reasoning, belief in the reliability of the evidence, belief in the reconstruction erected on the basis of the evidence. The position of Jesus is in principle no different from that of any other historical person.

This point is of some importance theologically. It is sometimes argued that faith ought not to depend on the results of historical research. The possibility of my trusting in Jesus should not be dependent on a historian proving to me that Jesus really existed and did certain things which entitle me to believe that he is a saviour. That would be to make faith dependent on historical research and to deprive it of its character as faith. But if our argument is valid, this objection falls to the ground. For what we have claimed is that there is an element of faith in the task of the historian. To greater or lesser extent the results which the historian obtains are matters of probability, and the historian has to exercise faith in the course of obtaining them. This means that it is wrong to distinguish faith and historical research, as if the one excluded the other. Rather, faith works in and through historical research, even though the believer may not be conscious that this is what he is doing.

DOES HISTORY REST ON RELIGIOUS FAITH?

However, this is by no means the whole story. The kind of

faith of which we have been speaking is that which is shown by any scholar who believes in the possibility of his type of research and in the conclusions which he draws from it. The effect of our discussion has simply been to show that faith is not excluded from scientific and historical enquiry. But such faith is perhaps not specifically religious faith. We must ask what difference this may make to our discussion.

Religious faith and secular faith

Perhaps we should begin by asking whether religious faith is different from the type of faith of which we have been speaking. We established earlier that it contained elements of intellectual belief, trust and commitment, and it is thus a more comprehensive attitude than the faith of the historian, although in a sense the historian can be said to commit himself to his belief in the historical method and to work on the basis of it. But there does not appear to be any difference of kind. If there is a difference, it is to be sought in two other directions. First, the object of Christian faith is God or the risen Lord. Is not this object sufficiently different from other objects of faith to make the character of faith itself different? But, it may be replied, is faith in *God* any different in character from faith in a human person? Is not faith in God often understood in terms of the analogy with faith in a person, as when a small child trusts its father or a wife trusts her husband? And is not the alternative to faith in God an attitude of faith in something else? It may be doubtful whether an atheist will confess to believing in anything, but he probably has some 'ultimate concern' (to use P. Tillich's helpful phrase) which serves as a substitute for God. Without going into detail, we may perhaps conclude that religious, or more specifically Christian, faith is not different in character from other types of faith simply because it is faith in God.

Second, Christian faith is said to be due to the work of the Holy Spirit in a man. The ordinary man, we are told, cannot receive or understand the things of God. It is only when his mind is illumined by the Spirit of God and his heart moved by the same Spirit that he is able to believe in God and in

Christ. The whole process of believing is the gift of God. [6]
Surely, then, religious faith is a supernatural occurrence, of a
different character from ordinary faith? But, granted all these
points, it is questionable whether they make religious faith
into something different in kind from other types of faith.
They ascribe its origin to divine influence, they make it clear
that no man is capable of such faith by his own efforts or on
his own initiative, but they do not indicate that the attitude
of man thus set in action by the Spirit of God is an attitude
different in kind from other human affections and attitudes.[7]
The attitude of the unbeliever is equally due to supernatural
influence, since his blindness and lack of faith are due to the
action of Satan. [8] Both belief and unbelief are affected by
factors on the supernatural level.

The result of these comments is to suggest that there is no
difference in principle between ordinary faith and Christian
faith which would affect the conclusion so far reached.

Faith and the historical Jesus

But the matter goes deeper. The Christian believer is one
who believes in the risen Christ; he accepts his spiritual
reality and has committed his life to him. He is thus aware of
the reality of the risen Christ by means other than historical
research. And it is tempting to argue backwards from belief in
this reality to belief in the historicity of Jesus. Thus it can be
argued that our belief in the historicity of the resurrection of
Jesus is shown to be true by our experience of the present
reality of the risen Lord. 'You ask me how I know he lives?
He lives within my heart' is a popular expression of this
outlook. And, therefore, even if the historical evidence for the
resurrection of Jesus were ambiguous, even if the evidence
were apparently against it, the Christian believer would still
profess his belief that God raised Jesus from the dead, staking
his belief on the fact of his spiritual knowledge of the risen
Lord. The point can be taken further. If there is doubt, for
example, about whether the historical Jesus could have
performed miracles, the believer in the risen Christ will assert
that the historical Jesus (who is identical with the risen
Christ) was able to perform them. [9] We thus appear to have a

path to the historical Jesus which is independent of historical research. The Christian believer has a type of faith which is not the same thing as the faith of the historian in the validity of his method and its results, and by means of this faith he appears to have an alternative means of access to Jesus. By virtue of his faith he is able to pronounce his belief in certain historical facts which might otherwise be regarded as very questionable.

Our discussion has indicated that it is especially the supernatural features in the biblical account of Jesus which are said to be guaranteed by faith, although 'ordinary' events such as the death of Jesus would also be guaranteed in the same kind of way. This makes the task of evaluating this approach all the more difficult.

Can belief in the reality of the risen Lord substantiate belief in the historicity of Jesus? Such an approach is certainly open to dangers. Thus there is a parallel between this attitude and that which was associated with some historians of the Hegelian school of philosophy who were not above saying what *must* have taken place in history in view of their philosophical principles, and who evaluated their principles more highly than the historical evidence. The Christian believer may appear to stand in the same dangerous situation of preferring what his faith tells him to what the facts testify.

At the same time, this kind of approach may be intensely subjective and individualistic. Because of *my* faith in the risen Christ I may believe certain things about the historical life of Jesus, but if somebody else does not share my religious faith he may not be able to share my view of history. If so, there is no way of persuading him open to me. Our attitude to the facts differs because of the different perspectives in which we examine them. Historical debate becomes impossible.

Moreover, we have to face the question of how we estimate the validity and relevance of our religious experiences. I may have an experience which I claim to be an experience of the risen Christ. But how do I know that this is the case, and more important, how do I know that this experience has any connection with the historical Jesus?

In short, this approach looks highly subjective and arbitrary. It is not surprising that some scholars argue that religious faith in the risen Lord has no relevance for the historical study of Jesus, and that such study must be carried out 'objectively' without reference to faith.[10] The whole nineteenth-century enterprise in search of the historical Jesus can be represented as an attempt to be objective, and to discover what picture of Jesus emerges when religious presuppositions are put aside.

Unfortunately, the laying aside of these presuppositions usually leads to their replacement by another set of presuppositions. The student of the historical Jesus comes up sooner or later against the supernatural elements in the story, and he judges these in the light of his presuppositions. If he judges that 'miracles cannot happen', then he will assess the historicity of the accounts in one particular way. If he is open to the possibility of miracles, he will assess them in a different way. But which of these two ways is right? There are many factors involved in discussing the historicity of such stories, factors which can perhaps be discussed without presuppositions entering into the debate, but sooner or later this fundamental question comes into focus. The point of entry may well be the accounts of the resurrection of Jesus. Did Jesus rise from the dead or not? But surely one of the relevant factors in answering this question is whether there is any evidence that Christ is alive today. Much of the evidence from the past consists of the testimony of various people who claimed that Jesus had appeared to them or that they were conscious of his living presence. The question then arises whether these experiences were real, and whether they can be accounted for by natural causes. And one relevant factor in assessing the situation is whether such a consciousness corresponds to anything in contemporary experience. If there is nothing quite like it, we may be tempted to dismiss the accounts of past experiences as delusions or hallucinations. If, however, there is some correspondence between modern experience and ancient experience, we shall look at things in a different light.[11]

Suppose, for example, that some accounts have come down to us relating how certain people in the ancient world had

unusual powers of guessing secret messages. If their powers
were beyond what is possible by ordinary rational means, or
what might be achieved by luck, we might be tempted to suspect that the stories were exaggerated or fictitious. But suppose now that there exist contemporary well-authenticated
cases of extra-sensory perception. If that is the case, we
should want to revise our opinion about what was and was
not possible in the ancient world. Things that could not be
explained previously may now be susceptible to explanation in terms of extra-sensory perception. And even if the
character of extra-sensory perception remains obscure, we
may still use it as a proper category of explanation for the
ancient events — until such time as a better explanation is
forthcoming.

In the same way, we shall be tempted to approach the New
Testament accounts of the resurrection in a different manner
if there is something comparable in our own experience. It
may be replied that we ought to subject our own experience
to the same rigorous 'objective' scrutiny as is needed in the
case of the New Testament narratives. Fair enough. But this
does not mean that these experiences will necessarily be
interpreted in naturalistic terms. A naturalistic explanation of
Jesus and of Christian experience is one that rules out the
possibility of the supernatural. It *may* be the right explanation. It is not necessarily the only one. The problem is
whether we are prepared to allow the possibility of a
supernatural explanation where this appears to be called for.

We are obviously in the area of presuppositions. The
question of the supernatural may indeed belong to the
category of absolute presuppositions, the kind which, according to R. G. Collingwood, cannot be verified but whose
usefulness depends on their logical efficacy. [12] In other words,
whether we accept an absolute presupposition depends on its
usefulness as a means of explaining the universe.

The dialectic of presuppositions and evidence

Suppose that a person who disbelieves in the possibility of
supernatural events comes up against some event for which
every explanation except a supernatural explanation seems to

be ruled out. What is he to do? He may resolve to hold on to his presuppositions and regard the alleged supernatural event as something which he cannot explain on these presuppositions; but he is not prepared to let it upset his presuppositions and therefore he suspends judgment upon it. It is always possible that some new evidence or explanation may turn up. This is a perfectly fair procedure. It is followed by many Christians who come up against facts in the world (*e.g.* the problem of suffering) which *prima facie* set a large question mark against their Christian theistic presuppositions. Very often they are content to admit that they cannot reconcile their belief in God with the problem of suffering, but they believe that ultimately some reconciliation will be possible, and that therefore they are justified in retaining their Christian world view.

On the other hand, the person may realise that the fact which he cannot explain knocks a fair-sized dent in his presuppositions, and therefore he is prepared to revise them, and if necessary alter them. Faced by the problem of the supernatural, the unbeliever may turn to theism; and faced by the problem of pain, the theist may turn to atheism. A third possibility is that in both cases the perplexed thinker may seek refuge in agnosticism, concluding that it is not possible for us to combine all phenomena in a satisfactory world view.

There is perhaps no way of determining how a person's mind is going to work in such a situation. But what our argument is meant to show is that presuppositions and evidence stand in a dialectical relationship to one another. We interpret evidence in the light of our presuppositions, and we also form our presuppositions in the light of the evidence. It is only through a 'dialogue' between presuppositions and evidence that we can gain both sound presuppositions and a correct interpretation of the evidence. The process is circular and unending. It demands openness on the part of the investigator. He must be prepared to revise his ideas in the light of the evidence, for ultimately it is the evidence which is decisive.

Some Christians would claim that the evidence for Christianity is unambiguous and that any honest investigator should be led to acknowledge its truth. Others admit that while they find it convincing it is not of such a character that all rational men will necessarily be persuaded by it. The fact that distinguished thinkers can examine the evidence for Christianity and fail to be convinced by it suggests that the second alternative must be accepted by Christians, at least as a working hypothesis. This does not mean that the believer is uncertain about his belief; for him the evidence points decisively in a particular direction. But he must allow other people the right to differ.

What this means for our present task is that both believer and unbeliever must approach the historical evidence regarding Jesus with open minds on the possibilities. The Christian comes with his particular world view, to which all kinds of experience have contributed, and therefore he approaches Jesus in a particular way, but basically his task is to ask what is the correct interpretation of the evidence, the correct interpretation being the one which provides a coherent explanation of all the evidence. He is prepared to let his world view be altered by the evidence, but his world view is part of the evidence, and cannot be simply laid aside. But he must allow the same liberty to the person who does not share his Christian outlook. There is, in other words, nothing illegitimate from the Christian point of view about a rationalist attempt to explain the evidence regarding Jesus. The debate regarding its validity will centre on whether it does justice to all the evidence, historical and otherwise.

The effect of this argument is to allow the Christian to bring his experience of the risen Lord into the picture. He has a right to bring his presuppositions into the discussion, provided that he is conscious of them, and that he is prepared to revise them in the light of the evidence.

But is experience of the risen Christ relevant to the question of the historical Jesus? Such experience of the risen Lord, which might otherwise be regarded as a 'spiritual experience' capable of being interpreted in various ways, is in fact tied closely to the historical Jesus. For the thing that gives rise to this spiritual experience is in fact the story of Jesus as interpreted in the New Testament. Present experience of the risen Lord is generated directly or indirectly by the biblical account of Jesus, and it therefore stands on a level with the experience of early Christians. It is not a case of a person having an experience of an unknown character and then resolving to call it an experience of the risen Lord; the experience cannot be had and be recognised as such apart from the hearing of the Christian message. Consequently, it is legitimate to appeal to modern experience as part of the evidence which must be examined in a study of the resurrection of Jesus. If the historical question of the resurrection is a relevant factor in determining the validity of a modern experience of the risen Lord, it would seem to follow that the reverse is also true, that modern experience must be a relevant factor in discussion of the historical facts regarding the resurrection of Jesus.

The fact that present experience of the risen Lord is generated by the biblical account of Jesus provides an adequate reply to the charge that to bring modern experience into the historical debate is as dangerous as the attempt to interpret history in the light of Hegelian presuppositions. In the latter case an alien element imported from philosophy is being used to understand historical evidence, and this element is not subjected to the controls imposed by the evidence or revised in the light of the evidence. But in the case of faith in the risen Lord, the experience arises out of the evidence and the character of the experience is shaped by the evidence. Certain forms of experience which might be regarded as experiences of the risen Lord may be ruled out of court because they do not conform to what would be expected in the light of the biblical evidence. The appeal to experience is corrected by the historical evidence. In this way the point of view which we have been defending escapes the criticism which is levelled against it.

If this defence is valid, it follows that it can be relevant to historical study to make use of the evidence of personal, spiritual experience in assessing evidence from the past, since the two are inter-related and form a unity. But the negative point must also be admitted. If a person fails to have a personal experience of the risen Lord, this may prove to him that the biblical evidence does not support belief in the resurrection of Jesus. What is essential is that both believer and unbeliever approach the evidence with a readiness to follow it wherever it leads, even if this means an upturning of their earlier ideas.

CAN FAITH REST ON HISTORY?

In the earlier part of this chapter we have in effect been asking the question: can historical study depend on faith? We have argued for two main points in reply to this question. Firstly, we have claimed that all historical study involves elements of imagination and faith in that the historian, possessed of only partial and sometimes enigmatic evidence, has to exercise a measure of faith in the reliability of the evidence, the validity of historical study, and the possibility of constructing a model which will account satisfactorily for the evidence. Unless the historian is prepared to take some leaps in the dark, he will not be able to make any progress at all.

Secondly, we have argued that in the particular case of the historical Jesus it is inevitable that a person's Christian faith or lack of it will be part of the total evidence which he must consider, and that it is right for the historian to bring this factor into consideration — provided that he is prepared to let the historical evidence and his faith enter into a kind of dialogue with the possibility that his faith will be at risk and may need revision in the light of historical study.

We may note in passing that this is not something peculiar to the study of Christian origins. Let a capitalist politician, for example, examine historically the development of his own political outlook in comparison with Marxism. He will find that it is impossible to make an 'objective' study from a point of view that transcends both outlooks. He will without doubt find himself compelled to make judgments about the thinking and actions of politicians and political groups. As a capitalist he will find himself saying that such-and-such a Marxist did politically foolish things. He judges them by a standard from which he finds it difficult to detach himself. But he may also see some actions of his own political group in a less favourable light. He may be led to challenge some of the traditional understandings of the history of his party. He may even be led to conclude that in the light of history his party has really made a poor showing, that its ideas were really inferior to those of its Marxist opponents, and so on. By doing historical study he may find himself undergoing a conversion. It is a risk that is inherent in historical study. The important point, however, is that it is impossible to discuss political history without one's own political attitudes becoming involved in the process.

But now we must try and look at the relationship the other way round. Can faith be dependent on historical study? This question arises directly out of the first one, for the implication of the preceding section is that if faith is dependent on the results of historical study, it becomes a very precarious affair. It may easily be upturned by shifts in historical conclusions.

There is something of a paradox here. On the one hand, there are people who tell us that we should not have a faith which is dependent on historical study, because this is in effect to replace faith by knowledge and to destroy the element of trust — and with it the element of risk — in real faith. [13] We have already done something to meet this argument by showing that faith is already involved to such an extent in historical study that the elements of trust and risk are certainly not absent. But, on the other hand, we may be told that this is precisely what is wrong with basing faith on history: it makes faith continually dependent on the uncertain conclusions of the historians and destroys any permanency that faith may have. It puts the simple Christian at the mercy of the historians and deprives him of direct access to the object of his faith. You only need to have a historian coming along and showing that the resurrection of Jesus did not happen — and faith is instantly deprived of its basis. An archaeologist may discover the bones of Jesus in a grave in Palestine, and if your faith is in the *physical* resurrection of Jesus, you've had it. (Of course, you can get yourself off the hook by switching to belief in some kind of *spiritual* resurrection).

What are we to make of this objection? Do the two objections in fact cancel each other out? Or are they directed against different understandings of Christian faith? Or are they attacks from opposite directions?

In the light of what has already been said, the correct answer may be to accept the point contained in the objection, in other words, to admit that faith is continually at risk because of the uncertainties inherent in history. But let us see what is involved in this.

To begin with, it could be argued that the same thing is true of the challenge presented to Christianity in other spheres of knowledge. If Christianity is dependent on some particular philosophical outlook, then it is at risk whenever philosophers produce arguments to show that the philosophical outlook in question is illogical or otherwise faulty. Thus Christianity implies a theistic understanding of the universe, and there can be a Christian philosophy which understands reality in theistic terms. Such a philosophy is a standing object for attack by philosophers. There is a set of philosophical arguments for the existence of God; one and all they have been declared incapable of proving the existence of God. It is an open question to my mind whether these attacks have succeeded. It is also possible for Christian philosophers to attack non-theistic interpretations of reality put up by non-Christian philosophers. Again it is an open question whether such attacks have succeeded. The point is simply that in this area, as in the area of history, Christian faith is open to attack and defence.

The same point could be made with regard to the age-old conflict between science and religion. It has been argued that science shows religion to be false, and the contrary position has equally been argued. Once Christian faith is related to any field of human knowledge there is the possibility of debate and conflict, and the risk of what appears to be an irresistible case against Christianity gaining the upper hand. And this is true, whether the area in question is one concerning the empirical universe or the universe of thought.

One might hope to escape this conflict by escaping into the world of mystical experience, but the validity of mystical experience can also be challenged, especially when different people have different kinds of experience, and it is suggested that the claims of Christian mysticism to mediate true religious experience are no better than those of Moslem or Buddhist mysticism.

The point which is being made is the simple one that the Christian faith is always open to attack when it claims dependence on any kind of human knowledge or makes statements about any field of human knowledge. The alternative is to have a form of Christianity which has no relationship whatever to human knowledge and experience. Some people have tried to produce such a type of Christianity, usually by casting off the moorings that tie Christianity to history, but the results are anything but satisfactory. First, the cutting of this particular set of mooring ropes still leaves others attached. Bultmann's non-historical brand of Christianity is firmly tied to Heideggerian existentialism — and who can be sure that this philosophy will prove to contain absolute truth? Secondly, the cutting loose of Christianity from its ties with the real world emasculates its character and produces a vague, unsatisfying religion which has nothing to say about human life. Maybe this is why much of contemporary Christianity makes so little impact in the Western world. Our cultured version of it, too smooth for its opponents to grasp hold of it, is also too smooth to make any impression on the world as it glides past.

Christianity, then, cannot help being vulnerable to attack so long as it says anything meaningful in respect of human knowledge and experience. However, it may be objected that the area of history is on a different level from the other areas to which we have alluded. For our knowledge of Christianity is mediated to us by means of historical events and their interpretation. Whereas attacks on the Christian faith by philosophers and scientists strike more at the fringe, attacks by historians strike at the centre of the faith, since it is only through history that we can perceive the central act of revelation in Jesus Christ. If we cannot know anything for certain about the historical Jesus or the other historical facts which are commonly regarded by Christians as the means of divine revelation, then the foundation of our faith is highly vulnerable and uncertain.

Lessing's famous claim that 'accidental truths of history can never become the proof of necessary truths of reason' is not strictly relevant here, since the Christian religion is not based on an attempt to derive truths of reason from truths of history; it is concerned rather with historical facts which can be seen as instruments of divine revelation, happenings in which God is active to reveal himself in judgment and salvation. Nevertheless, Lessing's argument can be reformulated as a claim that the acceptance of certain historical facts as means of divine revelation is weakly based if the historicity of the events in which God is believed to have revealed himself is in doubt. [14]

But it may be said in reply that the strength of the historical argument for Christianity is that of a piece of chain mail rather than that of a single chain. There are ever so many historical facts involved in the self-revelation of God in biblical history as a whole and in Jesus in particular, and the uncertainty of some of these does not cast doubt on the certainty of the others. To call one fact, or even several, about Jesus into question does not mean that other facts about him are also doubtful. The fact that a movie film may contain a number of badly-focussed or poorly-lit frames does not mean that the film as a whole is faulty or that the general sequence of the story is necessarily unintelligible. The possibility that every important historical fact about Jesus could be convincingly denied is highly remote.

But Lessing held that if there was *any* doubt at all about historical facts, he could not stake his life on them. This attitude of methodological doubt is, in fact, nonsensical. Lessing is able to maintain it only by drawing a distinction between past events, for which he is dependent on the testimony of others, and present events which he is able to observe for himself, and evidently he is prepared to act on the basis of the latter. But present facts are not necessarily any more reliable than past facts, and the evidence of one's own senses may be inferior to that of other observers. If Lessing was prepared to trust the one, he should have been prepared to concede that the other also offered a basis for belief and action. There is an inevitable risk in accepting any testimony, whether that of one's own senses and judgment or that of somebody else, but this does not stop us from taking the risk of belief. One suspects that Lessing was simply being 'thrawn' (as we say in Scotland), and that his difficulties arose more from his dislike of Christianity than from an alleged weak historical foundation.

In conclusion, it may be useful to remember that Christian faith is ultimately dependent upon what actually happened rather than upon the views of historians. A Christian who believes in the saving efficacy of the death of Jesus is saved by that death and not by theories of the atonement. The theories of theologians, like those of historians, are subject to change and uncertainty, but this does not affect the saving character of the cross experienced by the believer. In this situation the Christian may well believe that he is saved by the death of Jesus, even though he lacks full understanding of the process. But he seeks that full understanding; his situation is that of *fides quaerens intellectum*, 'faith seeking understanding'. He seeks understanding by means of theological study, so that his faith is active in his theological study, just as it must also be in historical study. The fact that he may not reach certain answers to his questions in theology or history does not take away the reality of his Christian experience or the objective significance of the cross. The real threat to faith would be if it could be proved historically that Jesus had never died, and that he could not have been the Son of God; but the former of these points lies beyond all reasonable historical doubt, and the latter is beyond the reach of historical disproof. Our faith thus rests on the historical event of Jesus to which testimony is given in the Gospels with their fusion of fact and interpretation.

Christian faith and historical study of the Gospels thus stand in a dialectical relationship. The Christian's faith has as its object the Jesus whose earthly life is a matter for historical investigation, but this investigation cannot be carried on in independence of faith. We have attempted to prove the nature of this relationship between faith and historical study and thereby to clarify the nature of both components, and have seen that it is possible to combine rigorous historical study with Christian faith. Certainly there is nothing in the relationship between history and faith which makes it impossible in principle for a person to confess 'I believe in the historical Jesus' — always bearing in mind, of course, that the Jesus of Christian belief is more than a merely historical figure.

NOTES

1 The *Concise Oxford Dictionary* offers the meanings: 'Have faith *in*, trust word of (person); put trust *in* truth of a statement...; give credence to...; be of opinion *that*'.

2 English word usage is, however, flexible. When a person says (echoing Job), 'I know that my redeemer lives', he is using 'know' as a strengthened form of 'believe', in order to indicate that he has the strongest possible grounds for his conviction.

3 The word 'know' cannot be easily used in this sense of commitment since this element of trust and commitment is lacking from the word. The oddity of 'believe' is that it combines the apparently contradictory motifs of doubt and trust. 'I believe in one God...' allows for the possibility that my belief may be falsifiable, but at the same time indicates my commitment to it.

4 For the biblical usage see R. Bultmann and A. Weiser's article in G. Kittel (ed.), *Theological Dictionary of the New Testament*, Grand Rapids, 1968, VI, 174-228; O. Michel's article in C. Brown (ed.), *The New International Dictionary of New Testament Theology*, Exeter, 1975, I, 593-606.

5 For this view of scientific method see the writings of K. Popper; a convenient introduction is provided by B. Magee, *Popper*, London, 1973.

6 See 1 Cor. 2:14; Eph. 2:8.

7 It is thus the fact that a person realises that it is *God* in whom he ought to trust which is due to divine illumination, and it is the ability to trust in God rather than in any other object of faith which is the gift of God.

8 See Luke 8:12; 2 Cor. 4:4.

9 This point would strictly confirm merely the possibility of miracles; it would not necessarily confirm the truth of any particular miracle story.

10 This approach is particularly associated with W. Marxsen who would reject the possibility of deducing the historical fact of the resurrection of Jesus from present-day spiritual experience: 'By means of spiritual perception no *event* is grasped, no historical fact, but merely the significance of a phenomenon open to others as well... If the question is raised how the facticity of Jesus' resurrection is established, this can only be answered in historical terms. The historical verdict cannot be refuted in spiritual terms.' ('The Resurrection of Jesus as a Historical and Theological Problem', in C. F. D. Moule (ed.), *The Significance of the Message of the Resurrection for Faith in Jesus Christ*, London, 1968, 15-50; citation from 21f.).

11 For this insistence that contemporary experience of the resurrection of Jesus is relevant to a historical assessment of the evidence see G. O'Collins, *The Easter Jesus*, London, 1973, pt. 2.

12 R. G. Collingwood, *An Essay on Metaphysics*, Oxford, 1940, 21-33.

13   'The historical Jesus as a proven divine fact is a worldly security with
     which the *homo religiosus* arms himself in his attempt to become
     self-sufficient before God, just as did the Jew in Paul's day by appeal
     to the law. Whereas the *kerygma* calls for existential commitment to the
     meaning of Jesus, the original quest was an attempt to avoid the risk
     of faith by supplying objectively verified proof for its "faith". To
     require an objective legitimisation of the saving event prior to faith is
     to take offence at the offence of Christianity and to perpetuate the
     unbelieving flight to security, *i.e.* the reverse of faith' (J. M. Robinson,
     A New Quest of the Historical Jesus, London, 1959, 44).

14   G. E. Lessing, 'On the Proof of the Spirit and of Power', in H.
     Chadwick, *Lessing's Theological Writings*, Cambridge, 1956, 51-56,
     citation from 53. For discussion see Chadwick's introduction, 30-35; G.
     W. Bromiley, 'History and Truth: A Study of the Axiom of Lessing',
     The Evangelical Quarterly 18, 1946, 191-198.

CHAPTER 6

The Search for
the Historical Jesus

IN A SENSE the whole of our discussion so far has consisted in clearing the ground. We have examined the nature of historical study and seen what is meant by the phrase 'the historical Jesus' as used by different writers. We have faced up to the problem caused by the possible supernatural elements in the story. We have discussed the relationship between faith and historical study, and argued that neither of these excludes the other. In other words, we have tried to establish on general historical and theological grounds the validity and the possibility of a historical study of Jesus.

Now we must look at the problems raised when such historical study is attempted. What happens when historians do study Jesus? At the very outset of this book we saw that some of them come to highly sceptical conclusions about the details of his life. Some of the reasons for such conclusions have already been discussed. A person, for example, who disbelieves in the ability of the historical method to establish any reliable facts is not going to accept the story of Jesus as history. But such a wholesale rejection of historical study is completely unjustified. A person who disbelieves in the supernatural may also want to reject large parts of the story of Jesus on the grounds that they cannot possibly be historical; but we have argued that the historian must at least preserve an open mind in this regard, and that if the historical evidence is good, and if a reasonable world view allows for the possibility of the supernatural, then the historian cannot rule it out as impossible.

But now we must face up to the question of whether we do have the evidence and the critical tools which the historian needs in order to construct a picture of the historical Jesus. In order to understand the problems involved it may be most useful to draw a historical sketch of the process of 'historical study of Jesus'.

THE NINETEENTH-CENTURY QUEST

The standard historical surveys of our theme, which are in number like the sand of the seashore, [1] usually follow the example of Albert Schweitzer in locating the beginning of historical study of Jesus in the writings of H. S. Reimarus (1694-1768) which were published posthumously by G. E. Lessing in 1778. [2] Reimarus was certainly not the first to raise the question of the historical Jesus, but he did so in such a way that his work can be seen as symbolising the beginning of the modern self-consciously critical era. What Reimarus did was simply to ask whether the real, earthly Jesus was the sort of person whom the Evangelists made him out to be. And he answered his own question in a decidedly negative manner. The real Jesus was 'a Jewish revolutionary who failed in an attempt to establish an earthly Messianic kingdom'; the Christ of the Gospels was by contrast 'a deception created by the disciples who stole the body of Jesus from the tomb and invented the doctrines of the resurrection and the parousia'. [3]

We shall not spend time in summarising the views of Reimarus's many successors in the nineteenth century. Many of them are little more than names today. But the re-publication in English of the most famous of these nineteenth-century studies, that of D. F. Strauss, [4] shows that the issues raised then are by no means dead today, and that the same kind of motives that inspired their approach are still active in twentieth-century study. What, then, were the issues that arose in this discussion?

One such issue was rationalism. Many of these investigators believed that the real Jesus must have been an ordinary person with nothing supernatural or divine about him. His life must have conformed to ordinary human patterns, and be explicable in purely human categories. For such people the phrase 'the historical Jesus' clearly meant a non-supernatural Jesus. They further believed that if the Gospels were examined critically, such a picture of Jesus would emerge from them, a picture somewhat different from that which had been uncritically accepted by the church.

A second issue that emerged was the way in which the Gospels must be studied. Orthodox Christians placed the Gospels upon a pedestal, regarding them as being entirely trustworthy, and thus in effect treating them differently from other historical sources. But now it was claimed that the Gospels must be subjected to the normal processes of historical study. Their reliability could not be taken for granted. It must be tested. They must be studied like any other books and not exempted from the rigours of historical investigation.

A third point is that it was firmly believed by many students that when the Gospels were examined in this kind of way it would be possible to obtain results. In other words, there was optimism that the critical study of the Gospels would lead to the desired goal, to a picture of 'the historical Jesus'.

On these basic assumptions the investigation got under way. Three results characterised many of the studies that appeared. The first was that many apparent contradictions and historical impossibilities were discovered in the Gospels. What was described in the Gospels often could not have happened, either because the different Gospels presented conflicting accounts, or because the sequence of events was historically incredible, if not downright impossible. The second result was that many apparently supernatural accounts were given rationalistic explanations: what appeared to be miraculous was not really so. The third result was that much material in the Gospels was explained as mythical in origin; it was a description of a perfectly ordinary Jesus in language that was inherently mythical, and behind which no historical events in fact lay.

It is important to recognise the various motives and methods that were characteristic of nineteenth-century scholarship, for they are by no means absent today, even if they are not always openly admitted. They deserve some comment before we proceed further.

We have already discussed the rationalist presupposition sufficiently. The important point to observe at present is that the re-definition of 'the historical Jesus' implicitly adopted by such scholars is purely arbitrary, and makes the assumption that the real Jesus must have been a person of such a kind. The question of whether the sources might not lead to a different kind of Jesus was never tackled.

The positive contribution of nineteenth-century scholarship, however, was that the Gospels must be studied historically. [5] This is a position which is not universally accepted, and many Christians still fight shy of biblical criticism and believe that it is inherently rationalistic in outlook. But this assumption is false. Criticism simply means 'examination', and the Gospels have to be examined in all possible ways that may shed light on them. The wisest of the orthodox Christians recognised that historical arguments must be met by historical arguments and not by protests that historical study is irrelevant. The finest example of this is possibly to be seen in the work of J. B. Lightfoot. When an anonymous writer published a set of essays entitled *Supernatural Religion* in which he attacked the credentials of the New Testament documents on historical grounds, the answer to him took the form of a careful historical enquiry by Lightfoot in which counter-arguments were developed. [6] There is no doubt to whom the prize in the contest should be awarded. But the point that we make here is simply that Lightfoot recognised the necessity of confronting the critic on his own ground. He himself wrote, 'The abnegation of reason is not the evidence of faith, but the confession of despair'. [7] There can be no retreat from this position.

As to the third point, the writers whom we are discussing believed that by this method of study they would be able to arrive at the historical Jesus. But unfortunately another presupposition of which they were largely unconscious affected what they were doing. In a famous metaphor G. Tyrrell compared their endeavours to those of a man who peers to see what is at the bottom of a deep well, but all that he really sees is his own image reflected in the water. Tyrrell was referring in particular to the work of A. von Harnack, and said of him, 'The Christ that Harnack sees, looking back through nineteen centuries of Catholic darkness, is only the reflection of a liberal Protestant face, seen at the bottom of a deep well'. [8] The point could be generalised, and was in effect generalised by Schweitzer in his chronicle of nineteenth-century research. In every case the picture of Jesus was of a Jesus clearly fashioned by a nineteenth-century artist. The process reached its climax in the so-called 'Liberal Jesus', a somewhat inoffensive teacher proclaiming 'the fatherhood of God and the brotherhood of man'. [9]

It was, of course, possible that their nineteenth-century background might have enabled these scholars to see Jesus more clearly than their predecessors and to remove layers of misinterpretation that had accumulated during preceding centuries. But the test of whether a historian's presuppositions help him to a better picture of a historical figure is simply whether they explain the evidence more adequately. It could certainly be argued that the pre-critical picture of Jesus produced a docetic figure who had little real connection with his Palestinian environment, a divine messenger who appeared as an alien in this world. But the Liberal picture fared no better, though for different reasons. The most damning criticism came from the pen of William Temple, Archbishop of Canterbury, who said quite simply, 'Why anyone should have troubled to crucify the Christ of Liberal Protestantism has always been a mystery'. [10] The Jesus of Liberal Protestantism simply fails to explain the evidence of the Gospels; he could never have been the founder of a new religion. In this way nineteenth-century study led into a cul de sac. Could the twentieth century do any better?

THE EARLY TWENTIETH CENTURY

Jesus' preaching of the kingdom

Inasmuch as it represents a swing away from the 'Liberal' view which became dominant at the end of the nineteenth century, we may perhaps regard the work of J. Weiss and

A. Schweitzer as marking a significant new stage. For where the trend in previous studies had been to see the message of Jesus in terms of the kingdom of God as a kind of moral universe brought about by the endeavours of men of good will inspired by religious motives, these two scholars presented a different picture of the message of Jesus. The earlier view was congenial to those who described it. But it had been obtained at the cost of ignoring or explaining away anything in the teaching of Jesus which pointed in a different direction. It was the merit of Weiss's approach that he gathered up the evidence which had been set aside and insisted on its importance for understanding Jesus. [11] For Jesus the kingdom of God meant God acting in apocalyptic fashion in the immediate future to set up his rule. The Jesus who preached this was more like a fanatical preacher warning men that the world might come to a sudden end at any time than an urbane teacher of general religious truths. In the same way Schweitzer saw Jesus as a deluded dreamer, longing for an end to history within his own lifetime, and dying in despair because nothing had happened. [12] These were highly uncongenial pictures of Jesus for modern rationalists who had hoped that Jesus might be to them as the Psalmist had thought God would be to him: a person like himself (Ps. 50:21). The significance of Weiss's and Schweitzer's work was that it raised the possibility that Jesus might be a figure different from modern men. But this was a hard lesson to learn, and it may be doubted whether we have learned it yet. For those who had the wit to see it, it raised the important question of what to do with a Jesus who was not readily identifiable as a figure whom modern man would wish to follow or even worship.

Are the Gospels history or theology?

About the same time another book was published which raised issues of a different sort. It was the work of William Wrede who drew attention to the way in which Jesus is presented as the Messiah in the Gospel of Mark, but as a Messiah who does his best to keep his identity a secret. [13] When he performs miracles, he commands that nobody should be told about them. When he gives teaching, he either couches it in parables which, according to Mark, were not meant to be understood by the people, or he speaks more directly and openly to his circle of close disciples, who for their part usually misunderstand it. What Wrede did was to examine the way in which Mark conveyed this motif of 'secret Messiahship', and to claim that it was historically impossible that Jesus could ever have acted in this way. The whole presentation was riddled with contradictions and wild improbabilities. How, for example, could the raising of Jairus's daughter be kept a secret, as Jesus commanded, when everybody knew that she had been dead or at the very least in a deep coma? What was the point of Jesus telling people possessed by demons to be quiet about his identity when they had already blurted out who he was? (And how could people allegedly possessed by demons know that he was the Son of God anyhow?) So Wrede argued that in fact Jesus had never claimed to be Messiah. But the early church believed that he was the Messiah, and Mark endeavoured to bridge the gap between the fact that Jesus was regarded as the Messiah by the early church and that the early church had no evidence for this belief in the actual facts of Jesus' ministry. Such a lack of evidence for the church's foundation belief must be overcome somehow. And Mark tried to fill in this lacuna in the church's title-deeds by claiming that the reason why Jesus was not thought to be Messiah in his lifetime was because he deliberately told his followers not to reveal this fact to anybody; nevertheless, according to Mark, he did know himself to be Messiah and he did reveal this secretly to his closest followers. In order to achieve this aim Mark played fast and loose with the history, deliberately falsifying it in the interests of theology.

What Wrede claimed with regard to this facet of Mark's Gospel could easily be generalised. The Gospels were not historical reports about Jesus which could be used as sources for the real facts about his life. They were theological fantasies from which history could be extracted only with the greatest difficulty.

Let us note carefully what is involved in this case. First, Wrede was applying 'historical criticism' to the Gospels. He was asking whether their contents could be regarded as historical, and he argued that this could not be the case because the accounts were self-contradictory and full of impossibilities. We may refer to this type of study as *Sachkritik*, criticism of the facts recorded in the Gospels, in order to see which are reliable and which are unreliable. It was by no means a new method. From the very beginning critics have drawn attention to difficulties in the Gospels and concluded that they must be unhistorical.

Second, Wrede made the important point that Mark was painting a theological picture in the guise of history. Mark imposed a theological theory on the material at his disposal and so reinterpreted and rewrote it, not in accordance with what happened, but in accordance with his own ideas. Thus Mark was seen to be both a theologian and a creative writer rather than simply a historian recording facts that he had diligently researched.

Third, Wrede believed that the actual character of Jesus was unmessianic. He did not claim to be the Messiah. His ministry did not have the supernatural features ascribed to it by the Evangelists.

Wrede's use of *Sachkritik* remains of tremendous importance. The problem whether a historical source is reliable is to be answered, in part at least, by seeing whether it tells a self-consistent and historically credible story. Whether or not Wrede's criticism of Mark in this respect is justified, the fact remains that he occupies an important place in influencing other scholars to accept the view that the Gospels cannot be regarded simply as historical documents. Even scholars who would criticise details of Wrede's work would agree that he has made out his case in general terms.

His case that Mark was a theologian rather than a historian can be traced in two ways in more recent scholarship. First, his view that the Gospels were not written as historical witnesses to the ministry of Jesus has been typical of much modern scholarship. If the Gospels were written for theological motives, then they cannot be historical. We cannot trust texts written primarily for propaganda purposes. But, second, Wrede's view that Mark himself was a theologian took longer to gain acceptance. Scholarship proceeded on the assumption that those who handed on the teaching of Jesus between his death and the writing of the Gospels altered it and rephrased it in the course of oral transmission. But the Gospel writers themselves were thought of as basically collectors and recorders of such traditions. It is only within the last twenty years that scholars have argued that the Evangelists themselves shaped and modified the traditions from their own individual theological viewpoints — which was what Wrede had already claimed on behalf of Mark. [14]

Finally, Wrede's case that the ministry of Jesus was unmessianic has continued to influence scholars. We may, however, raise the question whether Wrede reached this conclusion on the basis of the evidence or adopted it as a presupposition. In any case, it should be noted that more recent studies of the 'messianic secret' have come to almost the exact opposite of Wrede's conclusion: the original tradition about Jesus was 'messianic', *i.e.* it portrayed Jesus as the Messiah; and it was the later church which tried to play down the more showy aspects of Jesus' messiahship by claiming that he himself kept it as secret as possible and did not draw attention to it. In other words, although Wrede isolated a problem in the interpretation of the Gospels, it is by no means certain that his answer was the right one, and there is some reason to suspect that the answer which he adopted reflected a rationalist presupposition. [15]

So far, however, as the immediately following years were concerned, the work of Wrede was typical of a trend which claimed that the Evangelists were not trying to record the story of Jesus 'as it actually happened'.

Jesus in the light of his environment

During Wrede's lifetime another type of approach to the Gospels was gaining momentum. This was the approach of the so-called *religions-geschichtliche Schule.* [16] If the Gospels were to be studied 'like any other book', the proper way to understand them was to place them in their literary and religious environment in the first century, and see what light this shed on them. This would be a generally agreed principle of study. The thesis of the particular approach developed in

the early years of the century was that what was recorded in
the New Testament must be understood as part of the general
religious history of the time, and that it could be completely
understood in terms of its first century environment. The
first-century religious world was studied to find ideas and
concepts which were parallel to those in the New Testament
and which could be regarded as their sources. Christianity
could be explained without recourse to the theory of supernatural revelation; everything could be explained naturally
in terms of the effect of the religious forces which played
upon the early Christians. The writers who adopted this approach, among whom R. Reitzenstein and W. Bousset are the
best known, tended to look for their evidence in the Graeco-
Roman world and in the syncretistic religious sects of the
eastern Mediterranean which amalgamated Graeco-Roman
ideas with ideas drawn from the Middle-East. In doing so,
they tended to ignore the Jewish background of the New
Testament writers. Since orthodox Christians had never
doubted the influence of the Old Testament on Jesus and his
followers — they saw a continuity in divine revelation
between the old and new dispensations — this tendency to
explain Christianity in terms of non-Jewish influence appeared to them to be the fruit of scepticism. It is unfortunate,
therefore, that those who discovered a Jewish background to
New Testament ideas were thought of as conservative, while
those who looked more to the Graeco-Roman world were
thought of as radical in their approach. Issues were in danger
of being settled by party considerations rather than by
objective research. For, of course, the truth of the matter
is that the world of the New Testament was both Jewish
and Graeco-Roman, and it is hard to separate or compart-
mentalise these two types of influence. The presentation of the Gospel was inevitably coloured by both sorts of
background as Christian preachers tried to express themselves
in ways that could be understood by all kinds of hearers.
Moreover, it is wrong to think that because an idea
comes from the Old Testament it must necessarily be true,
while if it comes from the Graeco-Roman world it cannot
be part of revelation and must be false. Ideas can be true or
false whatever their source, and those from pagan sources

can be taken up and used by Christian writers as well as biblical ones.

Now that the smoke of the battle has subsided, however, and we are able to appreciate the value of the attempt to place the New Testament in its cultural, social and religious setting, we can ask more objectively what the religious-historical approach achieved. It must be admitted that its proponents did tend to look more to the Graeco-Roman world than to the Jewish for influence upon Christianity. Paul was seen as a Jew of the Dispersion, open to Hellenistic influences and untouched by Palestinian Jewish influences. His theology was thought to be deeply affected by the mystery religions which flourished in the Aegean area. Few scholars today would agree with so one-sided an interpretation of Paul. In the same way, the development of thought about the person of Christ was seen in terms of the use of Hellenistic categories such as 'Lord' and 'Son of God' taken over from pagan religions and applied to Jesus. Again there was the same tendency to play down the Jewish elements in christology and to explain everything in terms of alien influences.

So far as the historical Jesus was concerned, the religious-historical approach had two effects. First, by finding the main influence upon christology in the pagan world, it denied that Jesus himself had any great influence on later thought about his person. The roots of thinking about his person lay in the developing churches in their Hellenistic environment rather than in any seeds sown by Jesus himself. [17] This fitted in, of course, with a non-messianic view of Jesus as a teacher and prophet who could be accounted for in essentially human terms. Second, this school tried to account for the supernatural presentation of Jesus in the Gospels by showing that in the ancient world there were many accounts of 'divine men', half-legendary figures with strange powers of prophecy and clairvoyance and the ability to work miracles, men who claimed to be divine or semi-divine. Against this background, it was easy to understand that Christians would portray Jesus in this kind of way. Whatever Jesus himself may have done to spark off such thinking about himself, the early church proceeded to deck him in the robes of the 'divine man'. So the problem of miracles was solved: miracles were ascribed to Jesus simply because every great religious prophet was thought to be capable of performing them and Jesus must not be presented as being in any way inferior to his rivals. By the comparative method Jesus was reduced to the stature of an ordinary man, and a giant question-mark was placed against a substantial part of the Gospel story.

The 'form' of the Gospel traditions

Yet another approach was taken by a group of scholars who are usually called 'form critics'. [18] We may reckon among their number K. L. Schmidt, since he provided one of the basic principles on which they operated. [19] What Schmidt did was to examine the outline of the story of Jesus in the Gospels. He was able to show that the order of events varied somewhat from Gospel to Gospel. This raised the question of whether the order in any of the Gospels was historical. When he examined the framework in detail, he claimed that it had in fact no claim to being historical. It was a framework created by the Evangelists on which to hang their various stories about Jesus and the sayings ascribed to him. Many of the stories were recounted without any details of time and place, and the Evangelists strung them together to make a connected story as best they could. In some cases stories appeared to have been strung together because they had the same theme rather than because they were known to have happened one after the other: thus stories in which Jesus came into conflict with the Jewish religious authorities were brought together by this common theme rather than because they necessarily all happened in the same period of time. Schmidt also found internal inconsistencies in the framework of the story. He concluded that originally the story of Jesus was handed down in discrete units without any details of time or place, and that it was only at a comparatively late stage that people began to group the units together and attempt to establish some sort of chronological and geographical order in them. The framework of the Gospel narrative could, therefore, be set on one side as late and historically valueless. Only in a few cases had authentic information about the chronology of Jesus' ministry survived.

This case, if proved, led to the conclusion that scholars could not write an orderly biography of Jesus because the requisite chronological information had not survived. For most scholars, except those who did not read the book (it was never translated into English) or who chose to ignore its existence, it put paid once and for all to the idea of writing a biography of Jesus, and thus it made the hope of recovering 'the historical Jesus' in that kind of way a vain one.

But of course Schmidt did not mean that we had no historical information about Jesus, but only that we could not arrange that information chronologically. Once the framework of the story had been removed, there were still the pictures lying on the floor. Logically, the next step was to examine these. Historically, however, the two processes were being carried on simultaneously, and the credit for the first publication in this area belongs not to Schmidt but to M. Dibelius who published the first edition of *Die Formgeschichte des Evangeliums* earlier in 1919. [20] It was to be followed in 1921 by the more famous and more comprehensive work of R. Bultmann, *Die Geschichte der synoptischen Tradition.* [21] Both of these books continue in print, both in German and English, and have continued to exercise a decisive influence in the study of the historical Jesus. The significant feature in both books (and in others which appeared soon after) was the analysis of the various individual items of tradition about Jesus in terms of their form, rather than their content. It was realised that different stories and sayings of Jesus followed recognisably similar patterns. The aim of form criticism was to establish what these patterns were and to show how the different pieces of tradition fitted into them. This new approach was based on similar work which had already been carried out in the field of Old Testament study, especially by H. Gunkel, but also on similar studies in the general field of literary criticism. The application of form criticism to the Gospels was thus due to the example already set in other areas of literature, especially literature which represented the crystallising of oral traditions. For Dibelius the basic activity in the early church was preaching, and he tried to show how various types of material in the Gospels were related directly or indirectly to the task of preaching. He showed that numerous Gospel stories fell into the category of the 'paradigm', a brief story culminating in a decisive saying by Jesus which could be used in preaching. Longer stories, especially those containing accounts of miracles, were classed as *Novellen* or 'stories'. Yet another group consisted of *Legende*, pious stories about holy men. Other types of story current in the ancient world are also discussed. In addition Dibelius examined the story of the passion of Jesus which formed the one connected narrative of any length in the Gospels, and he also discussed the sayings of Jesus, but without making any detailed classification of them.

Dibelius's work could be regarded as an attempt to illumine the nature of the Gospel tradition from the life of the early church. The much more detailed work of R. Bultmann tended to work in the opposite direction; it analysed the tradition in order to gain insights about the nature of the church in which it was created and circulated. In particular, Bultmann paid much more attention to the sayings of Jesus than Dibelius. Both authors recognised that the 'paradigms' or 'apophthegms' (as Bultmann called them) were recounted primarily because of the teaching of Jesus that they contained. In addition Bultmann recognised five main types of sayings of Jesus: 1. *Logia* or sayings of Jesus as a teacher of wisdom. These were sayings of a proverbial character (*e.g.* Mark 7:15; Luke 6:43f.). 2. *Prophetic and apocalyptic sayings.* These were sayings similar to those of the prophets or the apocalyptic writers who painted detailed pictures of the future in vivid imagery (*e.g.* Luke 6:24-26; Mark 13:2). 3. *Legal sayings and community rules.* These are sayings which regulate the communal life of the disciples. (*e.g.* Matt 5:23f.; 6:2-4; 18:15-17). 4. *'I' sayings.* These are sayings formulated in the first person singular (or referring to Jesus in the third person as 'the Son of man') which sum up his calling and mission (*e.g.* Mark 2:17; Luke 19:10). 5. *Parables and related material.* These are sayings, often of some length, couched in the form of pictures, metaphors, analogies and parables (*e.g.* Mark 4; Matt. 25).

These systems of classification have been refined by subsequent writers, but the general picture remains unchanged.

Although some scholars, such as T. W. Manson, have claimed that the proper task of form criticism was simply to classify the Gospel material in this kind of way, [22] in fact Dibelius and especially Bultmann went considerably further than this and saw their task in a larger framework.

First of all, the form critics saw it as part of their task to attempt to write a history of the individual units of tradition. Granted that they were handed down by word of mouth before being incorporated in the Gospels, it was reasonable to assume that both stories about Jesus and sayings attributed to him would undergo some alterations in the telling. One has only to compare the final form of a rumour or a piece of gossip with the original form to realise that very considerable alterations can take place to material passed on by word of mouth. We might well assume that material about Jesus would be less prone to change than the idle chatter of gossip-mongers, but even so we must reckon with the possibility and indeed the probability of change happening. If the tradition was originally handed down as separate stories and sayings, there would clearly be some modifications of the wording when the various pieces were joined together in a consecutive narrative. But earlier still, when sayings and stories were being passed from person to person and used in church teaching and preaching, changes would inevitably occur. So Bultmann in particular saw it as an important part of his task to reconstruct the probable earliest form of any piece of tradition and show how it had developed to its present form. This is why his book is rightly called 'The History of the Synoptic Tradition', and why the subject is properly 'form history' (Formgeschichte) rather than 'form criticism'.

Second, the form critics saw their task as being closely related to sociological considerations. What kind of church was it which made use of these forms and developed them? Why was the material transmitted in these forms and not in others? Hence there developed the idea of the 'life setting' (Sitz im Leben), i.e. the typical situation in the early church in which particular forms of material were used. We have seen that Dibelius identified preaching as an important setting for the Gospel tradition. Bultmann for his part laid stress on situations of conflict and argument in which the church defended itself against its opponents. He tried to show how the material appeared especially relevant when seen against such a background.

Third, the form critics examined the Gospel material against the broader background of the ancient world and ancient literature. They observed, for example, that stories about the miracles performed by other figures in the ancient world bore a close resemblance in form to the stories about Jesus. Bultmann assembled a whole list of features which appear in both groups of stories — stress on the length of time the patient had been ill, the intensity of the illness, the failure of doctors to provide a cure, the efforts made by the healer, the use of gestures and commands to effect the healing, the proof that the person had really recovered, and the effects on the bystanders. In the case of the sayings it was not difficult to produce parallel forms from the Old Testament (*e.g.* for the wisdom and prophetic sayings) and from Jewish sources such as the rabbinical writings. Thus the types of tradition found in the Gospels could be illuminated from a variety of sources offering similar sorts of material.

Fourth, Bultmann in particular clearly did not believe in the possibility of the miraculous. Here he stood under the influence of nineteenth-century rationalism, and he was quite candid in stating that modern man (a term which included himself) could not accept the pre-scientific world view of the Bible. [23]

Fifth, Bultmann, who was much influenced by Wrede, had a strong tinge of historical scepticism in his make-up and would accept stories as historical only on the most firmly based evidence.

The effect of a study of the Gospels based on these factors was to call in question the historicity of much of their contents. Bultmann here went much further than Dibelius, who took a more moderate position. For the purpose of studying the historical Jesus, the Gospel of John was rejected from the outset as a late, imaginative work; its picture of Jesus was so different from that in the other three (Synoptic)

Gospels that both could not be true simultaneously, and the temptation was to reject the Gospel of John outright without seriously considering the possibility that it might contain occasional pieces of history. But within the Synoptic Gospels themselves the effect of Bultmann's work was pretty devastating. It went without question that all miracle stories were unhistorical. They were glorifications of Jesus made on the analogy of similar stories about other great men. The same was true of most of the stories about Jesus which contained 'legendary' features. One might expect that the 'apophthegms' would have better claims to historicity, but here Bultmann argued that in nearly every case the original element was the 'saying' ascribed to Jesus and that the 'framework' was a creation by the early church in order to make a little story out of the saying and give it a 'historical' setting in the ministry of Jesus. Great play was made with the concept of the 'ideal scene' — a description of the sort of scene that might have happened in the ministry of Jesus (*e.g.* the calling of disciples) but which was in fact only an imaginative reconstruction of a typical occasion.

What, then, of the actual sayings of Jesus? Here Bultmann was prepared to be more positive and to admit that some of the sayings were genuine. But a very large number indeed were either clearly the creations of the early church or Jewish maxims put on the lips of Jesus — or sayings that could be either from the early church or from Jesus, and in such cases Bultmann almost invariably gave the early church the benefit of the doubt. It was Bultmann who formulated the rule that if a saying ascribed to Jesus *could* have been said by some other Jew or could have been formulated in the early church, then we could not safely ascribe it to Jesus. [24] It is not a very big step from saying 'somebody else could have said it' to saying 'Jesus did not say it'. In particular, Bultmann was very sceptical about any sayings in which christological titles, such as 'Christ' or 'Son' or 'Son of man', which were used by the early church, were attributed to Jesus; he also rejected sayings of the 'I came...' variety, alleging that in these Jesus was made to look back on his career as a whole and that, therefore, they could not have been formulated until after the end of his career. It goes without saying that prophecies of

Jesus' fate at the hands of the Jews were dismissed without any argument: 'can there be any doubt that they are all *vaticinia ex eventu*?'[25]

The net result of all this was that for Bultmann nothing survived of the deeds of Jesus and very little of his teaching. The meagre harvest was gathered in a booklet translated into English as *Jesus and the Word*.[26] Another distinguished German scholar, E. Lohmeyer, drily remarked of it that it was 'a Jesus-book without Jesus', a description which it certainly merited.[27]

If A. Schweitzer had pronounced the obituary on the quest for the historical Jesus, Bultmann could be said to have laid its tombstone in place. The general effect of his work was to claim that the quest for the historical Jesus was impossible. Bultmann took the further step of declaring that the quest was illegitimate and unnecessary. This judgment was, of course, that of a theologian rather than a historian, and we have already devoted some attention to it at an earlier stage.

The conservative reaction

It is not surprising that various freebooters ignored Bultmann's embargo on their trade. In Germany itself there were scholars who claimed that the situation was not as desperate as Bultmann made it out to be. Of the greatest significance is the fact that M. Dibelius also wrote a book simply entitled *Jesus* and on the same sort of scale of treatment as Bultmann's popular work. He worked on the basis of form criticism, again like Bultmann, and he proceeded in a cautious manner, but the results of his study were considerably more positive than those of Bultmann. Thus he was prepared to write that 'the tradition that Jesus performed extraordinary deeds is as well guaranteed as such a fact can be guaranteed at all by means of popular reports', and he believed that 'Jesus knew himself to be the Messiah chosen by God' and that his appearance was closely related to the coming of the kingdom of God.[28] Such statements are extremely revealing for they show that it was not form criticism as such which led to the sceptical results produced by Bultmann.

In Britain also there were powerful voices raised in defence of the belief that it was possible to have considerably more historical knowledge about Jesus than Bultmann allowed. Here pride of place must be given to C. H. Dodd who challenged K. L. Schmidt's view that the Gospel writers had failed to preserve the historical outline of the ministry of Jesus. [29] It was not, however, until 1954 that Dodd gave a series of lectures in Aberystwyth which formed the basis of a book published in 1970 under the title *The Founder of Christianity*, and here Dodd gave mature expression to the study of a lifetime with a picture of the life of Jesus in which Dodd traced his character, his teaching and his career. We shall note the significance of these features at a later date. Let it be observed too that Dodd did not write in ignorance of form criticism (a preposterous suggestion!), but used it as a tool which could lead to positive results.

Next we must mention T. W. Manson who wrote a brief study of *The Servant-Messiah* (Cambridge, 1953), again based on an earlier series of lectures dating back to 1939. Here too a positive treatment of the historicity of the ministry of Jesus was given, and again by a scholar who had made several acute criticisms of form criticism. [30]

A third scholar whose work has not perhaps commanded the attention which it deserves is W. Manson, whose book *Jesus the Messiah* (London, 1943) bore the sub-title: *The Synoptic Tradition of the Revelation of God in Christ: with Special Reference to Form-Criticism*. The book does what it claims to do. Manson argues cogently that the Gospel tradition had not lost contact with history, and time and again he finds good reason to uphold the authenticity of material which had been rejected by Continental critics. The result is a powerful claim that the christology of the church ultimately rested on the impression made by the life of Jesus.

Finally, in this brief catalogue we should not forget V. Taylor. He was the author of what remains the best English exposition of the nature of form criticism, *The Formation of the Gospel Tradition*, a sympathetic and yet critical assessment of the new discipline. He also wrote a critical commentary on Mark, still unsurpassed for its thorough treatment. Against the background of this detailed preparation we can now place his book on *The Life and Ministry of Jesus,* which probably took the most positive view yet from the form-critical angle of the historical value of the Gospel material about Jesus. [31]

We deliberately draw attention to these four writers because they show that there were scholars in this country who, like Dibelius, refused to be brow-beaten by Bultmann into abandoning the quest for the historical Jesus. [32] Furthermore, their existence establishes conclusively that the so-called 'new quest' for the historical Jesus which came into being after the Second World War was by no means as new as its exponents may have liked to think. The impression of historical pessimism that might have been acquired by a student familiar only with the work of Bultmann would have been unjustified.

THE POST-WAR PERIOD

A 'New Quest'?

In 1959 J. M. Robinson published an influential book entitled *A New Quest of the Historical Jesus.* In it he reiterated the claim that the old quest of the historical Jesus was both impossible and illegitimate. His arguments were based on those of Bultmann before him. In particular, Robinson emphasised that any historical information about Jesus had survived only as *kerygma* or preaching, *i.e.* only because it fulfilled some function in the preaching and teaching of the church. There was no historical interest as such in Jesus, *i.e.* disinterested, objective effort to discover what had actually happened. What was recorded in the *kerygma* was interpreted material, sayings and stories that were adapted for use in the church. Only if the origin of a particular piece of tradition could not be explained in terms of the life of the church was it practicable to postulate a possible origin in the life of Jesus. Robinson clearly believed that not very much material could be traced back to the life of Jesus in this way. At the same time he underlined the illegitimacy of trying to work back to pure history. He argued, somewhat obscurely, that the historian's task has come to be seen 'to consist in understanding those deep-lying intentions of the past, by involving one's selfhood in an encounter in which one's own intentions and views of existence are put in question, and perhaps altered or even radically reversed'.[33] History is thus a matter of interpretation in which the interpreter may find himself being interpreted. The *kerygma* of the early church was to be understood in this way as an interpretation of the historical facts, and it is illegitimate to go behind it.

Robinson then posed the question of whether a renewal of the quest for the historical Jesus was possible. He reviewed three attempts to do so which in his opinion were failures. First, there was the possibility that the preaching of the early church contained a 'historical section'. As reconstructed by C. H. Dodd, the early sermons of the church contained a brief historical description of the ministry of Jesus. Robinson argued that any historical details in the preaching were scanty and irrelevant, since they were used purely as vehicles of theological interpretation and were not included to 'prove' that the interpretation was true. Second, there was the possibility that new historical sources might provide confirmation of the history behind the Gospels. Here Robinson argued that the use made of knowledge of the Palestinian background by J. Jeremias and others, and the use made of rabbinic references to Jesus by E. Stauffer, were part of the 'old quest' and in any case they could do nothing to disprove the fact that the Gospels were kerygmatic and not historical. Finally, there was the possibility that behind the Gospels lay a meticulously preserved tradition of the teaching of Jesus, analogous to the carefully preserved traditions of the teaching of the Jewish rabbis. Robinson dismissed this possibility virtually without argument.

Robinson then presented his own view of the possibility of a new quest for the historical Jesus. He claimed that modern historians saw as their task the bringing out of the 'selfhood' of the historical person being studied. In the record of the sayings of Jesus it was possible to discover something of his significance. If it was impossible to discover the chronological details of the ministry of Jesus, it was possible to work out the 'intention' of Jesus. The historian could uncover the *'Geschichte'* of Jesus, although the *'Historie'* remained inaccessible.

So Robinson argued that the historian could test the validity of the kerygma's identification of its understanding of existence by a comparison with Jesus' understanding of his existence. Robinson was prepared to allow that there were sayings attributed to Jesus in the Gospels which were unlike the teaching of the church and that the self-understanding revealed in these could be compared with the kerygma. In a brief excursion into this area of research Robinson was able to find in the teaching of Jesus and in the kerygma a sense of the coming of a new age. [34]

The followers of Bultmann

Robinson was writing about a new quest that was going on at the time when he composed his book. What he was trying to do in the last section of the book was to explain what was going on among some of the followers of Bultmann. By common consent the beginning of the new movement is to be found in a lecture by E. Käsemann in October, 1953, on 'The Problem of the Historical Jesus'.[35] It is not a lecture which is easy to understand — Käsemann is rarely easy to follow! — but it did utter the conviction that for all the dogmatic elements in the Gospels, for all the effort to clothe theological statements in the form of history ('historicisation'), nevertheless the Evangelists believed that they had access to historical information about Jesus and attempted to present it. On the basis of this belief Käsemann made some effort to spell out some basic facts about Jesus. Finally, he insisted that we cannot separate the Christ of faith from the historical Jesus: 'we also cannot do away with the identity between the exalted and the earthly Lord without falling into docetism and depriving ourselves of the possibility of drawing a line between the Easter faith of the community and myth'.[36] All this was expressed with immense caution and without going back on the stringent methodology with which Bultmann himself had approached the Gospels. The results achieved might, therefore, appear quite meagre, but the important thing was that a prominent member of the Bultmann 'school' had declared that knowledge of the historical Jesus was both possible and legitimate — and done so at a reunion of old students in honour of their teacher!

Only three years later the tender seed planted by Käsemann blossomed forth into a full-length study of *Jesus of Nazareth* by another distinguished pupil of Bultmann, G. Bornkamm. [37] Here again we see a scholar working with the utmost caution, careful not to outrun the evidence, but drawing a coherent picture of Jesus. Bornkamm particularly stressed the note of authority which was present in the ministry of Jesus. Whereas for Bultmann Jesus announced the future coming of the kingdom and called for present decision in the light of this existential challenge, Bornkamm shifted the emphasis and underlined the importance of the present element in the message: in Jesus the reality of God already faces men and calls them to decision. The new aeon is already bursting in, and the kingdom of God is being realised in Jesus' words and actions. And Bornkamm paid due attention to the kind of things that Jesus *did* in extending fellowship to tax-collectors and sinners. To be sure, Bornkamm made no attempt to write any kind of life of Jesus — an impossible task — but he was prepared to give some account of Jesus' pilgrimage to Jerusalem and what happened during his last days there. And, perhaps most significant of all, he did not stop at Good Friday but devoted some attention to the 'Easter faith' of the disciples; and although he claimed that the resurrection of Jesus lay beyond the scope of historical enquiry, nevertheless he stated quite factually that it was the appearances of Jesus and the word of the witnesses which provided the basis for the Easter faith.

The careful reader will discover that in basic essentials Bornkamm's book does not say anything new compared with the earlier one by M. Dibelius. Both books find the same degree of historical information in the Gospels, and the pictures painted of Jesus are very much the same. Consequently, judged in a broader context, there is nothing very novel in Bornkamm's book. The significant point is that from within the circle of Bultmann's followers somebody had dared to present a historical study of Jesus and to affirm that this Jesus is the object of Christian confession and faith.

Other followers of Bultmann took similar lines. Nobody could call E. Fuchs a clear writer; possibly there is no

contemporary German theologian who is harder to understand. But one thing he did affirm quite clearly, and this was
that Jesus' conduct is a means of divine revelation. His
fellowship with sinners was the communication of God's
forgiveness to them. [38] Yet another scholar to take a somewhat
more positive line was H. Conzelmann who wrote the article
on 'Jesus Christ' for the most recent edition of the standard
German Protestant multi-volume encyclopaedia, *Religion in
Geschichte und Gegenwart.* [39] And, finally, Robinson thought
that he could detect some shift of opinion in the thinking of
Bultmann himself.

Possibly the most influential disciple of Bultmann in the
English-speaking world and certainly one of the more sceptical, is N. Perrin, whose book, *Rediscovering the Teaching of Jesus,*
is controlled by the postulates that we cannot claim that any
Gospel narratives are other than possibly typical scenes from
the ministry of Jesus, that all settings given to sayings
ascribed to Jesus are editorial, and that in every case the
burden of proof lies on those who would uphold the
authenticity of any particular saying ascribed to Jesus; very
little historical material emerges through the filters of Perrin's
critical tests. [40]

Such was the new movement within the Bultmannian
camp. Its effect was to unleash a torrent of discussion *about* the
problem of the historical Jesus. It also played some part in
encouraging the equally great torrent of studies *of* the
historical Jesus to which we alluded at the beginning of this
book. The discussion was not confined to members of the
Bultmann school who took sides for and against the new
quest. Scholars of every outlook joined in the debate, and it is
probably no exaggeration to say that every continental New
Testament scholar of note (and not a few others as well) felt
impelled to write an essay on some aspect of the theme. At
least one enormous book of collected essays on 'The historical
Jesus and the kerygmatic Christ' appeared in German, some
of the contributions to which have also appeared in English. [41]

It is impossible to do justice to this volume of literature in
the present context. [42] Nor would anything be gained by
trying to summarise, if that were possible, so enormous a pile

of writings, many of which overlap considerably in the things that they say. It may even be too soon to attempt a considered evaluation of it. One thing which seems fairly certain is that Robinson's interpretation of the situation was not altogether accurate. Critics pointed out with some justification that he had exaggerated the differences between the old and the new quests. This happened because Robinson tended to attribute his own ideas regarding the nature of modern historiography to the 'new questers'. It is by no means certain that any of them would have said that they were doing precisely what Robinson thought they were doing. Robinson's understanding of Bultmann also came under fire. It was noted that Bultmann had never said that we could know absolutely nothing about the historical Jesus, so that there could now be talk of his being prepared to allow more history than previously. At the same time it was claimed that Bultmann did not in fact admit the legitimacy of the quest for the historical Jesus any more than he had done in the past. [43] The critics who made these attacks on Robinson's understanding of Bultmann were supported by a notable ally — none other than Bultmann himself, who joined in the discussion to reaffirm the views which, as he claimed, he had always expressed. He claimed once again that we cannot show that the actual life and work of Jesus were contained in the preaching of the early church or that the content of this preaching could already be seen in essence in the deeds and words of Jesus; in other words, there is no possibility of showing that the preaching is 'true' by establishing a basis for it in the historical mission of Jesus. For Bultmann there is a decisive difference between the preaching of Jesus and the preaching of the church. Jesus called men to decision, but the early church called men to faith in Jesus, something which Jesus himself did not require. (It is, of course, self-evident to Bultmann that sentiments such as those expressed in John 14:1 cannot be attributed to the historical Jesus). [44]

It will be clear that in this discussion questions regarding the possibility of historical knowledge of Jesus and questions regarding the theological significance of Jesus cannot be sharply distinguished. Our main concern just now is with the possibility of historical knowledge. Bultmann's claim is that we have virtually no historical knowledge of Jesus that would support the traditional view of his message; and even when we understand his message in existential terms it is still not possible for us to make a link between it and the message of the church.

Other points of view

At the opposite extreme from Bultmann and his followers there stands the figure of J. Jeremias, a scholar second only to Bultmann (if to anybody) in erudition. For Jeremias the basis of Christian faith lies in what Jesus actually said and did. Thus in his book on the parables of Jesus he stated that his aim was to recover the earliest attainable wording of the parables, and then he went on: 'It is to be hoped that the reader will perceive that the aim of the critical analysis contained in...this book is nothing less than a return, as well grounded as possible, to the very words of Jesus himself. Only the Son of Man and his word can invest our message with full authority.' [45] These words suggest that for Jeremias the historical backing for the Christian message is provided by a knowledge of what Jesus actually said, so far as this is accessible to the historian. Jeremias has been accused of reducing the basis of the Christian faith to the actual words of Jesus, or rather to the historian's findings on this score, but this is probably a misunderstanding: he would not dispute the revelatory significance of the New Testament as a whole, but what he does insist is that there is a fundamental historical basis for Christian faith in what Jesus actually said, and that this basis can be established by historical study.

The reader unused to biblical criticism who takes up Jeremias's book on the parables and labours through the first part of it, where the author attempts to work back from the present wording of the parables to the historical kernel of what Jesus actually said, may well be shocked by the degree to which Jeremias believes that they have been altered in transmission. Jeremias's procedures may appear quite radical, and he himself would claim that criticism must be quite rigorous. Nevertheless, in the constructive part of his book which follows he succeeds in making the parables come to life in the historical setting of Jesus' ministry and does provide a firm basis for Christian faith in the teaching of Jesus. No doubt there are many points where other scholars would want to modify or reject Jeremias's conclusions in detail, but the fundamental point is that he has demonstrated that the critical scrutiny of the Gospels can lead to positive results.

More recently Jeremias has published the first volume of his *New Testament Theology*, the whole of which is devoted to 'The Proclamation of Jesus'. [46] When it is observed that here 330 pages are devoted to the teaching of Jesus as a basic part of New Testament theology, whereas Bultmann allowed only thirty pages out of some 600 pages in his *Theology of the New Testament* to the same theme, the difference in outlook becomes obvious. Here we have a carefully reasoned reconstruction of the teaching of Jesus which shows that it is possible to put together a historically convincing picture of the ministry of Jesus, and that we are not confined to a few traces of what he said and did. While the picture presented is not convincing at every point, this work is perhaps the most important study of the historical Jesus to appear in the present century.

Our discussion is oriented to the English-speaking reader and tries to avoid undue reference to works not available or not yet available in English; and it is a fact that, while the main discussion of our theme has taken place on the Continent, the most significant works have been translated into English. [47] But we must take a few lines to refer to another work which backs up that of J. Jeremias. L. Goppelt, who died before his time in 1973, was able to complete the first volume of his *Theologie des Neuen Testaments* before his passing. This book, too, is devoted to the historical Jesus, but Goppelt sub-titled it significantly, 'The ministry of Jesus in its theological significance'. In other words, it is not just the message of Jesus which is theologically important, but also what he did, and Goppelt believed that we can know something about this.

A fairly positive line is also taken by the most recent major work to come from French-speaking scholarship. E. Trocmé has written *Jesus and his Contemporaries*, a book in which he takes up some half dozen different 'forms' of tradition which are found in the Gospels and examines each in turn to see what picture of Jesus is presented by it. Trocmé's case appears to be that, although we may not be able to bridge the gap between these early traditions and Jesus himself, nevertheless we can find in these traditions the kind of impact which was made by Jesus: we see his significance as it appeared to various groups of early Christians, and it can be claimed that this is sufficiently near to historical reality for our purpose. [48]

As for British scholarship it must suffice to mention two or three works which are typical of recent approaches. A very traditional type of picture of Jesus is presented by D. Guthrie in *Jesus the Messiah.* Although Guthrie is well aware of the methods of modern historical research, he tends to ignore them in this book and to take it rather for granted that we can read the Gospels more or less as they stand as straight historical sources for the life of Jesus. The result is that the reader who is puzzled by the historical questions will not find any help with his problems, and the insights which might be given by the application of historical methods are missing. The modern reader needs more help than Guthrie is prepared to give him and might mistakenly conclude that there are in fact no historical problems. [49]

At the opposite extreme stands the work of Peter de Rosa, *Jesus who became Christ.* The author is a Roman Catholic who is far from being bound by the traditions of the church, a biblical scholar with considerable literary powers, who is able to write in an effective and moving way, such as is rarely found in scholarly studies of Jesus. He squarely rejects the literal truth of much of the Gospel material, but believes that we can find some history in the Gospels. But the Evangelists were writing from the post-Easter situation, and so they present Jesus as the Christ. So we start with the stories of the birth of Jesus which can most easily be interpreted in poetical and mythical terms as attempts to express the religious significance of Jesus. What follows is not in any sense a life of Jesus but rather an attempt at a portrait of him as intensely human, and so as one who is divine in his humanity. At the other end of the story stand the resurrection legends which are the creations of faith that Jesus was risen; there is no proof that Jesus did rise, but the author holds that faith is impossible in the presence of proof, and that belief should not depend on proof. [50]

It may come as a surprise that one of the most notable attempts to wrestle historically with the Gospels comes from the pen of a Jew, expert in the Judaism of the first century. G. Vermes has presented a Jewish portrait of *Jesus the Jew*, a book which is a strange combination of rejection of current scholarly opinions and advocacy of new hypotheses which demand careful scrutiny.[51] Vermes is critical of Christian scholars who have (in his view) ignored or misinterpreted the Jewish background of the ministry of Jesus and failed to see that he was very like some of the charismatic Jewish prophets and wonder-workers in the first century. He offers some important evidence regarding the titles used in the Gospels for Jesus, and in general he attempts to bring fresh light on Jesus from Jewish sources — although the light is perhaps not always as fresh as he thinks. Of particular interest is his apparent acceptance of a kernel of historical truth in the stories of the empty tomb and the resurrection appearances of Jesus.

Even closer to a traditional Christian picture of Jesus is that offered by D. Flusser, a professor in the Hebrew University at Jerusalem, who shows a greater readiness to accept the evidence in the Gospels than many of his Christian colleagues, and finds, for example, no difficulty in believing that Jesus thought himself to be the Messiah. [52]

Here our catalogue must break off. [53] It has said nothing about the more sensational 'popular' accounts of Jesus which picture him in terms of a wild revolutionary and which fly in the face of all the evidence in so doing. If it can be objected that many of the Continental lives of Jesus regard much of the evidence as unreliable and dismiss it, here it is the case that small pieces of evidence are given arbitrary interpretations and the rest of the evidence is completely ignored. The case for Jesus being a revolutionary is non-existent. S. G. F. Brandon, a scholar who has particularly studied this area, [54] has been accused of arguing that Jesus was a Zealot, *i.e.* a Jewish revolutionary who favoured armed resistance, but he himself has explicitly repudiated this accusation, and pointed out that the fact that Jesus' group of disciples may have contained more than one erstwhile Zealot is no proof whatever that Jesus himself was a Zealot, and that the probabilities are against this hypothesis. [55] Similarly, M. Hengel who is perhaps the leading authority on Jewish revolutionary movements categorically denies that Jesus was a Zealot or favoured revolutionary policies. [56] The case for such outlandish interpretations of Jesus can safely be ignored without any prolonged discussion here.

Ignoring such more sensational presentations, the reader of this book is concerned to know what can be discovered about the historical Jesus by scientific criticism. What has emerged is that in the post-war period all points of view, ranging from fairly radical scepticism to fairly implicit trust concerning the Gospel accounts, is to be found. But the majority of serious New Testament scholars allow that something can be known about Jesus from the Gospels, even if the path from the Gospels to Jesus is a difficult one to trace. Within the Bultmann school there is agreement that some of the teaching of Jesus can be established with comparative certainty. Outside that school there is an increasing belief that a reasonably comprehensive picture of Jesus can be obtained from the Gospels.

If the pre-war period was characterised by the application of form criticism to the Gospels, the post-war period has seen a development of related methods which help to clarify the nature of the Gospels and their contents. We saw earlier that the form critics included in their task an attempt to write the history of the individual units of tradition which they isolated in the Gospels. The distinction between 'form criticism' and 'traditio-historical criticism' has now become clearer to scholars, and the contribution of the post-war period has been to lay greater stress on the need to work back to the earliest form of the tradition in attempting to find its historical core. At the same time it has been observed that the Evangelists themselves did not simply reproduce *verbatim* the traditions which they inherited but refashioned them in the light of their own total understanding of the significance of Jesus. 'Redaction criticism' is the name given to the study of the Gospels in order to distinguish between the contribution of the Evangelists and the traditions as they received them. Both 'traditio-historical criticism' and 'redaction criticism' are of great value in describing the theology of the early church and of the Evangelists. They are thus important for their own sakes. At the same time, however, they form essential steps in the task of working back from the Gospels to Jesus.

Our next task, therefore, must be to look carefully and critically at all of these methods of study and the results to which they lead. But already it can be said that the attempt to get back to the historical Jesus is hopeful of some success. We can know something about Jesus: but how much?

NOTES

1 See ch. 1, note 3. Also R. P. Martin, 'The New Quest of the Historical Jesus', in C. F. H. Henry (ed.), *Jesus of Nazareth: Saviour and Lord,* Grand Rapids, 1966, 25-45; J. S. Kselman, 'Modern New Testament Criticism', in *The Jerome Bible Commentary,* London, 1968, (II), 7-20; E. Trocmé, *Jesus and his Contemporaries,* 1-13.

2 A. Schweitzer, *The Quest of the Historical Jesus,* London 1950[3], 13-26. See H. S. Reimarus, *Fragments,* London, 1970.

3 J. S. Kselman *op. cit.,* 8.

4 D. F. Strauss, *The Life of Jesus Critically Examined,* London, 1972.

5 Note the insistence on this point in the magisterial study of W. G. Kümmel, *The New Testament: The History of the Investigation of its Problems,* London, 1973.

6 (J. A. Cassels), *Supernatural Religion,* London, 1874, 1902. J. B. Lightfoot, *Essays on 'Supernatural Religion',* London, 1889.

7 J. B. Lightfoot, *Saint Paul's Epistle to the Galatians,* London, 1865, 1896; the sentence is cited by Cassels at the beginning of his book, and one is tempted to comment, 'You have appealed to Caesar; to Caesar you shall go'.

8 G. Tyrrell, *Christianity at the Cross-roads,* London, 1909, 44.

9 A. von Harnack, *What is Christianity?* London, 1901. At worst, the liberals 'scaled down the imperial mind of Christ...to the level of a well-meaning Sunday School teacher' (F. R. Barry, *The Relevance of Christianity,* London, 1931, 98).

10 W. Temple, *Readings in St. John's Gospel,* London, 1939-40, 1945, xxiv.

11 J. Weiss, *Jesus' Proclamation of the Kingdom of God,* London, 1971 (originally published in 1892).

12 A . Schweitzer, *op. cit.,* 328ff.

13 W. Wrede, *The Messianic Secret,* Cambridge, 1971 (originally published in 1901).

14 In this way Wrede was the pioneer of what has more recently come to be known as redaction criticism.

15 See J. D. G. Dunn, 'The Messianic Secret in Mark', *Tyndale Bulletin* 21, 1970, 92-117; C. F. D. Moule, 'On Defining the Messianic Secret in

Mark', in E. E. Ellis and E. Grässer (ed.), *Jesus and Paulus,* Göttingen, 1975, 239-252.

16   On this and the various other types of approach discussed in the following pages see the appropriate essays in I. H. Marshall (ed.), *New Testament Interpretation,* Exeter, 1977.

17   W. Bousset, *Kyrios Christos,* Nashville, 1970 (originally published in 1913, revised edition in 1921).

18   Good surveys are available in V. Taylor, *The Formation of the Gospel Tradition,* London, 1935; W. Barclay, *The Gospels and Acts,* London, 1976.

19   K. L. Schmidt, *Der Rahmen der Geschichte Jesu,* Berlin 1919; Darmstadt, 1969. It has unfortunately never been translated into English.

20   Translated as M. Dibelius, *From Tradition to Gospel,* London, 1934; Cambridge, 1971.

21   Translated as R. Bultmann, *The History of the Synoptic Tradition,* Oxford, 1968[2].

22   See below, pp. 169-177.

23   Hence it was necessary for the biblical message to be 'demythologised'. See especially Bultmann's essay, 'The New Testament and Mythology', in H.-W. Bartsch (ed.), *Kerygma and Myth,* London, 1954 (originally written in 1941).

24   The principle operates throughout Bultmann's discussion. It is perhaps most clearly expressed in his comment on the similitudes used by Jesus: 'We can only count on possessing a genuine similitude of Jesus where, on the one hand, expression is given to the contrast between Jewish morality and piety and the distinctive eschatological temper which characterised the preaching of Jesus; and where on the other hand we find no specifically Christian features' (*The History of the Synoptic Tradition,* 205).

25   R. Bultmann, *Theology of the New Testament* I, 29.

26   R. Bultmann, *Jesus and the Word,* London, 1934; originally published in German in 1926.

27   E. Lohmeyer's review in *Theologische Literaturzeitung* 52, 1927, 438; cited at length by W. G. Kümmel, *The New Testament,* 375f. It is interesting that Lohmeyer went on to say, 'It is evident that what Bultmann tries to isolate as the historical content of Jesus' proclamation is nothing else than the apologia for his own religious position'.

28   M. Dibelius, *Jesus,* London, 1963 (originally published in German in 1939), 75, 88.

29   See below, pp. 165-168.

30   T. W. Manson, *Studies in the Gospels and Epistles,* Manchester, 1962.

31   V. Taylor, *The Formation of the Gospel Tradition,* London, 1935; *The Gospel according to St. Mark,* London, 1953; *The Life and Ministry of Jesus,* London, 1954.

32   The list could be considerably extended: *e.g.* H. E. W. Turner, *Jesus: Master and Lord,* London, 1953; *Historicity and the Gospels,* London, 1963.

33   J. M. Robinson, *A New Quest of the Historical Jesus,* 39.

34   The brief discussion of this area in the English edition of his book

was considerably expanded in the later German edition: *Kerygma und historischer Jesus*, Zürich/Stuttgart, 1967².

35   E. Käsemann, *Essays on New Testament Themes*, London, 1964, 15-47.

36   *Ibid.*, 34; *cf.* 45f.

37   G. Bornkamm, *Jesus of Nazareth*, London, 1960; originally published in German in 1956.

38   E. Fuchs, *Studies of the Historical Jesus*, London, 1964, originally published in 1960.

39   Translated into English as *Jesus*, Philadelphia, 1973.

40   N. Perrin, *Rediscovering the Teaching of Jesus*, London, 1967.

41   H. Ristow and K. Matthiae (ed.), *Der historische Jesus und der kerygmatische Christus*, Berlin, 1960; C. E. Braaten and R. A. Harrisville, *The Historical Jesus and the Kerygmatic Christ*, New York, 1964.

42   See further R. E. Brown, 'After Bultmann, What? — An Introduction to the Post-Bultmannians', *Catholic Biblical Quarterly* 26, 1964, 1-30.

43   For these criticisms see V. A. Harvey and S. M. Ogden, 'How New is the "New Quest of the Historical Jesus"?', in C. E. Braaten and R. A. Harrisville, *op. cit.*, 197-242. In the later, German edition of his book Robinson claims that his critics have misunderstood him.

44   R. Bultmann, 'The Primitive Christian Kerygma and the Historical Jesus', in C. E. Braaten and R. A. Harrisville, *op. cit.*, 15-42.

45   J. Jeremias, *The Parables of Jesus*, London, 1963, 9.

46   J. Jeremias, *New Testament Theology: Volume One: The Proclamation of Jesus*, London, 1971.

47   Among the most important of German works are two books by W. G. Kümmel, *Promise and Fulfilment: The Eschatological Message of Jesus*, London, 1957; and *The Theology of the New Testament according to its Major Witnesses: Jesus — Paul — John*, London, 1974.

48   E. Trocmé, *Jesus and his Contemporaries*, London, 1973.

49   D. Guthrie, *Jesus the Messiah*, London, 1972. For a conservative approach with a stronger critical grounding see R. T. France, *The Man They Crucified — a Portrait of Jesus*, London, 1975; C. Brown (ed.), *History, Criticism and Faith*, London, 1977. See also F. F. Bruce, 'Jesus Christ', in J. D. Douglas (ed.), *The New International Dictionary of the Christian Church*, Exeter, 1974, 531-534; C. F. D. Moule, *The Phenomenon of the New Testament*, London, 1967.

50   P. de Rosa, *Jesus who became Christ*, London, 1975.

51   G. Vermes, *Jesus the Jew*, London, 1973.

52   D. Flusser, *Jesus*, New York, 1969.

53   In the interests of simplicity the above survey has confined itself to a representative selection of significant works. Even so, much of importance has been omitted to avoid confusing the reader. Nevertheless, it would be misleading to omit all mention of the following: C. K. Barrett, *Jesus and the Gospel Tradition*, London, 1967; O. Betz, *What do we know about Jesus?* London, 1968; X. Léon-Dufour, *The Gospels and the Jesus of History*, London, 1968 (representative of French-speaking Roman Catholic scholarship); E. Schweizer, *Jesus*, London, 1971

(more a study of the significance of Jesus in the NT); E. Stauffer, *Jesus and his Story*, London, 1960.

54   S. G. F. Brandon, *Jesus and the Zealots*, Manchester, 1967.

55   S. G. F. Brandon, ' "Jesus and the Zealots": A Correction', *New Testament Studies* 17, 1970-71, 453.

56   M. Hengel, *Was Jesus a Revolutionist?* Philadelphia, 1971; *Victory over Violence*, London, 1975.

CHAPTER 7

The Nature of the Gospels

In the preceding chapter we attempted to chart the course of modern discussion of the problem of the historical Jesus in order to see what is the present status of the enquiry. It became apparent that the history of research was a history of the application of various methods of study to the Gospels in the hope that each of these in turn would unlock a few more doors and enable some further progress to be made in reaching back to the historical Jesus. In the days before the development of critical study of the Gospels it was assumed that the Gospels had been written by eye-witnesses of the events recorded, or at least by people who were in close touch with the eye-witnesses. Thus the Gospels of Matthew and John were assumed to have been written by disciples of Jesus who could draw on their own memories of what had happened. The Gospel of Mark was written by one who, according to early tradition, had been a close colleague of Peter, so that this Gospel was in effect 'The Gospel according to Peter'. As for Luke, he was an associate of Paul and it could be assumed that he had access to eye-witnesses of the ministry of Jesus in the early church; indeed he himself laid claim to have such dependable information at his disposal. [1] In various ways this simple picture of the situation has been shattered. As far back as 1924 B. H. Streeter, a distinguished English critical scholar, could affirm: 'We thus arrive at the quite simple conclusion: the burden of proof is on those who would assert the traditional authorship of Matthew and

John and on those who would deny it in the case of Mark and Luke'. [2] Since that time scholarship in general has rejected the traditional authorship of Matthew and John and has proceeded to do the same in the case of Mark and Luke also. The familiar figures of the four Evangelists have been replaced by shadowy ghost writers — or possibly even by groups of writers. The case that the Gospels are reliable because they were written by eye-witnesses seems to have evaporated. Even in its heyday it was sometimes not clear which way the argument was being directed: did the eye-witness character of the Evangelists guarantee the historicity of the contents, or was it the traces of what looked like eye-witness testimony (*e.g.* to particular times and locations in John) which proved authorship by an eye-witness?

A further point was that, even if the Gospels were written by their traditional authors, the material contained in them gave the impression of having passed through several stages of oral transmission: it was as if the original eye-witnesses told other people the stories of Jesus soon after they happened; they then passed them on to other people and so on until at last they came back to the original witnesses who then wrote them down in the rounded form which they had by now come to possess. Hence, even if the original apostles were writing the story, this was no guarantee that they themselves had not modified the facts in the course of repeated re-tellings by themselves and under the influence of the way in which other Christians recounted them.

As a result of these factors the material in the Gospels can be compared to a picture by an old Master which has progressively disappeared under a series of layers of varnish, touching-up paint and dust, and the task of the scholar is to remove the layers one by one with infinite care in order to recover the hidden masterpiece. [3] This simile is very much a simplification of a complex situation, since the material of the original picture has, as it were, become mingled with the succeeding layers of other stuff so that at every point the critic is concerned to separate off the original paint from that with which it has been mixed. Nevertheless, it will serve to give some idea of the situation and the complexity of the resulting task. How can we work our way down from the Gospels through the successive layers of tradition to the historical basis?

THE GOSPELS AND THEIR ORIGINS

First of all, we must look again at the question of the origins of the Gospels. To what extent can this help us in estimating whether they are likely to contain historical portraits of Jesus?

The Gospel of Mark

Streeter's claim that the weight of evidence was in favour of the traditional authorship of Mark and Luke has, as we noted, come under fire, and there is less of a consensus of opinion on this point today than there was in his day. [4] None of the Gospels actually names its author in the text. But the Gospels of Luke and John were undoubtedly written by people whose identity was known by their readers — Theophilus (Luke 1:3) and the circle of people who attested the origin of the Gospel of John (John 21:24); there is no reason to regard these passages as literary fictions. Nor is there any evidence that the writers of the other two Gospels deliberately concealed their identities. So far as Mark is concerned, a tradition dating from early in the second century and attributed to a man called Papias who had contacts with the followers of the apostles affirmed that he was some kind of assistant to Peter and that he wrote down Peter's account of Jesus. This tradition has been said to be unreliable for three main reasons. First, it dates from a time when the early church was attempting to secure respectable pedigrees for its documents by attributing them to the apostles or their associates. Since it was known that Peter had not written a Gospel (although a considerable number of books, including a Gospel, were written in the second century and attributed to him), it was natural to do the next best thing by attributing a Gospel to one of his colleagues, and 1 Pet. 5:13

suggested the appropriate name to use. Second, the character of the Gospel suggests that it reflects traditions handed down in the early church rather than a record of one man's story of Jesus. Third, the degree of theological reflection that has been uncovered in the Gospel is hardly consistent with a simple recording of an eye-witness testimony to Jesus. For these reasons many scholars are sceptical of the identification of the author of this Gospel as John Mark, or suggest that, although he may have borne the common name of 'Mark', he was not the Mark named in 1 Pet. 5:13. [5]

But this case, even in its more refined forms, turns out to be weak when tested. There is no clear evidence that at the time of Papias the church was seeking to establish apostolic origins for its documents, and, if it was doing so, there were several people who were better candidates for the position than Mark. Further, while it may be granted that the Gospel contains some community tradition, this does not rule out the presence of some Petrine material also, and the latter could well have attained some of the forms characteristic of oral material simply as a result of Peter's having often recounted his memories when he was preaching and teaching in the church. Finally, it is increasingly evident that there was much theological evaluation of the traditions about Jesus in the early church, and there is no reason why John Mark should have refrained from doing this himself. In short, the objections to Marcan authorship fall far short of proof. The question, then, is whether the case for Marcan authorship can be accepted. Can we advance from 'it is possible' to 'it is probable' that John Mark wrote the Gospel which now bears his name? It is here that the subjective element in historical study enters; scholars differ regarding the 'amount' and 'quality' of the evidence which is needed to make this shift from possibility to probability. An answer depends very largely on what we make of Papias's testimony. This has been carefully examined by R. P. Martin, and the impression which I gain from his comments is not that Papias was foisting an author's name on to an anonymous Gospel but rather that he was defending a known author against criticism of his unreliability. [6]

If so, the tradition was earlier than Papias himself, and this makes it the less likely that it was created for tendentious reasons. Later church writers saw no cause to reject it. The onus of proof still lies on those who would contradict them.

The Gospel of Luke

Acts (which is undoubtedly by the same author as the Gospel of Luke) contains some statements in the first person plural; these represent the narrator as a companion of Paul during part of his missionary career, and an examination of the names of Paul's companions suggests that Luke is the most likely of them. From the second century onwards there is a firm tradition that Luke was the author of the Gospel and Acts, although the earliest traces of this tradition are hard to establish. In this case, there is no problem caused by the presence of community traditions in the Gospel, since the author was confessedly dependent on earlier transmitters of the tradition (including eye-witnesses). The difficulties are whether the tradition is a reliable one. It has been argued that second-century Christians simply made the same deductions from the New Testament evidence as we ourselves have done, and that therefore their testimony has no independent value in corroborating the inferences which can be drawn from that evidence. Further, the evidence itself is of doubtful value: how do we know for certain that the author of the 'we' passages in Acts was Luke, and that he wrote the Gospel and Acts as a whole? May it not be that another writer incorporated extracts from a diary kept by an unknown companion of Paul, or may it not be that the use of 'we' is a literary device to vivify the story? Most important of all, it is claimed that the picture of the early church and of Paul in particular in Acts is so different from that which can be obtained from Paul's own letters that it can hardly be the work of a contemporary of Paul. [7]

It will be seen that the evidence in the case of Luke is all drawn from Acts rather than the Gospel. As in the case of Mark, the objections to Luke's authorship of his Gospel can be rebutted. Thus, in the first place, it is significant that the second-century Christians made the same identification of Paul's companion in the 'we' passages as appears most probable to many modern scholars, and that there is no indication that any rival candidate ever got any votes. There is some evidence that the tradition may go back to AD 120, but this point can be stated only with great caution. Second, since the author of Luke-Acts was a careful writer who had done his best to smooth out the differences in style between his sources, it is not probable that he left the 'we' passages in Acts standing without good reason; the view that they represent a literary device is quite unlikely, and it remains most probable that they indicate the final author's own presence in the scenes which he is describing. The third point is far-ranging in its scope; scholars of equal eminence are arrayed on both sides of the debate, but in my judgment the picture of the early church and of Paul in Acts is not incompatible with historical reality.

In the case of Acts we do have some internal evidence which leads to an identification of its author as Luke. Here the evidence in my opinion clearly justifies a 'probably' rather than a 'possibly', and a fairly strong 'probably' at that. [8]

A number of scholars would claim that at present the burden of proof lies on defenders of Mark and Luke as the authors of the Gospels associated with their names. In both cases, however, this burden can be taken up and sustained with considerable confidence. We must now turn to the two Gospels whose traditional authorship is in much greater doubt.

The Gospel of Matthew

The evidence for the traditional authorship of the Gospel of Matthew again depends upon statements made in the second century and traceable back to Papias who said that 'Matthew composed the *Logia* in the Hebrew tongue'. There is no internal evidence in the Gospel itself for or against ascribing it to Matthew. The case against Matthaean authorship reduces to two points.

First, if the Gospel was written by one of the twelve disciples of Jesus, it is hard to understand why its author incorporated in his account nearly the whole of the Gospel of Mark which was not by an eye-witness. It may be replied that an apostle might well have preferred the testimony derived from Peter to his own, but this explanation fails to account for the fact that there is no indication whatever in the Gospel that Mark's account has been supplemented by any material that bears the marks of independent eye-witness testimony. A more basic counter-reply is to question the hypothesis that Matthew was dependent for his information on the Gospel of Mark and to suggest that the present Gospel or an earlier edition of it in fact underlies the Gospel of Mark. This point will be examined below, but it will be found to be at variance with the facts.

The second argument against the tradition is that the interpretation of Papias's statement is uncertain. He does not say (in effect) that the Gospel according to Matthew was in fact written by Matthew, but rather that Matthew compiled the 'logia', and it is an open question what he meant by this word. [9] It need not have been the Gospel. Moreover, Papias says that the 'logia' were compiled in the Hebrew language, and this description will not fit the present Gospel which is dependent upon the Greek Gospel of Mark. This leaves open the possibility, however, that if Papias has got his facts right, Matthew may have been responsible for some earlier collection of tradition that lies behind the Gospels, and it is possible that Matthew's name came to be attached to one of the Gospels which contains this material. [10] This view may seem speculative, but its merit is that it explains the evidence adequately. If so, it gives some encouragement to the view that part of the Gospel tradition was compiled by an early disciple of Jesus. It is, of course, possible that Papias was mistaken in assuming that Matthew was responsible for compiling anything, but there is no positive reason for adopting this point of view. The conclusion is that it is unlikely that the Gospel of Matthew was compiled by Matthew but that there is reasonable evidence that Matthew did compile some record of the traditions about Jesus, which has been incorporated in the Gospel. [11]

The Gospel of John

Second-century tradition strongly associates John the apostle with the compilation of the Gospel ascribed to him. The Gospel professes to have been composed by a 'beloved disciple', and no identification of this anonymous figure is so probable as that John the apostle is meant by this designation. But the tradition is first clearly attested towards the end of the second century by Irenaeus, and the Gospel had something of a struggle for recognition in the church. This latter fact may well have been because the Gospel was accepted at an early stage by Gnostic Christians, and orthodox Christians may well have thought that anything which they believed to be a support for their position was necessarily false, even despite claims to apostolic authorship. It is, therefore, doubtful whether the Gospel's slowness in being accepted by the orthodox is an argument against its apostolic authorship. Alleged historical and geographical errors in the Gospel have been urged against its authorship by an eye-witness of the ministry of Jesus, but these cannot carry the burden of proof assigned to them. More weight attaches to the fact that the Gospel shows some evidence of use of earlier sources and that its thought, with its subtle blend of Jewish and Hellenistic ideas, seems to require a more learned and profound author than a Galilean fisherman. The Revelation is also ascribed to John the apostle, and it is difficult to believe that one mind produced both works, so different in language and character. These facts lead most scholars to conclude that John could not have been the author of this Gospel. However, the weight of the evidence for some connection between John and the Gospel is so strong that many scholars feel unable to deny that John had something to do with the Gospel. The tradition suggests that John dictated the Gospel, and this may well conceal the fact that John's memoirs of Jesus were

an important source for the Gospel, and that his influence lay behind the various Johannine works in the
New Testament. On the whole, therefore, it is improbable (although not impossible) that John himself wrote
the Gospel, but very probable that his influence lay behind
it. [12]

Our conclusion is that Matthew and John had something
to do with the traditions recorded in the Gospels ascribed to
them, although the extent of this influence cannot be
estimated. We are thus left with two Gospels which were
probably written by the men whose names they bear and two
which remain anonymous. This conclusion is not unimportant. Clearly we cannot argue from apostolic authorship to
reliable testimony in the old-fashioned way, but equally we
cannot simply dismiss the possibility of apostolic testimony
in the Gospels. When Luke says that he took pains to find
out what the eye-witnesses said, there is no reason at
all to suppose that he was uttering conventionalities or
that he was just a facile liar. Nor is there any reason to suppose that the other Evangelists did not exercise some degree
of similar care in the compilation of their Gospels. But
while this gives us some justification for believing that the
Evangelists honestly recorded what they believed to be
historical, it does not absolve us from the responsibility
of asking whether each individual piece of information in
their Gospels is reliable. At most we have some justification
for assuming that they were not wild romancers without
any historical connection with the origins of Christianity.
We have still to ask how they exercised their responsibilities and to what extent they made use of reliable information. Before we can take this step, however, it is necessary that we raise the question of the sources employed
by the Evangelists.

THE SOURCES OF THE GOSPELS

In the previous section we have seen that the Gospels were
written by men who stood at some remove from the events
which they were recording. [13] This fact immediately raises the
question of the sources of their information, and the first

possibility to be discussed is whether they made use of any written materials in the composition of their own works. When Luke tells us that many other people before him had attempted to compose narratives of what had happened (Luke 1:1), his statement gives us some justification for making this our starting point despite the fact that Jesus lived in a culture where there was greater reliance on oral teaching than on written records. The fact that any such oral teaching was committed to writing in the Gospels themselves makes us ask whether we can trace the beginnings of this process at an earlier date.

The Synoptic Gospels

After a century and more of discussion there is still dispute on the main lines of a solution to this problem. Nevertheless, a number of conclusions can be regarded as having a high degree of probability. First of all, scholars are agreed that the Gospels of Matthew, Mark and Luke display such great similarities among themselves in content and style that they must have shared some common sources of information. By contrast the Gospel of John is so different in content and style from the other three that its sources must be considered separately. With the first three Gospels it is possible to arrange their contents in parallel columns so as to give one picture (Greek *synopsis*; hence the use of the phrase 'Synoptic Gospels') of where they run in parallel and where they individually deviate from the general pattern.

Second, analysis of the contents and style of the Synoptic Gospels has led most scholars to the conclusion that Mark's Gospel lay before Matthew and Luke and was used by them as a primary source. The arguments for this are somewhat technical and cannot be reproduced in detail here. Suffice it to say that in matters of order and wording Matthew and Luke rarely agree with each other in differing from Mark in the passages which they have in common, and that comparative analysis of the wording of these common passages shows that Matthew and Luke are each independently editing Mark and adapting its contents to their own purposes. There are places where some other source material may have been known to both Matthew and Luke and may have influenced their wording in passages where they are each basically dependent upon Mark, but this does not significantly affect the main hypothesis. Again, it is possible that the copies of Mark used by Matthew and Luke were not identical textually with a modern text of the Gospel, but this too does not affect our conclusion.

I should be prepared to attach very high probability indeed to this conclusion. Nevertheless, it is only right to admit that it is not universally accepted. An earlier theory, which dates back to Augustine, is that Matthew is the oldest Gospel and that it was used by Mark and Luke as the basis of their Gospels. This theory still finds supporters today, particularly but not exclusively among Roman Catholic scholars. [14] While its proponents have shown that there are weaknesses in some aspects of the case that Mark was the earliest Gospel, they have not in my opinion succeeded in making this alternative theory at all plausible. Some scholars hold other, much more complicated theories which postulate a number of written sources behind all three Gospels, but these have not commanded any substantial assent.

Third, after allowing for those passages where Matthew and Luke have material in common with Mark, we are left with a further couple of hundred verses or so, principally containing sayings of Jesus, where Matthew and Luke again show parallelism with each other; in some cases their wording is virtually identical, whereas in others the same thoughts are conveyed in different wording. It can be argued that in these passages one of the Gospels has drawn upon the other, and the more popular theory of this kind is that Luke was making use of Matthew. [15] But this theory faces unsurmountable difficulties. If it were true, we should expect that Matthew would always have the more primitive form of wording in such passages, but literary analysis shows that this is not the case and that on occasion Luke's wording appears to be more original. Further, on this theory it is impossible to explain why Luke was never influenced by Matthew's wording when recording scenes also found in Mark. It is much more probable that Matthew and Luke were using some common source, now lost, for these sayings of Jesus. The symbol 'Q' is often used for this hypothetical source. But there is much less certainty about this postulated source than there is about the use of Mark as a source. The 'orthodox' view is that Q was a single written source, and recent scholars have offered detailed reconstructions of its original wording. [16] Their working assumption, which in their view is justified by subsequent investigation, is that Matthew and Luke had identical copies of the source before them, and the differences in wording between the two Gospels can be fully explained by the editorial activity of the two Evangelists. To other scholars, including the present writer, this is a forced explanation of various passages, and it is more likely that the copies of Q used by Matthew and Luke differed from each other in various places; in other words, editing of Q had started before the Evangelists carried the process a step further. [17] Yet another view is that there was no Q document at all, and that the Evangelists had access to various unwritten traditions. [18] This may well be the case with regard to some of the material commonly assigned to Q, although in my view it does not do justice to the evidence which shows that the two Evangelists were using sayings of Jesus which occur in such an order, with such common wording, and with such unity of subject-matter as to suggest that they had already been compiled in written form. The precise extent of Q is uncertain because we do not know whether each Evangelist included material from it that was omitted by the other. Despite these uncertainties, it seems very probable that Matthew and Luke had access to a written collection of (mainly) sayings of Jesus alongside Mark.

The establishment of these points creates the so-called 'Two-document' theory of the sources of the Synoptic Gospels. It clearly has its limitations. In the first place, it is only a hypothesis, the two parts of which have different relative degrees of probability. It is, however, a hypothesis which has proved to be a fruitful basis for study of the Gospels and its success in this regard gives what is perhaps the only kind of proof that can be expected for a hypothesis of this nature.

In the second place, this theory does not account for the sources of all the material in the first three Gospels. There remain considerable areas in Matthew and Luke which have no parallels in the other Gospels. Matthew contains a lot of the teaching of Jesus and some narratives which are peculiar to it. Some of this material may be from Q. Some of it may be from another compilation of sayings of Jesus used only by Matthew. The same situation holds in the case of Luke where again the Evangelist has probably drawn on Q material omitted by Matthew and on other sources of information. But there is no consensus of opinion among scholars as regards possible written sources for this material.

In the third place, the results of the investigation may seem meagre. We have accounted for a good deal of the contents of Matthew and Luke in terms of two written sources but so far we have done nothing about the problem of the sources used by Mark. Attempts to trace written sources used by Mark have so far not been successful. Many scholars would claim that Mark was in fact the first person to produce a written *Gospel*, although this is not of course the same thing as to say that he was the first person to put some *record* of part of what Jesus said and did into writing. In any case, we have gone as far in the detection of written sources as critical study can at present take us.

The Gospel of John

At the beginning of this section we laid John on one side, since it did not fall into the same category as the Synoptic Gospels. Did it have any written sources? This problem has been attacked from two main angles. First, there is the question of whether John knew and made use of any of the first three Gospels. Clearly he did not incorporate any of the other Gospels in his own record in the way in which Matthew and Luke used Mark. Nevertheless, he does show many contacts with them in points of detail — which perhaps should not surprise us unduly, since they were all writing about the same person. The question is whether these contacts arose from having read the other Gospels or from having independent access to the same traditions as lay behind them. Scholars are quite divided among themselves on this point. After a period during which the complete independence of John from the other Gospels was strongly favoured, there is at present something of a reaction in favour of the earlier view that John knew Mark and Luke. [19] But even if John did know the other Gospels, it seems most likely that he was not dependent on their information to any great extent, and that even where he records facts also found in them he was using independent sources of information. If this is the case, it is a fact of some significance, for it means that we have independent corroboration of some of the material in the Synoptic Gospels. [20]

The second angle of attack is to ask whether John used any other written sources for his Gospel. Even if he was familiar with the other Gospels, the major part of his own Gospel is quite different from them. Among recent scholars there is growing support for the hypothesis that John used a written account of the mighty works done by Jesus, and attempts have even been made to reconstruct its wording. [21] It is also possible that the teaching ascribed to Jesus in this Gospel comes from a source document, [22] although the evidence in this case is much weaker than in the case of the other possible source. Johannine source criticism is still in its infancy. [23]

THE CONTRIBUTION OF THE EVANGELISTS

Although the results of the preceding section have been somewhat meagre and hypothetical, we now have some information on the basis of which we can return to the question which was raised earlier: how did the Evangelists use the sources of information which were available to them? [24] This question can be answered with some assurance if we consider the use made by Matthew and Luke of Mark. Here we have a reasonably objective basis for drawing some conclusions which can then be extended, with all due caution, to other areas where we lack the original sources used by the Evangelists. With Mark before us we can actually see what Matthew and Luke have done with it in writing their own Gospels.

The results of such a comparison show that Matthew and Luke each incorporated most of Mark into their Gospels. In the main they preserved the order of the incidents in Mark, although they altered the order on occasion partly as a result of their use of other source material and partly in order to regroup the incidents in the interests of their own presentation of the ministry of Jesus. While they adhered fairly closely to Mark's wording, they exercised a fair degree of freedom in rewording their source. Mark's style is fairly simple and his narrative abounds in detail, sometimes to the point of prolixity. Both the other Evangelists considerably improve his style and abbreviate his stories. In general, a large part of their editorial activity can be described as clarification of their source in order to bring out its meaning more clearly for their readers. They tend to make most alterations at the beginning and end of stories (where they join on to other material), and they make least alteration in the actual sayings of Jesus. For the most part their alterations simply bring out the meaning implicit in Mark's text. At the same time, however, they have their own theological interests which they pursue, and they do amend Mark's account to express these. An interesting exercise in comparison is furnished by the parable of the sower and its explanation in Mark 4:3-9, 13-20. [25] When we examine the parallel accounts in Matt. 13:3-9, 18-23 and Luke 8:5-8, 11-15, it becomes evident that Matthew has highlighted the notion of *understanding* the word of God which is not present in so many words in Mark's version, although it is based on the intervening passage in Mark 4:10-12; in the same way Luke has emphasised the ideas of *believing* the word of God and *continuing faithfully* in discipleship despite temptations to fall away. In both cases the more developed teaching is in harmony with Mark's account, but it goes beyond what he actually says. But the extent of such rewriting of Mark is perhaps less than might be expected, and there can be no doubt that for the most part the essential substance of Mark's account has been retained by the later Evangelists. This point is worth making fairly emphatically, for some recent studies give the impression of almost uncontrolled, drastic rewriting of Mark by the later Evangelists.

It is true that there are some places where the original facts in Mark appear to have been obscured. In Matt. 8:28-34 it is surprising to find *two* demoniacs where Mark has only one, and the same thing has happened in Matt. 20:29-34 where blind Bartimaeus has acquired a companion who was unknown to Mark. Here and elsewhere it seems probable that Matthew has doubled the numbers without any historical basis in the stories themselves; it is possible that he was trying to indicate that Jesus performed more healings of the same kind than he had space to record as separate incidents. We have, therefore, to allow for the introduction of features which are not strictly historical into some of the incidents, but it is clear from the existence of Mark's version of the stories that Matthew had a firm basis in his source for the basic kernels of the stories. Similar problems arise in Luke; although in general Luke follows Mark's stories with little change, there are one or two places where he recounts incidents remarkably similar to those in Mark but with considerable difference in detail. In such cases (*e.g.* Jesus' visit to Nazareth, Luke 4:16-30; compare Mark 6:1-6) there is some debate as to whether Luke was freely rewriting Mark's story to make his own point in it, or was in possession of a different story or a different version of the same story in another source. On the whole, the latter set of possibilities is the more likely, but this simply shifts the historical problem back from Luke's version in relation to that of Mark to the version in Luke's source in relation to that in Mark.

In the same kind of way we can compare Matthew and Luke's treatment of Q material in order to detect their characteristic emphases, although here the enquiry is less objective since we do not know for sure the wording of their common source. It is, however, possible to proceed on a statistical basis to establish some probabilities. From study of their use of Mark it is possible to draw up a list of words and constructions favoured by each Evangelist in rewriting Mark. When a word typical of Luke in his revision of Mark turns up in a Q verse where Matthew offers a different word which is not typical of Matthaean style in his revision of Mark, the chances are that in this case Matthew has preserved the original wording of Q and Luke has introduced the alteration. In this situation, however, we are dealing with statistical probabilities and not with objective comparisons of the Gospels with extant sources, and therefore the process must be conducted with very great caution. It is probable that in the first flush of enthusiasm for this type of study scholars today are altogether too sanguine in the certainty with which they express conclusions that should be regarded as only tentative. There is a tendency to read too much significance into each and every detail where Matthew and Luke differ from Mark or from each other, and here too (as in many other aspects of New Testament study) they are often credited with the ruthless consistency of a computer. In the same way there is a strong temptation to claim as redactional what may well be traditional. Scholars have not reckoned sufficiently with the probability that the thinking of the Evangelists was moulded by the traditions which they inherited; apparent idiosyncrasies of Luke may be the idiosyncrasies of his traditions.

When these warnings are borne in mind, we have in 'redaction criticism' a method of study which can be fairly certain in its results when Matthew and Luke are compared with their extant source, Mark, and which can work to a fair degree of probability in assessing the editorial activity of Matthew and Luke in relation to Q.

If, however, Matthew and Luke have exercised creative editorship upon their written sources, the implication is presumably that any earlier compilers of written sources also exercised the same kind of editorial activity. It is a fair inference that Mark and the compiler of Q also edited the material available to them. [26] The same will also of course be true for the author of John, who, as we have already noted, may have made use of written sources. In all three cases, it is true, the compilers may have been using oral traditions as well as, or instead of, written sources; if this is so, it would presumably be the case that an even greater degree of editorial activity must be postulated, since the reduction of oral material to writing, especially if it is composed of independent units, affords greater scope for the compiler than the rewriting of existing documents.

But it is just here that the method becomes highly speculative. In the two earlier cases which we have examined, it was a case of comparing two Gospels with an extant source or of comparing two Gospels with a source whose wording could be established with some considerable probability by a comparison of the Gospels. But now we have, on the one hand, the cases of Mark and John, and, on the other hand, of Q. In the first of these two cases we have the texts of the documents in which we are trying to distinguish tradition from redaction, but in the second case we are dealing with a hypothetical document whose wording can be established only to a certain degree of probability. The second case is clearly going to produce much more speculative results than the former. In both cases, however, the method must work by means of estimating the characteristic vocabulary, style and motifs of the redactor, and this depends on the use of statistical probability already mentioned in connection with Matthew and Luke. The result is that the method is highly speculative when applied in cases where we simply have the text of the redactor before us and have to work out the presence of traditional elements in it. Needless to say, the dangers involved in the method have not prevented scholars from tackling the problems. One does not wish to be unduly pessimistic or over-cautious in estimating the validity of this method, but it must be emphasised that at the present moment it is still in its infancy and that the results obtained by different investigators show that there is a considerable element of subjectivity in its application. Most of the work which has been carried out in this area has been in the German-speaking world, and its results have not yet trickled through into English literature to any great extent. [27]

Consequently, there is something of a gap in our investigation at this point. We have managed to peel off the top layer of paint from our picture, but so far there has been only limited success in peeling off the next layer. Fortunately, the layers of later varnish and touching up of the original picture are not of uniform thickness and have been applied somewhat piecemeal. Even if one cannot totally remove a layer of varnish, one can see through it with reasonable clarity, and there are some places where it has not been applied at all. As a result, it is still possible to see what is below it without too much distortion, and we can proceed to explore at a deeper level in order to see if by the use of other methods we can make further progress towards our objective.

NOTES

1 This traditional view of the authorship and sources of the Gospels is still held today by some scholars who are fully abreast of the critical problems but urge that no compelling reason has been produced for abandoning it; see D. Guthrie, *New Testament Introduction*, London, 1970.
2 B. H. Streeter, *The Four Gospels*, London, 1924, 1953, 562.
3 The simile is borrowed from the publisher's blurb on the dust cover of J. Jeremias, *The Parables of Jesus*, London, 1954.
4 Nevertheless, Streeter's view can still find supporters, *e.g.* R. H. Fuller, *A Critical Introduction to the New Testament*, London, 1966.
5 For details of recent discussion of Mark see R. P. Martin, *Mark: Evangelist and Theologian*, Exeter, 1972.
6 R. P. Martin, *op. cit.*, 80-83.
7 For the case against Lucan authorship see, for example, W. G. Kümmel, *Introduction to the New Testament*, London, 1966, 102-105, 123-132.
8 For the case for Lucan authorship see, for example, E. E. Ellis, *The Gospel of Luke*, London, 1974, 40-51.
9 The word *logia* (plural of Greek *logion*) means 'oracles' and could refer to sayings of Jesus, stories about Jesus, or even a collection of prophetic 'oracles' from the Old Testament.
10 An association of Matthew with the hypothetical Gospel source 'Q' was defended by T. W. Manson, *The Sayings of Jesus*, London, 1949, 15-20.
11 See D. Hill, *The Gospel of Matthew*, London, 1972, 52-55.
12 See, for example, R. E. Brown, *The Gospel according to John*, London, 1971, I, lxxxvii-civ.
13 The question of how far the Evangelists stood from the life of Jesus is not unimportant. G. A. Wells, who has a vested interest in dating the Gospels as late as possible, sums up by saying that 'The latest of the four gospels existed by AD 125 and the earliest of them was written between AD 70 and this date...the evidence allows that [Mark] was written about the middle of this period' (*Did Jesus Exist?* 92). He

is right about the upper limit, which is fixed by the existence of a papyrus fragment of John (generally reckoned to be the latest of the Gospels). But although many scholars would also regard AD 70 as the lower limit, there is reason to suspect that it is too high and that some of the Gospels may have been written earlier (B. Reicke, 'Prophecies on the Destruction of Jerusalem', in D. E. Aune [ed.], *Studies in New Testament and Early Christian Literature*, Leiden, 1972, 121-134). Certainly in the case of Mark, there is good reason to date it close to AD 70; Well's arguments for a later date are not cogent. The first three Gospels were most probably written within thirty to fifty years of the death of Jesus. While this may seem a long period, it must be remembered that the traditions contained in them can be traced back to a much earlier point. The nature of the traditions indicates that they have undergone a lengthy process of transmission, so that their origins considerably ante-date the Gospels. For an early dating of the Gospels see J. A. T. Robinson, *Redating the New Testament*, London, 1976.

14   The case is best presented by W. R. Farmer, *The Synoptic Problem: A Critical Analysis*, London, 1964. For a confrontation of the two main theories see the essays by D. L. Dungan and J. A. Fitzmyer in D. G. Miller (ed.), *Jesus and Man's Hope*, Pittsburgh, 1970, I, 51-97, 131-170.

15   M. D. Goulder, *Midrash and Lection in Matthew*, London, 1974.

16   The best work of this kind is still T. W. Manson, *The Sayings of Jesus*. The more recent works, to which the criticisms made in the text are more relevant, are D. Lührmann, *Die Redaktion der Logienquelle*, Neukirchen, 1969; P. Hoffmann, *Studien zur Theologie der Logienquelle*, Münster, 1972; S. Schulz, *Q — Die Spruchquelle der Evangelisten*, Zürich, 1972.

17   G. Bornkamm, *Jesus of Nazareth*, 217.

18   J. Jeremias, *New Testament Theology* I, 37-41.

19   C. K. Barrett, 'John and the Synoptic Gospels', *Expository Times* 85, 1973-74, 228-233.

20   For the presence of independent tradition in John see especially C. H. Dodd, *Historical Tradition in the Fourth Gospel*, Cambridge, 1963.

21   R. T. Fortna, *The Gospel of Signs: A Reconstruction of the Narrative Source underlying the Fourth Gospel*, Cambridge, 1970.

22   R. Bultmann, *The Gospel of John*, Oxford, 1971.

23   D. M. Smith, 'The Sources of the Gospel of John: An Assessment of the Present State of the Problem', *New Testament Studies* 10, 1963-64, 336-351.

24   The study of the Evangelists' own contribution to their Gospels has come to the forefront of scholarly activity under the name of 'redaction criticism' since the 1950s. See the survey by J. Rohde, *Rediscovering the Teaching of the Evangelists*, London, 1968, and S. S. Smalley's essay in I. H. Marshall (ed.), *New Testament Interpretation*.

25   For a detailed study of this passage see I. H. Marshall, 'Tradition and Theology in Luke (Luke 8:5-15)', *Tyndale Bulletin* 20, 1969, 56-75.

26 Hence there is much interest at present in the theological outlook of
    the compiler of 'Q'. See G. N. Stanton, 'On the christology of Q', in
    B. Lindars and S. S. Smalley (ed.), *Christ and Spirit in the New Testament*,
    Cambridge, 1973, 27-42.
27 See, however, N. Perrin, *What is Redaction Criticism?* London, 1970, for
    application of the method to Mark.

CHAPTER 8

The Form of
the Gospel Tradition

IN THE PREVIOUS chapter we discussed the Gospel writers and the ways in which they used the written sources and other traditions which they had at their disposal. Now that we can, as it were, set their contribution on one side, we can try to proceed backwards in time by examining the nature of the traditions incorporated in the Gospels. This part of our enquiry will cover two chapters. In the present chapter we shall be concerned with questions that have basically to do with the *forms* in which the traditions have been handed down, and in the following chapter we shall look at the ways in which the *contents* of the traditions may have been affected in the course of transmission.

We saw that the isolation of possible written sources behind the Gospels did not wholly account for the material incorporated in them. Our task now is to look at the nature of the material which was incorporated either directly into the Gospels or indirectly via their written sources, and which was probably handed down by word of mouth. To some extent the task of compilers editing traditions and putting them in written form and of transmitters of tradition consciously or unconsciously reshaping the material which they passed on are similar, and the line between these two types of activity is somewhat fluid; nevertheless, it should be noted that a number of recent scholars have begun to question whether written and oral traditions are transmitted in the same ways. [1] We must, therefore, be cautious in our study of this particular aspect of the sources concerning Jesus.

THE FRAMEWORK OF THE GOSPEL NARRATIVE

In our historical survey we saw that the starting point of form critical study lay in the twin postulates that the framework of the Gospel narrative was secondary, and that the original, oral tradition about Jesus was handed down in discrete units. The implication of these two propositions is that we have no basis for a chronological outline of the ministry of Jesus. These postulates have seemed so self-evident to scholars since they were stated by K. L. Schmidt that they have received little scrutiny.

In a brief, but significant, article C. H. Dodd made a response to Schmidt. He claimed that while much of the tradition was handed down in short units, Mark had nevertheless managed to place them in a broadly correct order. While certain items appeared to have been associated for topical reasons, Dodd suggested that this was because certain topics were uppermost in the teaching and ministry of Jesus at particular times. He then separated off the material in the early chapters of the Gospel which appeared to represent 'editorial framework' rather than traditional units, and suggested that when this was viewed as a whole it gave the impression of a reasonably coherent narrative which had not been tailor-made as a setting for the various incidents incorporated in it. Finally, he observed that the early preaching of the church probably contained a rough outline of the ministry of Jesus. Hence he concluded that Mark had available to him not only independent units of tradition but also some groupings of items and a rough outline of the ministry, and on this basis he created an account partly chronological and partly topical. [2]

Dodd's thesis was subjected to detailed criticism by D. E. Nineham, [3] and in the light of his and other comments needs reappraisal.

Nineham claims that it is unlikely that the early church had an outline of the ministry of Jesus since there is no plausible 'life setting' for its use; he mentions only to dismiss the fact that Luke portrays both Peter and Paul (Acts 10:37-41; 13:22-31) as including a bare outline of the ministry of Jesus in their preaching. But it is in fact highly probable that the early church did explain who Jesus was by making some historical reference to him in the course of its preaching, and Nineham's suggestions that nobody showed any historical curiosity in the matter, and that such an account had no theological significance, are quite unconvincing. It is, of course, possible that the material attributed to Peter and Paul by Luke is his own creation, based on the Gospel of Mark rather than upon independent tradition, but there are some grounds for suspecting that traditional material lies at the base of Luke's account here. [4]

It is generally accepted among scholars that the passion story existed in the form of a continuous narrative from an early date. [5] Here we have a collection of incidents which were arranged in their probable historical order — an order dictated by circumstances which allowed little play for imagination. It is not clear whether any earlier parts of the ministry of Jesus were also remembered in the same kind of way. There is certainly a case that some of the collections of stories in Mark were already grouped before they reached the Evangelist. One such example, noted by Schmidt, is the story of a typical day's ministry in Mark 1:21-39. The other examples usually cited (Mark 2:1-3:6; 11:27-12:44), however, may represent collections of stories with the same common theme of conflict between Jesus and the Jews rather than incidents which happened in series.

It is possible, however, that although chronological sequences of this kind are hard to attest, there may nevertheless be a broadly chronological outline of the material in Mark. The general sequence of Jesus' baptism by John, a ministry in Galilee, a journey to Jerusalem, a period of activity there, and his death and resurrection is attested beyond all doubt. Within this very broad framework the Marcan picture of the Galilean ministry with its initial success, the calling of the Twelve and their missionary work, the feeding of the multitude, and thereafter a concentration by Jesus on instructing his disciples — this picture has impressed numerous scholars by its historical plausibility. [6] It can be argued that historical plausibility is not the same as historical accuracy, but there is good reason to hold that in this case the outline can be trusted.

One important critic at this point is W. Marxsen who has drawn attention to the different historical pattern in John where Jesus moves to and fro between Galilee and Jerusalem; he suggests that the simple Galilee/Jerusalem pattern in Mark is due to the Evangelist who wished to stress the theological significance of Galilee as the place of Jesus' ministry and Jerusalem as the place of his passion. [7] But Marxsen's case is palpably weak. Indisputably original elements in the tradition firmly anchor much of his ministry in Galilee and (of course) his death in Jerusalem. The Johannine material reflects the practice of Jesus, as a pious Jew, in regularly visiting Jerusalem on the occasion of religious festivals, and at various points Mark and John supplement, rather than contradict, each other's accounts. [8]

The weakest element in Dodd's case is perhaps his argument that the connective tissue in Mark forms a continuous outline of the Galilean ministry. Nevertheless, the arguments adduced against it are not conclusive. Thus it can be objected that it is largely composed in Mark's own vocabulary and style. But this objection holds water only if it can be assumed that a text in an author's characteristic idiom *must* have been created by him; it is also possible that he may have rewritten source material in his own words, and this would be especially possible when reworking the connective material to incorporate fresh units of narrative. More weight must be attached to Nineham's argument here that the connective tissue represents Mark's own picture of the ministry so well that he surely could have created it. On the other hand, when Nineham takes up Dodd's admission that Mark did not fit his material too neatly into this outline and tries to use this against him by suggesting that Mark can hardly have possessed a traditional outline when he treated it with so little respect, it looks as though he is trying a 'Heads I win, tails you lose' type of argument; either the outline fitted Mark's purpose or else it didn't, and Nineham cannot have it both ways.

There may, therefore, be something in Dodd's claim at this

point, although it is perhaps more likely that Mark's 'connective tissue' contains some traditional elements rather than
that it was a continuous outline of the ministry. The point is
one that needs further investigation. But, regardless of how
we judge this point, the evidence as a whole suggests that
Dodd was right in holding that 'in broad lines the Marcan
order does represent a genuine succession of events, within
which movement and development can be traced'. The
events appear to have been placed in broad chronological
order, even though it must remain doubtful whether the
actual wording of a pre-Marcan historical framework can be
traced in the Gospel.

THE FORM OF THE GOSPEL NARRATIVES

From the framework of the Gospel narratives we must now
turn to the narratives themselves and examine the contribution of form criticism to the question of their origin and
historical worth. At an earlier point we gave an outline of the
analyses of the narratives into their different types made by
Dibelius and Bultmann. Subsequent writers have attempted
to take their work further at various points, usually by
making subdivisions in the various types of sayings found in
the Gospels. For example, S. Schulz has examined the
'prophetic' sayings which he finds in some of the 'Q' material
and notes five particular forms of saying that are found:
sayings introduced by 'I say to you' which represent authoritative utterances by early Christian prophets; blessings
which promise future blessings to certain people; woes
which contain messages of judgment; expressions of an 'eschatological *ius talionis*', *i.e.* sayings which draw a comparison
between how men behave in this world and how they will
be judged by God; 'which of you?' sayings which lead
men to think seriously about the character and actions of
God in comparison with those of men. [9] Such refinements
as these make the classification more exact and serviceable.
The question to be asked is how this classification helps
us to work back from the present *form* of the tradition to
its earlier stages. This question is virtually inseparable
from the question of the *content* of the tradition, but we

shall try to keep the two issues separate for the purposes of exposition.

If we consider first the types of narrative about Jesus, we can observe straightaway that the classification is not very exact. The two forms of story which stand out clearly are the pronouncement story and the healing miracle story. These have both been examined fairly thoroughly by scholars and their characteristics are clear enough. But the other types of story — 'novels', 'legends' and such like — do not emerge anything like so clearly from form-critical study, and it would be better to speak of 'novelistic' and 'legendary' motifs being found in such stories. A pronouncement story has little interest in filling out an incident with detail, whereas other stories may contain much more detail which does not contribute materially to the main point of the story.

Next, we must take note of T. W. Manson's statement:

> Strictly the term 'form criticism' should be reserved for the study of the various units of narrative and teaching, which go to make up the Gospels, in respect of their form alone... But a paragraph of Mark is not a penny the better or the worse for being labelled, 'Apothegm' or 'Pronouncement Story' or 'Paradigm'. In fact if form criticism had stuck to its proper business, it would not have made any real stir. We should have taken it as we take the forms of Hebrew poetry or the forms of musical composition. [10]

There are two things to observe here. First of all, Manson wrote at a time when 'form criticism' was a term used in practice to mean more than the mere classification of forms of tradition; it included various other things including the history of the development of the tradition. More recent scholarship has begun to refer to the latter as 'tradition criticism', and this has allowed the original term to be defined in stricter terms, though perhaps not as strictly as Manson would have wished.

Second, so far as Manson's limited definition of the scope of form criticism is concerned, his estimate of its use in historical criticism remains standing: '*a paragraph of Mark is*

*not a penny the better or the worse for being labelled, "Apothegm" or
"Pronouncement Story" or "Paradigm"'*. I was tempted to describe
this as Manson's famous statement, but it is not sufficiently
famous among practitioners of the art of form criticism, and
therefore I make no apology for repeating it and emphasising
it. The form of a story is no guide to its historicity. [11] Why,
then, was it ever thought that it was? The answer is bound up
with the questions of the content and 'life setting' of the
stories.

Form and historicity

We may make some progress here by asking the question,
which came first, the pronouncement story with its lack of
detail or the fuller type of story found in the 'novels' and
'legends'? Is detail a mark of primitive or developed tradition? R. Bultmann stated that details, such as the use of
proper names, are accretions to the earlier form of stories. But
the truth is that we cannot tell for certain. This has been
demonstrated by E. P. Sanders in a careful study in which he
examined the evidence in areas where control was possible
and concluded that

> There are no hard and fast laws of the development of
> the Synoptic tradition. On all counts the tradition deve-
> loped in opposite directions. It became both longer and
> shorter, both more and less detailed, and both more and
> less Semitic... For this reason, *dogmatic statements that a
> certain characteristic proves a certain passage to be earlier than
> another are never justified.'* [12]

Sanders allowed that some general tendencies could be
detected, and that some criteria were stronger than others,
but his fundamental point was that such evidence by itself
cannot prove anything; it can only establish a balance of
probability.

Essentially the same point was made by A. M. Ramsey,
former Archbishop of Canterbury and himself a biblical
scholar. He protested warmly against the assertion of R. H.
Fuller that a couple of passages in the Gospels in their present

form 'must be judged by the rules of traditio-historical criticism to be reflections of the church's Christology':[13] 'What rules?' he said. 'Historical science does not have rules, and the suspicion arises that the rules here may be more those of a game than a science.'[14] Sanders makes the same point when he notes that the 'laws' by which tradition develops are statements of what has happened, expressing probabilities; they do not constitute rules which the transmitters of tradition were bound to obey, and any individual transmitter could easily break them. They are, in other words, statistical summaries of observable trends, and *not* norms which people were required to obey. [15] And Sanders' book shows that the extent to which they were observed varied considerably.

The point which emerges from all this is that we cannot claim that one 'form' of story is necessarily earlier or later than another 'form', simply on grounds of form.

But this is not the end of the story. If we have a pronouncement story, the 'pure form' contains a single statement ascribed to Jesus as its climax. If there are two or more such statements, the critic will tend to argue that one or more must be additions to the original statement. In the story of Jesus going through the cornfields on the Sabbath there are no less than three statements made to justify his conduct and that of his disciples (Mark 2:25f., 27, 28). [16] Critics are not happy until they have got rid of two of these from the original story, although one might well claim that the arguments for regarding each particular saying as 'late' tend to cancel one another out. In the present case there may well be reasons for considering some statements to be additions to earlier forms of the story, but there can be no wholesale rejection of all such 'additions' purely on grounds of form.

The question of the 'life setting'

R. Bultmann claimed that in many cases the original element in pronouncement stories was an isolated saying of Jesus, handed down by itself; only later did someone (in effect) ask the question, 'When and why did Jesus say this?', and proceed to come up with a suitable answer. On this view many of the settings of the sayings of Jesus are inventions by the early church. Bultmann was prepared to admit that many of these scenes *could* have happened in the ministry of Jesus, but he thought it more likely that the descriptions of them rested on a general memory of the sort of situations in which Jesus was involved rather than on a historical memory of particular scenes. Consequently, he spoke of them as 'ideal scenes'. He also regarded some of them as mirroring situations faced by the early church in its own conflict with the Jews. Thus, if the disciples were faced by Jewish critics questioning their conduct on the Sabbath, this was mirrored in the kind of scene created by the early church to act as a frame for the saying of Jesus which they quoted as the authority for their conduct ('And the Pharisees said to him, "Look, why are *they* doing what is not lawful on the Sabbath?"').[17] Bultmann was thus claiming that the settings of incidents in the Gospels reflect the *Sitz im Leben* or 'life setting' of the early church. This technical phrase properly refers to the sociological situation of the church *in general terms* in which particular types of material in the Gospels were found to be relevant or were created. It is often used less precisely to refer to a *particular* situation in which a story about Jesus was used, and then by extension scholars have spoken of a *Sitz im Leben Jesu* to refer to a particular occasion on which Jesus himself spoke or acted in a given manner.[18] Scholars have been tempted to assume that if there is a *Sitz im Leben* in the life of the church for a particular story, then this story was created in that setting. The extreme step in this direction is taken by N. Perrin who says that many of the narratives in the Gospels have been freely created within the early church, and that 'the most that the present writer believes can ever be claimed for a Gospel narrative is that it may represent a typical scene from the ministry of Jesus'.[19]

Such scepticism is thoroughly unjustified. The weak point logically is the claim that because a certain story was appropriate for use in a particular situation in the early church, then it is probable, if not certain, that it was created in that situation and for that purpose. But it is obvious that this is not a compelling argument. The fact that something is found to be useful in a particular situation does not mean that it was necessarily created in that situation. Preachers, for example, do not usually invent the illustrations in their sermons. The world is full of things made for one purpose and found to be useful (sometimes even more useful) for other purposes.

Further, if Jesus was in any way the inspiration of the early church, it is highly probable that the same sort of conflicts would have arisen in his life-time as in the time of the early church. If we take one example, that of 'Sabbath-breaking', we can make the point even more strongly. On the one hand, D. Daube has shown that Jewish rabbis were held responsible for the behaviour and teaching of their pupils. [20] Hence, the fact that Jesus is asked about his disciples' conduct rather than about his own is not a sign of lateness in the construction of the narrative; on the contrary, if the event had actually happened, this is how it would probably have happened. On the other hand, it is very questionable whether the problem of Sabbath-breaking was a live issue in the early church in Palestine which appears to have been fairly law-abiding. [21] Both of these points make it probable that the setting of the Sabbath conflict stories goes back to the ministry of Jesus. If so, we are justified in asking why the settings must be assumed to be typical rather than actual. We need to be given some *evidence* that this is the case, and sweeping generalisations will not do instead. The generalisations are not unimportant, and will be examined in due course, but even if valid they do not prove the point.

Stories of healing

Let us turn our attention now to the stories of the healing miracles of Jesus. Here again the question of form has been thought to be relevant to historicity. In the first place, stories about healings fall into fairly regular patterns: there is a description of the situation requiring a cure, an account of what the healer does, and a description of the effects of the healer's action both in terms of the actual cure and in terms of the reaction produced in any observers. This pattern is found in non-biblical stories of healings as well as in the Gospels. The fact that stories fall into this pattern is clearly as irrelevant to their historicity as is the fact that accounts of accidents in policemen's notebooks tend to fall into a stereotyped pattern. ('At 8.45 a.m. we received news of an accident on the A 123 X miles north of Sumtown, and immediately proceeded to the scene where we found a blue sportscar, registration no. XYZ 234P, lying in the ditch...'). The points made earlier about the presence or absence of details also apply in this connection.

In the second place, the case is sometimes made that the 'form' of miracle stories arose in a 'Hellenistic environment' when the early church was portraying Jesus in terms of a Hellenistic 'divine man' with unusual powers, and had to show that he surpassed any possible rivals. Although Bultmann allows that such stories were told about Jesus in the earliest, Palestinian church, he holds it as being much more probable that such stories were told in the Hellenistic church (*i.e.* churches in places like Antioch exposed to a wider, non-Jewish culture). [22] The presence of the kind of details found in pagan miracle stories suggests that the Gospel narratives arose in this environment.

But the picture is by no means as simple as this might suggest. Even in the case of a story which appears to resemble Hellenistic stories fairly closely, the healing of the widow's son at Nain (Luke 7:11-17), the story is couched in the language of the Old Testament and has close similarities to the stories of Elijah and Elisha. There is a considerable Old Testament element in other stories also, often interwoven in a fairly subtle manner. Moreover, similar stories were told in rabbinic Judaism about great rabbis, including some who were contemporary with Jesus, so that the likelihood of a Palestinian background for the stories about Jesus is increased. [23] Finally, we cannot use the presence of Hellenistic elements in stories about Jesus as a sign of their late development outside Palestine because Hellenistic culture had penetrated Palestine fairly thoroughly and affected the thinking of both Judaism and early Christianity. [24]

These points show that the case for the miracle stories being late constructions on account of their form is very questionable. Once again we have found that the form of Gospel material does not offer a safe criterion for estimating the historicity of what is related in it. In the case of the other types of narrative material recognised by form criticism, the 'formal' features are much more difficult to identify, and we have a rather miscellaneous collection of items. Here it is even more difficult to draw any historical conclusions from the form of the stories.

THE FORM OF THE SAYINGS OF JESUS

From the stories about Jesus we turn now to his sayings. Here we are likely to be in closer touch with primitive tradition, since it is fairly generally agreed that sayings of Jesus are likely to have been preserved more faithfully than stories about him. When the Evangelists were telling stories about Jesus, they obviously felt free to vary the wording to quite a considerable extent. But when they were recording his sayings, they were much more restrained in their handling of the wording. It is probable that there was considerable reverence for the sayings ascribed to Jesus, although this did not prevent modifications being made in their wording. And if the Evangelists acted in this way, there is strong probability that their predecessors were equally faithful in their attitude to the tradition which they handed on. This, however, is a point to which we must return later.

Of the five main categories of sayings recognised by Bultmann the one which has the highest claims to historicity is the parables. Yet here too questions of form have sometimes been made the basis for sceptical verdicts regarding the authenticity of some of the parabolical material. It has been claimed that 'parables' make one basic point, and that stories whose details are capable of allegorical interpretation are not true parables and therefore cannot go back to Jesus. [25] Why Jesus, however, should have been incapable of using allegory, although both the rabbis and the early church did, is a postulate which defies proof. Some parables have been

disallowed to Jesus on the grounds that they make *two* points
(as in the parable of the prodigal son), [26] and again the
argument is basically of the quite unconvincing form: since
Jesus usually told parables in form A, he can never have told
any in form B. Similarly, preachers who usually preach
three-point sermons could never preach two-point or
four-point sermons without breaking the 'rules' of form criticism.

These points are trivial enough. More serious problems
arise when critics note that the various Gospels contain their
own characteristic types of parables and proceed to argue
that Jesus could only have told one type, the other types
being creations of the Evangelists or their sources. [27] In
this case, arguments from form are allied with arguments
from source criticism and thus carry greater weight. When
a particular form of material appears only in one source,
there is some degree of probability that it was created
by the compiler of that source, but 'some degree of probability' is not the same thing as 'certainty', and other
factors must be taken into consideration in reaching a
verdict.

So far as the other forms of sayings are concerned, here we
run into the difficulty that the classification is based on
content rather than on form. The one apparent exception to
this statement is the 'I' sayings. Although one can isolate a
group of sayings which all have this form, their contents are
spread over the remaining three main categories of wisdom,
prophetic and legal sayings. Bultmann argued that in general
this particular group of sayings all looked back on the
ministry of Jesus as a completed whole, and therefore they
must come from the time after Easter when the early church
looked back and summed up the nature of Jesus' ministry.
Since so many could be explained in this way, Bultmann was
tempted to regard *all* such sayings with suspicion, even when
there was nothing particularly suspicious about their contents. [28] Here is a clear misuse of the argument from form.
The fact that Bultmann suspected the authenticity of some,
even of most, sayings of this kind because of their content, is
no argument for suspecting the authenticity of others simply
because they manifest the same form. Moreover, on this view

it would have been impossible for Jesus ever to have begun a saying with 'I...' and for such a saying to have been remembered. But the suggestion that Jesus never used 'I' is so utterly ridiculous that further comment on this travesty of form criticism is not needed.

The three remaining groups of wisdom, prophetic and legal sayings are differentiated from one another more by content than by form. Analysis of their form is not of much help in tracing the history of the tradition. But one negative point must be made. Sayings of all three kinds are to be found in the Old Testament and are characteristic of the three divisions in the Hebrew Bible: the law, the prophets and the writings. These forms lived on into New Testament times in the activity of the scribes, prophetic figures, and teachers in the wisdom tradition. There would be nothing strange in the use of any or all of these forms by Jesus and his disciples. The question of form cannot take us back with any assurance to Jesus, but at least we can say *with certainty* that the forms of the sayings do not give us a criterion for denying any of them to him. A saying of Jesus is not a penny the better or the worse for being labelled, 'prophetic saying' or 'apocalyptic saying' or...

If the arguments advanced in this section are sound, they indicate that form criticism is a tool which must be used with extreme caution in making historical judgments about the traditions in the Gospels. As a method of analysing the material and showing how it was handed down and used in the early church it has its obvious merits. It can teach us how the early church used the traditions about Jesus — and perhaps suggest how they should be used to-day. But when it is used as a means of passing negative historical judgments on the tradition, we may be tempted to conclude that it is being put to what is often an illegitimate use.

NOTES

1   E. E. Ellis, 'New Directions in Form Criticism', in G. Strecker (ed.), *Jesus Christus in Historie und Theologie*, Tübingen, 1975, 299-315; G. N. Stanton, 'Form Criticism Revisited', in M. Hooker and C. Hickling (ed.), *What about the New Testament?* London, 1975, 13-27. The basic

study is E. Güttgemanns, *Offene Fragen zur Formgeschichte des Evangeliums*, München, 1971².

2   C. H. Dodd, 'The Framework of the Gospel Narrative', *Expository Times* 43, 1931-32, 396-400 (reprinted in the author's *New Testament Studies*, Manchester, 1953, 1-11).

3   D. E. Nineham, 'The Order of Events in St Mark's Gospel — an examination of Dr Dodd's hypothesis', in D. E. Nineham (ed.), *Studies in the Gospels*, Oxford, 1955, 223-239.

4   G. N. Stanton, *Jesus of Nazareth in New Testament Preaching*, Cambridge, 1974, 67-85.

5   Against recent denials of this hypothesis see R. Pesch, 'Die Überlieferung der Passion Jesu', in K. Kertelge (ed.), *Rückfrage nach Jesus*, Freiburg, 1974, 148-173.

6   T. W. Manson, *The Servant-Messiah*, Cambridge, 1953, 65-79; V. Taylor, *The Gospel according to St Mark*, London, 1953, 145-149.

7   W. Marxsen, *Mark the Evangelist*, Nashville, 1969. This work, originally published in German in 1956, was one of the first expressions of the redaction-critical approach.

8   A. M. Hunter, *The Work and Words of Jesus*, London, 1973², 51-68, 131-138.

9   S. Schulz, *op. cit.*, 57-63.

10 T. W. Manson, *Studies in the Gospels and Epistles*, 5.

11 'The fact is, apart from the parables, form is rarely a decisive criterion for authenticity', R. H. Fuller, *A Critical Introduction to the New Testament*, 93.

12 E. P. Sanders, *The Tendencies of the Synoptic Tradition*, Cambridge, 1969, 272. Sanders was particularly concerned with the relation of the synoptic Gospels to one another, but his conclusions have some application to the development of the tradition.

13 R. H. Fuller, *The Foundations of New Testament Christology*, London, 1965, 111.

14 A. M. Ramsey, 'History and the Gospel', in F. L. Cross (ed.), *Studia Evangelica* IV, Berlin, 1968, 75-85, citation from 78.

15 E. P. Sanders, *op. cit.*, 272f.

16 See the survey in F. Neirynck, 'Jesus and the Sabbath. Some Observations on Mark II, 27', in J. Dupont (ed.), *Jésus aux origines de la christologie*, Gembloux, 1975, 227-270.

17 R. Bultmann, *The History of the Synoptic Tradition*, 48.

18 The terminology has been clarified by H. Schürmann, *Traditionsgeschichtliche Untersuchungen*, Düsseldorf, 1968, 47f.

19 N. Perrin, *Rediscovering the Teaching of Jesus*, 29.

20 D. Daube, 'Responsibilities of Master and Disciples in the Gospels', *New Testament Studies* 19, 1972-73, 1-15.

21 J. Roloff, *Das Kerygma und der irdische Jesus*, Göttingen, 1970, 85f.

22 R. Bultmann, *op. cit.*, 239f.

23 G. Vermes, *Jesus the Jew*, 58-82.

24 See below, pp. 182-186.

25 Writing in 1908, when the views of A. Jülicher about parables having

only one point were gaining currency, J. Denney commented sarcastically that the use of allegory by Jesus was 'a supposition which is nothing short of distressing to many honourable men' (*Jesus and the Gospel*, London, 1908, 315).

26 J. T. Sanders, 'Tradition and Redaction in Luke xv. 11-32', *New Testament Studies* 15, 1968-69, 433-438.

27 M. D. Goulder, 'Characteristics of the Parables in the Several Gospels', *Journal of Theological Studies* 19, 1968, 51-69.

28 R. Bultmann, *op. cit.*, 155f.

CHAPTER 9

The History of
the Gospel Tradition

IF THE ANALYSIS of the forms of the tradition has little to contribute to historical study of Jesus, the situation is very different with regard to 'tradition criticism', the study of the development and change in the tradition as it was handed down in the church. It is here that the question of the historicity of the tradition becomes most acute.

The historian's difficulty, says M. Bloch, is that he is like a soldier at the rear of a marching column, 'in which the news travels from the head back through the ranks. It is not a good vantage-point from which to gather correct information. Not so very long ago, during a relief march at night, I saw the word passed down the length of a column in this manner: "Look out! Shell holes to the left!" The last man received it in the form, "to the left!" took a step in that direction, and fell in.' [1]

This transformation was due to an error in oral transmission. On a more serious level, a story or saying which is passed on orally by several people will undergo changes in content, both deliberately and unconsciously. If the traditions about Jesus were transmitted orally in the early church, obviously they can have been affected in this way. If so, can we work back scientifically to the earliest forms of the tradition?

THE EARLIEST CHRISTIAN COMMUNITIES

We may begin by noting that an examination of a tradition

may reveal something about the community in which it was transmitted and thus enable us to allow for those aspects in which it has been modified or created by the community. A historical account may sometimes reveal more about the historian than about the event which he is describing. In the same way, a study of the Gospel tradition may tell us something about the church which formed it and thus enable us to 'subtract' elements which are not historical.

A vicious circle?

The application of this principle obviously demands that we know sufficient about the community which handed on the tradition in order to be able to recognise the effects of its character and situation on the transmission of the tradition. Otherwise, we are in danger of arguing in a circle, determining the character of the community from the character of the tradition, and then analysing the tradition in the light of those characteristics of the community which have been deduced from the tradition itself. Without some outside control on the procedure this method is open to considerable subjectivity. While a proponent of the method may argue that the circle need not be a vicious one, and that the success of the method in analysing the tradition provides justification for its employment, the objection still remains valid. This point has been made with considerable force by F. G. Downing who has claimed that if we want to find out about the historical Jesus we must begin with a clear knowledge of the historical early church; in fact, however, we know as little about the early church as we do about Jesus. He sums up: 'We have to admit that we do not know enough about Jesus to give us a clear start in our reconstruction of the story of the primitive Church. *And we do not know enough about Jesus to allow us to construct a clear account of the primitive church because we do not know enough about the primitive church to allow us to construct a clear account of Jesus.*'[2] Downing's conclusion is one of agnosticism concerning the possibility of detailed, reliable knowledge about either Jesus or the early church. His argument is undoubtedly an over-statement (since we do know something about the early church from elsewhere in the New Testament), but there is sufficient force in his objection to traditio-historical method to make us cautious in applying it. We must be wary in drawing conclusions about the early church from the Gospel tradition and then using them in traditio-historical criticism of material about Jesus without some corroboration from other sources.

Palestinian and Hellenistic Christianity

One particular hypothesis about the early church has been made the basis for the study of the Gospel tradition. It is recognised that 'the early church' is an umbrella term, covering a number of different communities with their own characteristic backgrounds and outlooks. It is possible to be more specific by assigning them to various categories, and a classification involving three categories has commended itself to many scholars. In Acts 1-6 we are confronted by the earliest church in Jerusalem, and it appears that there were two groups within it, the so-called 'Hebrews' and 'Hellenists'. Some kind of division between the two is apparent from Acts 6 where we hear of a dissension over care for the poor which, in the opinion of many scholars, may hide some more fundamental differences. Originally, then, the early church was composed of Jewish Christians, native to Palestine and speaking Aramaic (and/or Hebrew). They were fairly close to traditional Judaism in outlook. Alongside them there developed a group of Jews whose background lay in the Jewish Dispersion and who spoke mainly Greek; they were more open to the broad, Hellenistic culture of the time, and hence they were less hidebound by traditional Judaism. It was this group of Christians, associated with the name of Stephen, who saw that the new Christian religion demanded a break from the law of Moses and the worship of the Temple, and who realised the missionary implications of Christianity. They carried the Gospel to Antioch and further afield. We may call the first group 'Palestinian Jewish Christians' and the second group 'Hellenistic Jewish Christians'. At a still later stage the church began to include groups whose members were increasingly Gentile rather than Jewish in race and who were thus more free from Jewish influence. This third group may be called 'Hellenistic Gentile Christians'. Here, then, we have a scheme which corresponds geographically to the widening spread of the church from Jerusalem to Antioch to the wider Gentile world, and also chronologically to the development of the Christian mission from evangelism confined to Jews to evangelism of Gentiles.

It is now possible in theory to plot the material in the Gospels on this chart of development. We may recollect how Bultmann assigned most of the miracle stories to the 'Hellenistic' stage of development. In the same way, teaching ascribed to Jesus but written in Hellenistic language will belong to one or other of the Hellenistic stages, whereas teaching in strongly Palestinian Jewish terms will belong to the first stage. In some cases the material may be regarded as having been created at one of the later stages. In other cases it may have been created at an earlier stage and have remained unaltered. In yet other cases it may be possible to show how a saying or story has passed through two or even three stages of development and has received characteristic modifications at each stage. Analysis of the Gospel material by means of this scheme has been practised especially with regard to the titles ascribed to Jesus. [3] Its possible scope is obviously much wider. For example, such a saying as Matt. 10:5f., 'Go nowhere among the Gentiles, and enter no town of the Samaritans, but go rather to the lost sheep of the house of Israel', must surely represent a Palestinian Jewish saying which has survived unaltered at later stages in transmission. Its limitation of the mission of the disciples to Israel could hardly have been created at a later stage in the church, since by then the duty of mission to the Gentiles had been accepted. [4] On the other hand, such a saying as Mark 13:10, 'And the gospel must first be preached to all nations', betrays a later origin, since the earliest church does not appear to have been aware of a command to universal mission.

Difficulties in distinguishing Palestinian and Hellenistic elements

Although this scheme seems very plausible at first sight,

there are serious objections to using it for precise traditio-historical analysis of the Gospel material. [5] These boil down essentially to the fact that the scheme itself is not, and cannot be, precise. It draws lines between different types of background influence on the early church — Palestinian Jewish, Hellenistic Jewish and Hellenistic Gentile. But the truth is that *ideas* cannot be as sharply differentiated as this scheme suggests. The ancient world contained a rich mixture of ideas from different sources, and it is not possible to sort these out and classify them. For example, the philosophy of the time was eclectic in character, so that thinkers of different schools might share many ideas in common. Again, the religions of the time each drew upon many sources for their inspiration, so that different religions often had common characteristics. In particular, Judaism had been strongly influenced by pagan culture, religion and philosophy, and while this was especially the case with Judaism outside Palestine it was also the case in Palestine itself. While we would expect Palestinian Judaism to be more defensive against the infiltration of Hellenistic outlooks than Judaism in the Dispersion, it was certainly not free from such influence. [6] As a result, we cannot claim that certain aspects of Christian tradition reflect backgrounds that can be precisely separated from one another.

Nor again can we precisely distinguish the separate stages in the development of the church. It is doubtful whether there were any purely Gentile churches in the period under consideration; and it is virtually certain that there were none involved in the production of the Gospels and the traditions behind them. For the most part the church was composed of Hellenistic Jewish Christians and Hellenistic Gentile Christians. We can draw a rough line between Palestinian Jewish Christians and Hellenistic Jewish Christians: the church in Antioch would be composed principally of the latter. But in Jerusalem, the one place where we could expect to find a purely Palestinian Jewish church, there were Hellenistic Jewish Christians right from the start, and it is unlikely that these two groups formed tight conventicles with no influence on each other.

These arguments show that a rigid division between the

different strata in the early church is simply not possible. And if this is the case, it follows all the more strongly that we cannot attempt any precise classification of the Gospel material on this basis. There are cases where some material is obviously Palestinian rather than Hellenistic and vice-versa, but very little can be safely based on this distinction. This does not mean that we must simply abandon the classification and conclude that nothing can be done. It means that we must try to find some other way of producing a classification which will avoid the deficiencies of the present one; at the moment there is no indication that any better alternative exists. The truth is rather that we have to reckon with a number of early Christian communities about whose detailed beliefs we are almost completely ignorant; while we know the general shape of early Christian belief fairly clearly, we just do not know what variations existed within particular groups, or how Christian belief developed within them.

This conclusion may be regarded as a help or a hindrance in our search for the historical Jesus. The conservative scholar will be quick to point out that the failure of the method under discussion forbids us from disallowing certain elements in the gospel tradition to Jesus simply on the grounds that they are 'Hellenistic'. The radical scholar will point out that, if the classification is useless, we have no means of discriminating between authentic and inauthentic elements in the tradition; the whole tradition stands under suspicion of being created and modified by the early church, and we have no means of ascertaining the relative age of its various parts. The truth, however, probably lies between these two extremes. We have to ask how elements that may reasonably confidently be labelled as 'Palestinian' and 'Hellenistic' are distributed in the tradition and see whether any conclusions can be drawn regarding the tradition. Is there any evidence, for example, that would enable us to conclude that Jesus spoke in Aramaic, so that sayings which represent fairly literal translations from Aramaic will have better claims to authenticity than sayings which could be translated back into Aramaic only with great difficulty? Again, can we find pieces of teaching which existed in both 'Palestinian' and 'Hellenistic'

forms and hence draw any conclusions about the development of the tradition? It so happens that there is one good
example of this process. In Mark 10:45 we have the saying,
'The Son of man also came...to give his life as a ransom for
many'. This saying has a parallel in 1 Tim. 2:6 which speaks
of 'the man Christ Jesus, who gave himself as a ransom for
all'. The similarities between the statements are striking, and
the latter is a re-writing of the former in 'better Greek', *i.e.* in
a Hellenistic form. [7] What emerges is that the author of 1
Tim. did not create this form of words, as might well have
been supposed if we did not possess the parallel; and that this
form of words follows remarkably closely the wording in
Mark 10:45, so that the essential force of the saying ascribed
to Jesus is preserved with little change. Hellenistic language
can conceal a saying originally couched in a more Jewish
form. The use of Hellenistic language is no proof of creation
by the early church. At the same time, this process can lead to
modification of an earlier form of a saying.

What emerges from this is that the criterion of Palestinian
and Hellenistic elements in the tradition is a rather blunt
tool, but one which can on occasion be of some use.

THE INFLUENCE OF THE CHURCH'S 'SITUATION'

If we can identify particular factors in the life of the church
which may have been responsible for moulding the tradition,
this will help us to analyse the tradition accordingly. Thus, to
repeat an earlier example, Bultmann claimed that the early
church was frequently involved in conflict with the Jews;
consequently stories or sayings which present Jesus in situations of conflict with the Jews will have been used by the
early church to give it guidance in its own conflicts with the
Jews. But Bultmann went further and claimed that such
situations reflected the situation of the early church, and even
that the sayings of Jesus which were critical of Judaism were
often creations by the early church to justify its own conduct.
Now it is possible that this kind of activity went on. In a
number of passages in the Gospels there is reported a saying
of Jesus to the effect that 'Whoever divorces his wife and

marries another, commits adultery against her' (Mark 10:11). In Matt. 5:31f. a form of this saying is found, preceded by the words, 'But I say to you that'; this saying of Jesus is thus sharply contrasted with the preceding verse, 'It was also said, "Whoever divorces his wife, let him give her a certificate of divorce."' Here the teaching of the Jews and the teaching of Jesus are placed in sharp contrast, and over against the 'It was said' of the Jewish law stands the authoritative 'But I say to you' of Jesus. When we observe that this pattern of 'It was said... But I say to you' is repeated half a dozen times in Matt. 5 it is not implausible that sayings of Jesus like Mark 10:11 have been wrought into a carefully constructed pattern which reflects the church's controversies with the Jews, and in such a case the simpler form of the saying in Mark 10:11 presumably stands nearer to what Jesus actually said.

But we must tread carefully at this point. What this illustration has shown is the possibility that the early church took existing sayings of Jesus and compiled them in such a way as to be useful in controversy. It does not exclude the possibility that Jesus himself engaged in such controversy, so that the church was basically using the sayings in the kind of way in which Jesus himself had used them. In the present instance few critics would doubt that Jesus actually spoke about divorce in these terms. [8] But there are many cases where critics such as Bultmann would attribute both the imaginative creation of the setting and the creation of the saying of Jesus itself to the early church. How can we decide whether this is the case? The position is that Jesus may have engaged in certain controversies with the Jews, and the early church may also have done so. How can we decide, then, whether a particular narrative is historical or reflects the situation of the church? Nor should we forget the third possibility, that the narrative is both historical and a reflection of the church's situation. The basic answer to the question is that we cannot tell. There is no general rule that will enable us to do so. We need to know that a given controversial situation was typical of the life of the church and could not have happened in the lifetime of Jesus. Without this knowledge in each individual case Bultmann's generalisation cannot be applied.

But the procedure must be questioned at a deeper level. There are two assumptions at work in it. The first is that the interest of the early church in Jesus was moulded more or less completely by its own *Sitz im Leben*. The second is that the early church was capable of creating 'sayings of Jesus'. Each of these must be considered in turn.

Historical interest in Jesus

The first assumption is that in general the early church's interest in Jesus arose out of its own situation, and it remembered or created the traditions about Jesus because these were useful to it in its own situation. Purely historical interest was absent. The church was motivated theologically, and there was no sense of disinterested historical enquiry. The *Sitz im Leben* created and moulded the tradition.

If the arguments stated in the preceding paragraph seem at all illogical, it is not because we have deliberately misquoted the opinions of those who told them but because the arguments are inherently weak and even illogical. Of course it is true that the early church's interest in Jesus arose out of its own situation and was motivated by the desire to know more about Jesus for its own purposes and benefit. But this statement ignores three things.

First, if the church was interested in Jesus, this happened only because the church came into being as a result of the activity of Jesus and because it already knew something about him. A theory which explains *all* that the church knew about Jesus in terms of its own conscious interests is self-stultifying; and equally a theory which holds that only a very tiny amount of information about Jesus was handed down to the early church is incapable of explaining the rise of the church and of its traditions. Even if the event which brought the church into being was the resurrection, it was the resurrection of *Jesus*, and it must have carried with it some knowledge of who Jesus was and what he taught if it was not to be a freak event, lacking in the intellectual content to establish the church. In short, the creation of the church is inexplicable apart from the existence of knowledge of Jesus.

Second, the statement assumes too narrow a definition of 'useful'. Even if pure mathematicians may voice the toast: 'Here's to pure mathematics; may she never be of any use to anybody', the fact is that pure mathematics is of use and interest to them — not to mention that the toast is made with tongue in cheek. To know about Jesus for his own sake was interesting and useful for the early church. To suggest that the early church invoked his memory only when it had a problem on its hands is wildly unlikely. This statement could, it is true, be regarded as a generalisation that needs to be supported with evidence. But the evidence has been supplied by various writers. The German scholar J. Roloff has analysed in detail a number of stories in the Gospels and has shown that various features in the way in which the stories were told indicates that the interest was not in telling what Jesus did as a guide to the church in its own situation but rather in explaining what Jesus did for its own sake; its aim was to proclaim Jesus rather than to reflect on its own problems. [9] Even more thorough-going is the work of G. N. Stanton who has demonstrated, again by minute examination of the material, that not only the Evangelists but also the transmitters of the tradition were interested in both the life and the character of Jesus. [10]

Third, the statement assumes that theological purpose and disinterested historical research are incompatible with one another. Since the Evangelists were writing Gospels, and since the transmitters of the tradition were concerned with the proclamation of Jesus, they cannot have been writing accurate history; rather, their accounts must be regarded as suspect at every point, since they could have been moulding the facts to fit the theology all along the way. But this is blatant nonsense and needs to be clearly labelled as such. It is certainly not what Luke thought he was doing. He regarded himself as establishing a reliable account of what happened as a basis for Theophilus to believe the story of Jesus, and there is no reason to suppose that he saw any incompatability between his research into 'the things that had happened' and

his evangelistic and edificatory purpose. Nor is there any
reason to suppose that his predecessors thought any differently. M. D. Hooker quotes a comment by N. Perrin on
a book on the theology of Mark written by E. Best; he describes it as 'a strange book in that the author combines
redaction criticism with the assumption "that Mark believes
the incidents he uses actually happened"!' She goes
on:

> Now this is really an extraordinary statement. Why should
> the fact that Mark is a 'theologian' preclude him from
> writing about events which he thought had happened?
> Can a 'theologian' write only about imaginary events? This
> is obviously sheer nonsense. Against Perrin, we must quote
> Perrin himself: 'Mark has the right to be read on his own
> terms.' And what is the most obvious thing about Mark's
> method of writing? It is that he presented his theology in a
> form which 'misled' generations of scholars into believing
> that he was writing an historical account. [11]

This criticism is entirely valid. The antithesis of 'history *or*
theology' is a false one, both with regard to the final
compilation of the Gospels and with regard to the transmission of the traditions which lie behind them.

Ah, but the point goes deeper, we shall be told. It is not just
a question of what the transmitters of the tradition thought
that they were doing, but rather of whether they were
unconsciously led by their theological bias into presenting the
facts from a particular point of view. Earlier in this book we
noted how modern historians cannot rid themselves of bias
even when they try to present the past objectively; how much
more must this have been the case in the ancient world where
writers were much more open to rewriting the evidence in the
interests of their didactic purposes and much less aware of the
need to examine and allow for their own prejudices. Did
Christian writers not exaggerate the miraculous elements in
the stories of Jesus? Did they not mould stories in the light of
Old Testament patterns and prophecies? Did they not hold to
a world view in which things that would be regarded as
natural phenomena were regarded as having supernatural

causes? Are their writings not riddled with bias through and through?

Well, of course, there was bias. Faced by it, the historian must do two things. On the one hand, he must allow for its presence, and take note of its effects where it can be shown to be present. On the other hand, he must determine whether the presence of bias is so pervasive as to render the search for historical facts impossible (or almost impossible). It is too often assumed that the latter is the case. But we have the right to ask those who hold this view for the evidence which supports their case. And often the only evidence which we are given is the fact that the transmission and recording of the traditions were theologically motivated. That, however, is not evidence that the tradition was distorted. It is only evidence that it may have been distorted. We need 'hard' evidence of actual distortion, and then we must estimate the degree of distortion that may be present. Not only so, but we must determine at what stages in the process distortion took place. It may have taken place early or late (or both). Thus in the case of John it is fairly clear that the wording of the teaching ascribed to Jesus is to a considerable extent the product of the Evangelist's own mind working on the tradition which he had inherited. The style of the discourses in the Gospel is so uniform and so similar to that in passages in the Gospel and 1-3 John where the Evangelist himself is speaking that it is impossible to avoid the conclusion that he has given a stylistic and theological reshaping to the tradition. But when the discourses are examined critically, it emerges that at their base there is a tradition of sayings of Jesus very similar in character to those found in the other Gospels. [12] We can, therefore, say that behind the 'developed' discourses in John there can be traced a 'primitive' tradition of the sayings of Jesus which stands on the same footing as the tradition in the Synoptic Gospels. Whether or not this 'primitive' tradition has been interpreted, is then a question which must be answered in the same kind of way as the corresponding question with regard to the material in the Synoptic Gospels. In short, the fact that interpretation can be seen in John does not mean that the tradition as a whole has been affected at every level; if we can separate off the tradition from the redaction (which admittedly is not an easy matter), the position of the Johannine tradition is no better and no worse than that of the synoptic tradition. Moreover, the effect of this enquiry is to show that, despite their differences in treatment, the same kind of traditions lay behind the Synoptic Gospels and John.

The question still remains of whether this primitive reservoir of tradition contains pure, unsullied water or has already been contaminated. All that we have shown so far is that there is no basis for an *a priori* condemnation of it all as impure. What is now needed is some evidence to help us to estimate its worth.

DID EARLY CHRISTIAN PROPHETS UTTER 'SAYINGS OF JESUS'?

It is at this point that we must turn our attention to the second of the two assumptions mentioned above, namely that the early Church was capable of creating 'sayings of Jesus'.

In the course of our discussion we have seen that the early church did modify and rephrase the sayings of Jesus. The evidence for this fact is written in the Gospels and may be ascertained by comparison of the sayings as they are recorded in the different Gospels. Here we are dealing with observable facts. There are also places where it is probable that the early church placed appropriate sayings on the lips of Jesus and other characters in the story. In Luke there are a number of passages where statements of Jesus follow a question or interjection from one of the members of his audience, and in each case the question or other remark is absent from the parallel account of the same incident in Matthew. [13] Either Matthew has systematically removed all such remarks, or Luke has added them to his source, and the probabilities (based on the Lucan style of the remarks) suggest that in some cases the latter hypothesis is to be preferred. But these cases, while showing the possibility of such imaginative creation of sayings, are of marginal importance. The vital question is whether sayings belonging to the main substance of the tradition were created in the early church.

It is often assumed that Christian prophets spoke on behalf of the risen Lord; their utterances were spoken as if by Jesus himself, just as the Old Testament prophets spoke as the mouthpieces of God. They were not regarded as a separate category from the earthly sayings of Jesus, and hence both types of saying were mixed up in the tradition. [14] The task of the critic is, then, to separate off the sayings of the earthly Jesus from the sayings of his prophets. There has been much analysis of the sayings in the Gospels based on the assumption that many of them can be attributed to Christian prophets. Thus a recent discussion of the 'Q' source assigns much of its earliest material to sayings either used or uttered by Christian prophets. [15]

If these two possibilities are accepted, it follows that the church was perfectly capable of creating sayings of Jesus, and that we must examine each saying individually to try to see into which category it falls. But should they be accepted? When we look for evidence for them, we find that part of the evidence consists of features in individual sayings which are held to reflect the period after the death of Jesus; we shall return to this point. The other part of the evidence is the assumption that there were early Christian prophets, that they spoke as if they were mouthpieces of the risen Lord, and that the early church received their utterances as if they were sayings of Jesus and absorbed them into its collection of sayings of Jesus. By now the reader of this book will have guessed what our next move will be. We ask, what is the *evidence* for this assumption? And we shall ask in vain. For the assumption is — an assumption. The evidence which has been produced in its support is meagre, and it dwindles away under examination. Writing about one particular type of saying ascribed to such prophets, D. Hill comments: 'It is our impression that the position and the necessary presuppositions are simply affirmed, or re-affirmed, virtually without argument of any kind'. [16] He goes on to say:

Indeed, the evidence produced and repeated in support

of the contention that the Christian prophets played a
creative rôle in respect of sayings later attributed to the
earthly Jesus proves, on examination, to be lacking in
substance and authority... If it is to merit further consideration, the case for the attribution to Christian prophets of a
creative rôle in respect of *logia Iesou* requires validation by
new and convincing arguments. Repetition alone cannot
persuade'.[17]

These statements are made at the end of an essay which
examines the evidence with care and shows that it lacks
substance. It can be taken as certain that the case for this rôle
of Christian prophets has not been made out.

Moreover, it has been shown by F. Neugebauer that it is
unlikely that the church would have accepted such sayings of
prophets as sayings of Jesus. He has pointed out that in the
Bible generally prophecies are never anonymous, but are
almost always ascribed to some named person. It is therefore
unlikely that messages from the Lord were published without
the author's name. When we do hear of visions and prophecies in Acts, we always learn who received them. Further,
although there were prophets in the early church, the decisive
place was assigned to the apostles, and apostolic tradition was
placed on a higher level than prophetic inspiration. Neugebauer draws the conclusion that although the church
might erroneously have confused prophetic sayings with
sayings of Jesus, it did not mix the two categories deliberately. Since the theory we are criticising postulated deliberate
mixture, it is clear that the presupposition for its validity
is lacking. [18]

These considerations show that while it is possible that
occasional prophetic sayings were introduced into the tradition of sayings of Jesus, the evidence for wholesale activity of
this kind is lacking.

There remains the possibility of deliberate creation of
sayings of Jesus by persons who made no claim to prophetic
inspiration. What we must now ask is whether there are any
other considerations which may be relevant to determining
whether substantial portions of the Gospel tradition were
created in this way.

THE POSSIBILITY OF A TRADITION
STEMMING FROM JESUS

The Scandinavian contribution

In 1957 a Swedish scholar, H. Riesenfeld, opened up a new approach to the problem of the Gospel tradition. He argued that we lack evidence that the original source of the Gospel tradition was mission preaching and communal instruction in the early church. Rather, the tradition about Jesus was handed down by a fixed circle of people, the apostles, and it was handed down in a manner analogous to the transmission of rabbinic tradition. The latter was transmitted with great fidelity, each pupil learning accurately by heart what he heard from his teacher, and then passing it on. There was, on this view, little scope for the wild developments and additions to the tradition which had been envisaged by some scholars. Riesenfeld argued that if the tradition was treated in this sacrosanct manner, the explanation must be that it could be traced back to Jesus himself and so was regarded with particular reverence. [19]

Riesenfeld's case was developed by B. Gerhardsson who examined minutely the way in which rabbinic tradition was handed down and provided, as it were, the footnotes for Riesenfeld's article. [20] The publication of his book aroused considerable controversy, which was not unnatural since it appeared to represent an outflanking attack on form criticism. It was not, of course, a denial of the validity of the form-critical method properly practised; but it was an attack on the concept of the tradition held by some form critics. The hypothesis was seen to be vulnerable at two main points.

First, it was claimed that the evidence for the rigidity of rabbinic tradition was comparatively late, and that the attempt to read back the same attitude into first-century Judaism was unsuccessful. Thus M. Smith claims: 'to read back into the period before 70 the developed rabbinic technique of 200 is a gross anachronism'. [21] Although this criticism comes from a rabbinic scholar of high standing, it is probably an over-statement; the rabbinic attitudes current in AD 200 did not stem from nothing. If there is little evidence from before AD 200 to support the theory, there is equally little to disprove it.

More important is the second criticism: how far is it legitimate to draw an analogy between rabbinic tradition and Christian tradition? Scholars have pointed out that Jesus was not a rabbi, and his followers were not rabbinic pupils. The rôle of the apostles as the guardians of a sacred tradition is very questionable.[22] Despite these criticisms, it seems probable that the Scandinavian thesis does shed some light on the transmission of the Gospel tradition; it suggests that the tradition was handed down in a context where considerable importance was attached to the accurate memorisation and transmission of Jewish traditions, and that the onus of proof is on those who would postulate free creativity on the part of the church. It is significant that, after the detailed criticisms which he made of Riesenfeld and Gerhardsson's approach, W. D. Davies could go on to say:

> By bringing to bear the usages of contemporary Judaism, in a fresh and comprehensive manner, on the transmission of the Gospel tradition, they have forcibly compelled the recognition of the structural parallelism between much in Primitive Christianity and Pharisaic Judaism. This means, in our judgment, that they have made it far more historically probable and reasonably credible, over against the scepticism of much form criticism, that in the Gospels we are within hearing of the authentic voice and within sight of the authentic activity of Jesus of Nazareth, however much muffled and obscured these may be by the process of transmission. [23]

The tradition started before Easter

A second important step was taken by the German scholar, H. Schürmann. [24] He argued that form criticism had wrongly limited its scope to the period after Easter. It explored the *Sitz im Leben* of the Gospel tradition in the early church, but, said Schürmann, it had ignored the possible existence of a *Sitz im Leben* before Easter. It is important not to misunderstand the point which is being made here. As we noted earlier, '*Sitz im Leben*' denotes not a historical circumstance but a sociological situation. Schürmann was not concerned with the historical circumstances in which Jesus might have uttered a particular saying. (For example, he was not concerned with establishing the historicity of such a concrete situation as that in Luke 13:1 where Jesus replies to a specific comment about a historical occurrence). He was concerned with the possibility of a situation before Easter in which sayings of Jesus were used and transmitted, just as they were used and transmitted after Easter by the church because of its particular situation and needs. His case was that such a *Sitz im Leben* did exist. There was a group of disciples of Jesus during his lifetime. Their 'inner' life was controlled by their 'confession' of Jesus; if they regarded him as teacher or prophet, or something more than this, they must have had some relationship to what he said, for a teacher or prophet is nothing without his teaching or prophecy. But the disciples also had an 'outer' life in terms of their relationship with other people. Even if Jesus had never used them as helpers in his mission, they would still have had to defend themselves as his followers to people who questioned them. But they were in fact actively involved in the work of Jesus, and it is inconceivable that he did not instruct them for their task. The teaching of Jesus about the kingdom of God, for example, must have been used in their missionary preaching, especially since it does not seem to have figured prominently in the preaching of the church after Easter. Both teaching for outsiders and guidance for the inner life of the group of disciples were required during the ministry of Jesus. Here we have a plausible situation for the beginning of the Gospel tradition, and with it the possibility of carrying back form-critical study into the period before Easter.

This thesis may seem to afford a dazzling glimpse of the obvious, but the fact remains that it had not previously been taken up in form-critical study. The result was that form criticism had fixed an artificial horizon for itself. It is questionable whether even yet Schürmann's thesis has been taken sufficiently seriously.

Characteristics of the earthly Jesus

A third point must now be placed alongside these consider-ations. J. Jeremias has drawn up careful lists of characteristic ways of speaking which are to be found in the sayings of Jesus. Some of these are Aramaic forms of expression which occur with considerable frequency in the Gospels, while others are expressions which appear to be found only, or almost exclusively, in sayings attributed to Jesus. The presence of these linguistic and stylistic characteristics consti-tutes some solid evidence that the sayings in the Gospels can be traced back to Jesus. [25]

Stated thus baldly, the argument is open to criticism. On the one hand, it can be objected that the presence of Aramaisms merely points back to the Aramaic-speaking church as the source of the sayings rather than to Jesus himself. Even if this were all that was to be said, we should still have a useful tool to hand for separating off material that certainly came from the earliest church from material that might have originated at a later stage. Again, on the other hand, it can be objected that the style in question was that of early Christian prophets rather than that of Jesus; if Jesus did use some of these expressions, his followers could have imitated his style of utterance. Hence we have no sure criterion for distinguishing between Jesus and his followers. But these objections miss their target. Jeremias's point is that here we have a combination of stylistic peculiarities which testify to the particular manner of speaking of *one* person. There is sufficient evidence for us here to isolate a group of sayings which have these characteristics, and we can then examine them from other points of view to see whether the core of the group of sayings makes the best historical sense if it is attributed to Jesus.

The effect of the last three points which we have made is to indicate that there are sound reasons for believing that the Gospel traditions contain carefully preserved reminiscences of what Jesus actually said. In other words, having examined the arguments which suggest that the tradition is tendentious through and through, we have now offered some arguments for believing the contrary. The arguments have been largely concerned with the sayings of Jesus, but they also apply to some extent to the stories about him. We have now reached the point where we can try to draw a general conclusion about the nature of the tradition, and then proceed to examine a further aspect of the problems which it raises.

ASSIGNING THE BURDEN OF PROOF

In his discussion of the Gospel tradition N. Perrin argues that in order to arrive back at the teaching of Jesus we must begin by reconstructing the history of the tradition in order to establish the earliest ascertainable form of any given saying. We have accepted the correctness of this procedure. 'What next?' asks Perrin. 'Well, clearly, we have to ask ourselves the question as to whether this saying should now be attributed to the early church or to the historical Jesus, *and the nature of the synoptic tradition is such that the burden of proof will be upon the claim to authenticity.* This means in effect that we must look for indications that the saying does not come from the church, but from the historical Jesus. Actually, our task is even more complex than this, because the early church and the New Testament are indebted at very many points to ancient Judaism. Therefore, if we are to ascribe a saying to Jesus, and accept the burden of proof laid upon us, we must be able to show that the saying comes neither from the church nor from ancient Judaism. This seems to many to be too much to ask, but nothing less will do justice to the challenge of the burden of proof. There is no other way to reasonable certainty that we have reached the historical Jesus'. [26] The significant element in this quotation is that Perrin claims that the nature of the Gospel tradition is such that we require positive proof to demonstrate that any given saying stems from Jesus and not from the early church. Be it noted that this requirement applies even when everything that could be regarded as having been created at a fairly late point in the development of the tradition has been eliminated; we are concerned here with the *earliest* form of any saying in the tradition. Perrin's statement is not an original one; similar claims have been made by other scholars. [27]

Over against this statement may be placed the principle enunciated by J. Jeremias: 'We are justified in drawing up the following principle of method: In the synoptic tradition it is the inauthenticity, and not the authenticity, of the sayings of Jesus that must be demonstrated'. [28] This principle is stated in conscious opposition to the view of Perrin and others, and it too can claim distinguished scholarly support. [29] It is not too much to say that the basic problem in historical study of the teaching of Jesus is to be found here: which of these two fundamentally opposed principles are we to follow?

On the one hand, we have the historical principle of 'methodological scepticism'. The reports of all witnesses must be treated with scepticism unless they can be shown to be reliable. [30] Along with this principle of method goes the generalisation that the circumstances in which the tradition was produced militate against its reliability as a historical source for the teaching of Jesus. On the other hand, we have examined the case for the tradition being fundamentally tendentious, and we have concluded that the case is lacking in conviction. On the contrary, there is good reason to suppose that for the most part the tradition contains historical reminiscence of what Jesus said. If this is the case, then we are bound to adopt the principle stated by Jeremias as a working hypothesis. A tradition which purports to be recording what Jesus said must be reckoned to be doing precisely this unless there are clear signs to the contrary; in general these signs are lacking. What we must now do is to see whether there are any criteria for separating off inauthentic elements from authentic elements.

FROM THE TRADITION TO JESUS

In the preceding sections we have been discussing 'tradition history', *i.e.* the development of the tradition from its earliest forms to the point at which it was put into writing and found its way into the Gospels. Having seen that the tradition is based ultimately on what Jesus said, and did, we must now ask whether we can proceed back from what the early church thought that Jesus had said and done to what he himself actually said and did. Our attention will be primarily concentrated again on the teaching of Jesus, since this is the area where most discussion has taken place and where there is the best hope of progress.

The criterion of dissimilarity

A number of possible criteria for assessing the tradition of Jesus' sayings have been assembled by scholars. In the quotation from N. Perrin given above we find a clear statement of what has come to be called the criterion of 'dissimilarity'. According to this criterion only whatever can be regarded as not stemming from Judaism or the early church can be ascribed with any certainty to Jesus. This is a negative criterion, used by Perrin to filter off all possibly secondary matter and to leave a residue of material behind which must be from Jesus since it cannot be from either of the two other possible sources. [31] It is a criterion which can be regarded as establishing an irreducible minimum of authentic tradition. Sometimes it is stated as if it also established the maximum possible amount of tradition that can be ascribed to Jesus, but in this form it is plainly false. [32] In its more moderate form it is open to considerable criticism.

First, it assumes that we know with sufficient certainty what could have been said by contemporary Jews or by the early church. But there is considerable uncertainty about both of these factors, especially the latter. We are in effect dealing with two unknowns rather than one, so that we cannot establish one category merely by subtracting all that belongs to the second. We must not forget F. G. Downing's repeated warning that we are involved in 'the quest of the historical early church' as well as in 'the quest of the historical Jesus'.

Second, this view forgets that the early church derived at least some inspiration from the teaching of Jesus, and that he in his turn derived inspiration from his Jewish environment. But the operation of this principle would instantly cut out all such material where there is overlap between Judaism and Jesus and between Jesus and the early church.

Third, this criterion can only produce what was 'distinctive' of the teaching of Jesus rather than what may well have been characteristic or even central. It can produce only the bizarre features, sayings without a context and therefore misleading. It assumes that sayings have meanings in themselves and ignores the fact that their meaning is partly drawn from their context. D. G. A. Calvert rightly concludes: 'A rigorous application of these two criteria (*sc.* relation to the early church's teaching and relation to contemporary Judaism) would rule out most of the teaching of Jesus. Taken together they suggest that the teaching of Jesus was unique, and yet had no influence on the future ideas of the Church. Jesus' teaching is in a vacuum — no connection with Judaism; no connection with Christianity'. [33] In short, this criterion throws out the baby with the bath water. More seriously, it dictates its own conclusions from the start. M. D. Hooker has argued convincingly that it begs the question of the real character of Jesus by assuming that the irreducible minimum is what was unique, and then trying to produce a coherent picture on the basis of what may at least have been marginal. She further observes that it is in fact virtually impossible to apply:

> To be acceptable as genuine, a saying of Jesus must at one and the same time be 'dissimilar' from contemporary Judaism, and yet use its categories and reflect the language and style of Aramaic. In other words, authentic sayings must not be reflected in Judaism (as far as it is known to us) but must sound as if they could have been spoken at that time. [34]

These criticisms demonstrate quite clearly that if this criterion is applied indiscriminately to the tradition it will produce phoney results. Nevertheless, there may be occasions on which it can legitimately be used. Thus D. R. Catchpole has examined the saying of Jesus about divorce found in Mark 10:11 (*cf.* Luke 16:18), and concludes:

> By the criterion of dissimilarity, the divergence from Judaism (Deut. 24:1-4) points in its favour towards authenticity. And in so far as anything within the Gospels can be

said to diverge from Christian insights (which is, incidentally, highly doubtful) these sayings again do well, for we
can at least trace on a broad front a tendency to tone down
their sharpness... It is consequently thoroughly defensible
for anyone to claim that Mark 10:11 and Luke 16:18 fit
neatly inside the teaching of Jesus.[35]

Here is a case where the criterion can be legitimately
applied. But the circumstances must be carefully noted. First,
this criterion is here used alongside other criteria (yet to be
discussed) and is not made to bear the weight of proof by
itself. Second, a comparison is made between the saying in
question and other teaching on the same subject; the
comparison suggests that the present form of the saying is the
most primitive. [36] In this case, therefore, we have material for
comparison which permits some kind of verdict.

The criterion of multiple attestation

A second criterion is that of multiple attestation in the
sources. In this case a saying may be found in more than one
of the earliest Gospel sources established by critical study. For
example, a saying about saving and losing one's life is found in
a variety of forms in Mark 8:35 (cf. Matt. 16:25; Luke 9:24);
Matt 10:39; Luke 17:33 and John 12:25. The evidence
indicates that it figured in at least three sources — Mark, Q
and the source used by John. Moreover, the differences in
wording make it unlikely that all the various forms of the
saying can be traced back to one single source. [37] In such a
situation it may be claimed that the saying has multiple
attestation, and this gives us some guarantee that it goes back
to Jesus.

Here again, however, the argument must be used with
care. A saying attested only in one source may be just as
authentic as one attested in several. Nor do we always know
sufficient about the inter-relationship of the sources to be
absolutely sure that the various versions of a particular saying
do not stem ultimately from the same source in the early
church. Further, it can be objected that this argument only
takes us back to an early stage in the tradition and not to

Jesus himself. N. Perrin is sceptical of the value of the criterion, and says, 'If we cannot accept the basic presupposition that to take one step behind the sources is to arrive at a firm historical tradition about Jesus, then this criterion becomes much less effective'. [38] But why cannot this basic presupposition be accepted? Only for reasons that we have already shown to be faulty. In fact the strength of this argument is that it may enable us to trace back some saying by several routes to the earliest ascertainable form of tradition, and therefore to state all the more firmly that it belongs indubitably to the early tradition of what Jesus said. Such sayings which appear in several sources must have been important for the early church and their importance strongly suggests that they were spoken by Jesus. The same point will apply to narratives about Jesus from different sources which illustrate the same motifs in his activity.

The argument may be considerably strengthened at this point by a modification. We have spoken in terms of *sources*. But it is also possible to find the same basic motifs attested in a variety of *forms*. This point was made most forcefully by C. H. Dodd who drew attention to several characteristics of the ministry of Jesus which are found not only in different sources but also in different types of material. [39] Thus Jesus' friendship with tax-collectors and sinners is attested not only by stories of his behaviour but also by sayings of more than one form-critical category. [40] The point is that, whereas with the previous criterion it could be argued that all sources ultimately draw on the same tradition, here we are dealing with forms which cannot be derived from one another; we have independent attestation of basic motifs from a number of categories of tradition, and this can hardly be explained in any other way than by postulating historical reminiscence. Even Perrin must admit this fact, although he claims that it has restricted usefulness since there is not much material of this kind. The reader, however, may be more relieved to find a criterion that actually does work even in a limited area.

The criterion of coherence

A third criterion is that of coherence. If a basic irreducible minimum of authentic material has been established, other material may be added which, although it does not fulfil the first criterion, nevertheless fits in with the minimum so as to give a set of sayings free from internal contradictions. Thus material not dissimilar from contemporary Judaism or the early church's teaching may be admitted at this stage provided that it coheres with the already established genuine teaching. I have stated this criterion in the form in which it is used by scholars who operate with the criterion of dissimilarity and try to move out beyond it. [41] But we have already shown that the criterion of dissimilarity leads to some odd results. It may indeed give such a one-sided picture of Jesus that other material in the tradition may not seem to cohere with it at all. In other words, errors resulting from criterion 1. will be magnified in the application of criterion 3. On the other hand, if something corresponding to criterion 1. is not used to establish the 'irreducible minimum', the objector may well ask, 'coheres with what?' To this objection there are two possible replies. First, it may be possible to find some replacement for criterion 1. which will enable us to establish an indubitable core of genuine material. Or, second, it may be argued that several sayings are internally consistent with one another, and that such consistency is a mark of common origin. When Dodd finds the same motif expressed in a variety of traditions, the indications are that one common historical event lies behind them all. Certainly, internal consistency can be the mark of the successful novelist who constructs characters with consistent personalities. But there are no grounds whatever for supposing that at the basis of the Christian tradition there is to be found a remarkably successful novelist. On the contrary, we have a set of traditions, and it is the basic agreement between them which requires to be explained. It is the self-consistency of the traditions which points to their common origin in the ministry of Jesus.

The criterion of unintentionality

A fourth type of criterion has been developed by various scholars. Its origins go back to P. W. Schmiedel who drew attention to various pieces of evidence which had survived, as it were, contrary to the intention of the tradition. Thus the early Christian tradition plainly attached great importance to the aspects of Jesus' character which indicated that he came from God and had a supernatural character; all the more remarkable, therefore, are those points where the real humanity of Jesus shines through without any conscious intention on the part of the Evangelists to draw attention to it. [42] In the same way, we may look for places in the tradition where elements have survived that did not serve the particular purposes of the tradition and which may even stand in a certain tension with it. C. F. D. Moule has assembled a number of pieces of evidence of this kind. Perhaps the most striking is the attitude of Jesus to women.

> It is difficult enough for anyone, even a consummate master of imaginative writing, to create a picture of a deeply pure, good person moving about in an impure environment, without making him a prig or a prude or a sort of 'plaster saint'. How comes it that, through all the Gospel traditions without exception, there comes a remarkably firmly-drawn portrait of an attractive young man moving freely about among women of all sorts, including the decidedly disreputable, without a trace of sentimentality, unnaturalness, or prudery, and yet, at every point, maintaining a simple integrity of character?'

Moule goes on to argue that the environment in which the traditions were preserved was hardly favourable to such a portrait, and claims that this portrait would 'seem to have fairly forced its way through an atmosphere...alien to it'. [43] One can rightly say that his conclusion is 'certain' rather than merely 'probable'.

It will be observed that with this particular illustration we have moved over into the sphere of Jesus' actions and are not confined merely to his sayings. The truth is, of course, that his words and actions cannot be rigidly separated from each other; the same message can be present in both. In the case of his sayings, we have some justification in claiming a pre-Easter *Sitz im Leben* for their use by the disciples; in the case of his actions this is less probable, although the missionary preaching of the disciples before Easter may well have included reference to what Jesus did as justification for the message which they themselves preached.

The criterion of traditional continuity

To these commonly accepted four criteria we now want to add a fifth one. In effect we have before us a tradition of what Jesus said and did, and we have analysed this to arrive at its earliest ascertainable form as tradition handed down by the followers of Jesus, whether after his death or even (in some cases at least) before it. The question which the historian must ask at this point is: what historical cause must be postulated in order to explain the origin of this tradition? In some cases circumstances within the church may be an adequate origin. But this is certainly not the most obvious origin in view of the fact that the tradition claims to be reporting what Jesus said and did. Must we not postulate the ministry of Jesus as the necessary cause for the creation of the tradition, so that the basis for a reported saying of Jesus in the tradition will be an actual saying of Jesus, and the basis for a story about Jesus will be an action of Jesus?

In general terms, such a postulate would appear to be strongly justified. In terms of time, the gap between the earliest forms of the tradition and the ministry of Jesus is comparatively short. In terms of geography, the traditions developed in the same linguistic and cultural environment as that in which Jesus lived. In terms of personnel, some of his followers during his ministry were involved in the foundation of the church. In terms of content, the message of the early church must have borne a close relationship to that of Jesus himself. These considerations strongly support the view that we can adopt a criterion of 'traditional continuity'. That is to say, in each particular case we must ask what cause must be postulated to explain the creation of the tradition, and bearing in mind the factors just mentioned we are justified in arguing that we ought to accept the obvious explanation — the ministry of Jesus — unless there are factors which render this explanation unlikely. Historical credulity would in fact be stretched to the limit if some other explanation than the influence of Jesus were to be invoked for the development of the tradition.

After all, what is the alternative? It is to suppose that the influence of Jesus on his followers was minimal, and that it was comparable to the original reaction in a nuclear explosion which releases forces far greater than itself. In that case, we would have to ask what other forces were present in the environment to catalyse the massive chain reaction. Historical study has not produced any plausible answers to this question. The evidence for a group of Christian prophets at the base of the tradition is non-existent. And even if we postulated a group of such people, what could have led them to commence their activity? The only possible cause was Jesus and a belief in his resurrection. But the less scope we afford to Jesus, the less likely is his activity to have led to belief in his resurrection or to belief in the importance of his teaching and the desire to expand it.

Some readers may have recognised in the formulation of this point the development of an argument originally put forward by C. H. Dodd. In a discussion of the new understanding of the Old Testament found in the early church he wrote: 'This is a piece of genuinely creative thinking... To account for the beginning of this most original and fruitful process of rethinking the Old Testament we found need to postulate a creative mind. The Gospels offer us one. Are we compelled to reject the offer?' [44] What Dodd claimed with respect to the early church's interpretation of the Old Testament (found largely outside the Gospel tradition) can be claimed all the more confidently in respect of the contents of the Gospel tradition itself. Historical honesty forces us to attempt an explanation of the origins of the tradition, and only very good reasons can lead us to reject the answer given by the tradition itself. [45] In respect of each single item we must ask, what historical cause led to the production of this piece of tradition?

One important objection which could be raised to the validity of this criterion is that it leads to a set of different pictures of Jesus at the base of the several types of tradition which we possess. In one set of traditions Jesus is a miracle worker, in another he is like a teacher of wisdom, in yet another he is like the rabbis with whom he engages in dispute, and so on... E. Trocmé suggests that in fact we finish up with half a dozen different pictures of Jesus rather than one single picture. Faced by this problem, Trocmé offers two important suggestions. First of all, he looks for common features to be found in the various different pictures, and he finds such features to be the way in which Jesus constantly takes the initiative in various circumstances, the extraordinary zest which gives depth to the portraits, and the way in which he accepted the various conceptions which people had of him so that they became avenues of approach to one who was greater than any of these conceptions of his person. [46] Second, Trocmé suggests that what we have in the various types of tradition is in each case 'the total impression made by the Master on his disciples'.[47] Even if we cannot be sure of the precise reconstruction of the details of his ministry, yet the traditions enable us to grasp the impressions which Jesus made on his followers.

The second of these suggestions is worth noting. Trocmé's point is that even if we cannot be absolutely sure exactly what Jesus said and did on every occasion we still know what impression he made on his followers. But, we may well ask, is there so very much difference between what Jesus actually said and did and the impression which it created? Even if we are as cautious as Trocmé is — and he is undoubtedly over-cautious — must we not say that the cause of the impression cannot have been so very different from the impression itself? The impression made by a die-stamp is not so very different from the face of the stamp itself. Of course this is an imperfect analogy, since the impact made by a person on other persons and through them on a tradition is not static like that of a stamp on a piece of paper. Nevertheless, within limits, the point remains valid, namely that even if we were unable to get further back by historical means than to the impression made by Jesus, this would not be very far from getting back to Jesus himself.

This point is important. There are cases where it is impossible to work back with a high degree of probability to what Jesus actually said and did. In such cases Trocmé's point is that the tradition still gives us the impression made by Jesus on his followers, and this will not be so very different from the actual history.

Trocmè's other suggestion, however, is very open to criticism. He is mistaken in regarding the different types of tradition as conveying different impressions of Jesus. He speaks as though each 'form' of tradition had a separate origin. But this is a mis-statement. It is more likely that any one Christian community had several forms of tradition in its possession, and that these different forms were used for different purposes. Difference in 'form' is due to difference of function rather than to difference of origin. Thus the different pictures of Jesus found by Trocmé in different forms of tradition are artificial constructions. Furthermore, this approach makes the mistake of assuming that a given community has preserved all that it knew of Jesus. But the view that any Christian group must have put all its eggs into one basket, and that the basket has survived intact, is not realistic. To assume, for example, that the compiler of the Q traditions only had access to what he included in that source and that our reconstruction of Q represents the maximum of material contained in it is quite unsubstantiated. It follows that the different forms of tradition isolated by Trocmé may well have been more closely related to one another than he suggests. The coherence between the traditions, as analysed by C. H. Dodd, goes much further than Trocmé allows.

For these reasons the approach of Trocmé may be assessed negatively as being over-sceptical and creating non-existent distinctions between different aspects of the impact of Jesus. Positively, however, he offers an important supplement to our discussion above, since he makes it clear that even where we cannot work back confidently from the tradition to the historical reality of the ministry of Jesus we can still rest assured that the tradition faithfully reflects the total impression made by Jesus.

The result of our discussion is thus fairly positive. We have claimed that once we have worked back to the original form of the tradition we have a combination of criteria which when used in conjunction with one another, enable us to work back still further and see whether it reflects the historical sayings and deeds of Jesus. [48] Over against the scepticism of radical scholars we have been able to show that the tradition can be viewed in a positive way, and that there is good reason to regard it as reliable unless the contrary can be clearly shown. Even though the tradition was created by Christians whose purpose was to proclaim Jesus, nevertheless the tradition can be regarded as having a historical basis.

This approach admittedly carries with it the possibilities that in some cases it may not be possible to *prove* that the tradition has a historical basis, and that on occasion what is reported about Jesus may not correspond with historical reality; sayings ascribed to Jesus may turn out to have been created or modified by the early church as it recorded the impression which Jesus had made on it and presented him afresh to successive generations. These possibilities must be frankly admitted, even if we may suspect that the amount of such activity was slight.

The historical study of the Gospels is thus not a fruitless enterprise. We possess the evidence and the tools with which to assess it. To undertake the task of historical study is not to embark on a forlorn venture, bound to lead to ignorance and scepticism. On the contrary, historical study can be the servant of faith.

NOTES

1 M. Bloch, *The Historian's Craft*, 51f.
2 F. G. Downing, *The Church and Jesus*, London, 1968, 51.
3 See especially F. Hahn, *The Titles of Jesus in Christology*, London, 1969; R. H. Fuller, *The Foundations of New Testament Christology*.
4 See F. Hahn, *Mission in the New Testament*, London, 1965, 54f.
5 See my essay, 'Palestinian and Hellenistic Christianity: Some Critical Comments', *New Testament Studies* 19, 1972-73, 271-287.
6 M. Hengel, *Judaism and Hellenism*, London, 1974; see especially I, 105.
7 J. Jeremias, *New Testament Theology* I, 293f.
8 See the careful study by D. R. Catchpole, 'The Synoptic Divorce Material as a Traditio-Historical Problem', *Bulletin of the John Rylands University Library of Manchester* 57, 1974-75, 92-127.
9 J. Roloff, *Das Kerygma und der irdische Jesus*.
10 G. N. Stanton, *Jesus of Nazareth in New Testament Preaching*.
11 M. D. Hooker, 'In his own Image?' in M. Hooker and C. Hickling, *What about the New Testament?* 28-44, citation from 36.
12 C. H. Dodd, *Historical Tradition in the Fourth Gospel*.

13   For example, Luke 11:45; 12:41; 13:23; 14:15.

14   R. Bultmann, *The History of the Synoptic Tradition*, 127f.

15   S. Schulz, *Q — Die Spruchquelle der Evangelisten.*

16   D. Hill, 'On the Evidence for the Creative Rôle of Christian Prophets', *New Testament Studies* 20, 1973-74, 262-274, citation from 272.

17   *Ibid.*, 274.

18   F. Neugebauer, 'Geistsprüche und Jesuslogien', *Zeitschrift für die neutestamentliche Wissenschaft* 53, 1962, 218-228.

19   H. Riesenfeld, *The Gospel Tradition and its Beginnings*, London, 1957.

20   B. Gerhardsson, *Memory and Manuscript, Oral Tradition and Written Transmission in Rabbinic Judaism and Early Christianity*, Uppsala, 1961.

21   M. Smith, review in *Journal of Biblical Literature* 82, 1963, 169-176.

22   C. K. Barrett, review in *Journal of Theological Studies* 14, 1963, 445-449.

23   W. D. Davies, 'Reflections on a Scandinavian Approach to "The Gospel Tradition"', in *The Setting of the Sermon on the Mount*, Cambridge, 1964, 464-480, citation from 480. *cf.* W. Wiefel, 'Vätersprüche und Herrenworte', *Novum Testamentum* 11, 1964, 105-120.

24   H. Schürmann, 'Die vorösterlichen Anfänge der Logientradition: Versuch eines formgeschichtlichen Zugangs zum Leben Jesu', in *Traditionsgeschichtliche Untersuchungen*, 39-65.

25   J. Jeremias, *New Testament Theology* I, 3-37.

26   N. Perrin, *Rediscovering the Teaching of Jesus*, 39.

27   See above, p. 125, for Bultmann's statement of this position. Probably the most influential version in recent years has been that of E. Käsemann: 'In only one case do we have more or less safe ground under our feet; when there are no grounds either for deriving a tradition from Judaism or for ascribing it to primitive Christianity, and especially when Jewish Christianity has mitigated or modified the received tradition, as having found it too bold for its taste' (*Essays on New Testament Themes*, 37).

28   J. Jeremias, *New Testament Theology* I, 37.

29   W. G. Kümmel, *The Theology of the New Testament.*

30   So especially V. A. Harvey, *The Historian and the Believer*, ch. 2. The principle goes back at least to R. G. Collingwood, *The Idea of History*, Oxford, 1946, 256. See the criticisms of it made by F. F. Bruce, 'History and the Gospel', in C. F. H. Henry, *Jesus of Nazareth: Saviour and Lord*, 89-107, especially 99f.

31   Sometimes the principle is employed in a positive manner: see D. G. A. Calvert, 'An Examination of the Criteria for distinguishing the Authentic Words of Jesus', *New Testament Studies* 18, 1971-72, 209-218.

32   The statement by R. H. Fuller, *Interpreting the Miracles*, London, 1963, 26, is open to this misinterpretation.

33   D. G. A. Calvert, *op. cit.*, 212. See further R. S. Barbour, *Traditio-Historical Criticism of the Gospels*, London, 1972.

34   M. D. Hooker, 'Christology and Methodology', *New Testament Studies* 17, 1973-74, 480-488, citation from 482f.; *cf.* 'On Using the Wrong Tool', *Theology* 75, 1972, 570-581.

35   D. R. Catchpole, *op. cit.*, 113.

36 Something like this point is made by D. G. A. Calvert, *op.cit.*, 214, following H. E. W. Turner, *Historicity and the Gospels*.

37 C. H. Dodd, *Historical Tradition in the Fourth Gospel*, 338-343.

38 N. Perrin, *Rediscovering the Teaching of Jesus*, 46.

39 C. H. Dodd, *History and the Gospel*, Cambridge, 1938, 86-103.

40 Mark 2:14-17 (a pronouncement story); Luke 19:2-10 (Luke's special source material; a story about Jesus); Luke 7:36-48 (the same); John 7:53 — 8:11 (a story about Jesus from tradition preserved outside the Gospels); Luke 15:4-7 (Probably 'Q'; a parable); Luke 18:10-14 (Luke's special source material; a parable); Matt. 11:16-19 ('Q'; 'I' saying); Matt. 21:32 (Matthew's special source material).

41 N. Perrin, *Rediscovering the Teaching of Jesus*, 43-45.

42 P. W. Schmiedel, 'Gospels', in *Encyclopaedia Biblica*, London, 1899-1903, II, cols. 1761-1898, especially cols. 1881-1883.

43 C. F. D. Moule, *The Phenomenon of the New Testament*, London, 1967, 63, 65. See further R. N. Longenecker, 'Literary Criteria in Life of Jesus Research: An Evaluation and a Proposal', in G. F. Hawthorne (ed.), *Current Issues in Biblical and Patristic Interpretation*, Grand Rapids, 1975, 217-229.

44 C. H. Dodd, *According to the Scriptures*, London, 1952, 109f. See also D. R. Catchpole, 'Tradition History', in I. H. Marshall (ed.), *New Testament Interpretation*, 177f.

45 It should be noted that this formulation of the criterion of traditional continuity avoids the objection that might be raised by F.G. Downing with his claim that we are as much in the dark about the historical early church as about the historical Jesus and therefore cannot usefully discuss the continuity (or discontinuity) between them. In the present case we are dealing with a known factor — namely the tradition — and attempting to work back from this to its basis. The uncertain factor is the reconstruction of the earliest forms of the tradition, but we can be sufficiently sure about this in many cases to make the historical step backwards with reasonable confidence.

46 E. Trocmé, *Jesus and his Contemporaries*, 121-126.

47 *Ibid.*, 36; *cf.* 39.

48 For further discussion of the criteria for evaluating the tradition see K. Kertelge (ed.), *Rückfrage nach Jesus*.

CHAPTER 10

The Historical Jesus

FROM THE PRECEDING chapter it will be clear where the central issue in the problem of the historical Jesus is to be located. In the end, philosophical questions about the legitimacy and possibility of historical study do not seem to make much difference to the fact that historians carry on studying the past and writing books about it. In the same way, discussions about the philosophy of science, unfinished as they are, do not hinder scientists from pursuing their calling. Such discussions certainly help to clarify what the historian or scientist is doing and will enable him to do his task more effectively and accurately; he would be foolish to ignore them. But when all is said and done, the real problems lie in the area of actually carrying out the research, in finding out the right methods and in applying them to the subject-matter. The question of the historical Jesus is ultimately a question of historical evidence and the means of assessing it.

In the previous four chapters we tried to show how the process has been carried on by modern scholars and to assess the methods which have been used. Our enquiry was concerned with the two questions of whether we possess evidence that can tell us something about the historical Jesus and whether we possess critical tools that enable us to proceed from the evidence to the historical facts which lie behind it. The upshot of our discussion was that, although the critical problems are difficult, we do possess in principle the means to gain knowledge of the historical Jesus.

It might be expected that on the basis of these results we

would now proceed to a reconstruction of the historical Jesus which would afford some justification of the principles which we have adopted. Space alone would forbid this procedure, since the amount of evidence involved is so great and the critical discussion required is so intricate as to be beyond the scope of the present book. Nor would it be possible simply to present the results of such an investigation, since a justification of the principles would require some clear indication of the path from the evidence to the historical hypothesis that was being offered.[1] We must, therefore, be content with some more limited objective. Just as an archaeologist, confronted by a vast site, must begin by digging trial trenches which will give some insight into the character of the site as a whole, so we must restrict ourselves to some trial soundings in areas which we have reason to believe to be significant.

THE BARE MINIMUM OF INFORMATION?

It may be useful to begin by observing what sort of picture of Jesus is obtained by scholars who work on more sceptical principles than those outlined in this book. Among recent scholars who operate basically with the criterion of dissimilarity, both N. Perrin and R. H. Fuller have set down briefly what they believe can be established about the ministry and teaching of Jesus. The former scholar is the more rigorous in his approach. He offers this general statement about the life of Jesus:

He was baptised by John the Baptist, and the beginning of his ministry was in some way linked with that of the Baptist. In his own ministry Jesus was above all the one who proclaimed the Kingdom of God and who challenged his hearers to respond to the reality he was proclaiming. The authority and effectiveness of Jesus as proclaimer of the Kingdom of God was reinforced by an apparently deserved reputation as an exorcist. In a world that believed in gods, in powers of good and evil, and in demons, he was able, in the name of God and his Kingdom, to help those who believed themselves to be possessed by demons.

A fundamental concern of Jesus was to bring together

into a unified group those who responded to his proclamation of the Kingdom of God irrespective of their sex, previous background or history. A central feature of the life of this group was eating together, sharing a common meal that celebrated their unity in the new relationship with God, which they enjoyed on the basis of their response to Jesus' proclamation of the Kingdom. In this concern for the unity of the group of those who responded to the proclamation, Jesus challenged the tendency of the Jewish community of his day to fragment itself and in the name of God to reject certain of its own members. This aroused a deep-rooted opposition to him, which reached a climax during a Passover celebration in Jerusalem when he was arrested, tried by the Jewish authorities on a charge of blasphemy and by the Romans on a charge of sedition, and crucified. During his lifetime he had chosen from among his followers a small group of disciples who had exhibited in their work in his name something of his power and authority.

That, or something very like it, is all that we can know; it is enough.

After this brief sketch, Perrin lists four areas of the teaching of Jesus where we can come close to his actual words. These are:

1. The Proclamation of the Kingdom of God (Mark 1:15a; Luke 11:20; 17:20f; Matt. 11:12).

2. The parables (*e.g.* Matt. 13:44-46; Luke 10:30-36; 16:1-9, 19-31; 14:7-11; 14:28-32; 11:5-8; 18:1-8; other parables could be added to this list).

3. The proverbial sayings: the most radical sayings (Luke 9:60a; Matt. 5:39b-41); the eschatological reversal sayings (Mark 8:35; 10:23b,25; 10:31; Luke 14:11); the conflict sayings (Mark 3:27; 3:24-26); and the parenetical sayings (Luke 9:62; Matt. 7:13f.; Mark 7:15; 10:15; Matt. 5:44-48).

4. The Lord's prayer (Luke 11:2-4).

5   As an appendix Perrin adds that some kind of future expectation is attested in the Lord's prayer and in a group of parables (Mark 4:3-9; 4:30-32; Matt. 13:33; Mark 4:26-29).[2]

It can be said with confidence that there are very few elements in the summary presented by Perrin which would be considered inauthentic by even the most sceptical of scholars. It must also be said that the summary is extremely meagre, and one might feel that this 'historical Jesus' is not much more of a tangible reality than the 'historical Asyncritus': we do not know enough about him for him to rank as a historical figure. It is only fair to say that other radical scholars who adopt fairly similar historical criteria to those used by Perrin allow that a greater amount of historical information is present in the Gospels. Thus R. H. Fuller gives a very much longer list of genuine sayings of Jesus, and since he specifically calls it a 'representative' list, we may presume that he would be willing to extend it.[3]

But have we grounds for providing a more detailed picture of Jesus, based on reliable evidence? The fact is that the 'minimal' picture is inherently unstable. An important criterion of whether the picture of Jesus is historical is whether it is sufficient to account for the creation of the subsequent tradition. Judged by this standard, this minimal account is plainly inadequate. We are seriously being asked to believe that a man who was credited with some twenty miscellaneous sayings and a dozen or more parables could have provided the impetus for the growth of a tradition which regarded him as the greatest of teachers and prophets. One possible answer is that the early church took this step under the influence of the resurrection. But here we come across a difficulty of a comparable kind. It is safe to say that the majority of scholars who are sceptical about the historicity of the Gospel tradition are also sceptical regarding the resurrection as a historical event; the most that they will allow is that some members of the early church believed that they had seen visions of Jesus, and the number of stories of such visions which they regard as having some historical basis are very few. R. Bultmann, for example, quite clearly does not accept the fact of a physical resurrection of Jesus, and his statement that Jesus 'rose into the kerygma'[4] suggests that he does not believe in any kind of 'spiritual' resurrection either. But if there was, for these scholars, no resurrection event worthy of the name, how can they account for the development of the tradition from these puny beginnings to the magnitude which it came to possess? The argument is admittedly *ad hominem*, [5] since there is good

historical evidence for the resurrection event, but we are
completely justified in putting it in this form: if there was no
resurrection, what was it that led the first disciples of an
insignificant wandering teacher to ascribe to him the worth of
a great prophet and more?

The criticism, of course, goes deeper than this. The early
church did not merely esteem Jesus as an outstanding teacher
and prophet. It regarded him as the Messiah and Son of God.
But it seems impossible that a figure who was no more than
Perrin makes him out to be could have been elevated to such
a status, even if we allow for the effect of his resurrection;
Perrin's 'historical Jesus' can hardly bear the weight of the
theological interpretation which was put upon him by the
early church. Why was it that this Jesus was understood as
the Christ of faith? Perrin's view accentuates the discontinuity between the Jesus of history and the Christ of faith to
such an extent that it becomes impossible to explain the
continuity that was undoubtedly traced by the early Christians. It is historically unsatisfying because it fails to make
sense of the rise of the early church's faith in Jesus. [6]

We may note in passing that the contemporary Christian
believer also would find it difficult to believe that this picture
of Jesus can support his own faith in him as the Son of God.
The Christian who is convinced of the reality of the Christ of
faith can well argue on the basis of his faith that the historical
Jesus must have been more than Perrin's picture suggests.

One might, of course, attempt to counter this objection
with the reply that a historical reconstruction such as Perrin's
merely gives us what can be known with some confidence
about Jesus *now*, and that it does not necessarily show us what
the early church knew about him, which may well have been
considerably more. But it is far from obvious that this is what
Perrin intends. When he says 'That, or something very like it,
is all that we can know; it is enough,' presumably he thinks
that it would have been enough for the early church, as well
as for us; but our case is that it would have been as
insufficient for them as it is for us. Nor, in view of their
discussion of the actual Gospel tradition, can one avoid the
impression that Perrin and other scholars of similar outlook
do not simply state that certain sayings and deeds attributed

to Jesus are historically uncertain but that they are definitely unhistorical. For example, the claim is made, not that it is doubtful whether Jesus spoke about the Son of man, but that he most probably did not speak about him. Consequently, there can be little doubt that, while it is admitted that much about the historical Jesus must remain obscure, he was not so very different from the modern historian's reconstruction of him. Thus our point remains standing, namely that such a minimal portrait of Jesus cannot account for the rise of the church's faith in him.

Second, it is historically incredible that Perrin's summary represents all that could have survived of historical worth about Jesus. Here is a person who ranks as the great leader of the disciples, and we are seriously being asked to believe that this is all that could be remembered about him. On any account Jesus had some followers. Did they forget all that he ever did? Had they no memory for what he said in the course of a ministry that must have been spread over some period of time? Did they distort the tradition so thoroughly that next to nothing of what he actually said and did survived? The suggestion is ludicrous. Over against such nonsense must be placed the commonsense statement of V. Taylor: 'If the form critics are right, the disciples must have been translated to heaven immediately after the resurrection'. [7] Attempts have been made to weaken the force of Taylor's point, [8] but they have not in any way succeeded in doing so. If Jesus meant so much to his followers, then it is overwhelmingly improbable that they remembered so little about him, or that they so completely refashioned the content of their memories. [9]

A third point is that the minimal picture leads to absurd consequences. For example, on the evidence cited, Jesus simply announced the imminent coming of the kingdom of God, and left no room for the coming of the Son of man. Consequently, it has to be denied that sayings referring to the coming of the Son of man are genuine. They cannot be sayings about Jesus' own future coming (since this would be to attribute messianic ideas to him), and they cannot be sayings about some other figure whose advent he expected. Hence a number of scholars have to argue that *all* of the Son of man sayings were created by the early church. [10] What has happened is that abuse of the criterion of dissimilarity to identify what Jesus taught has produced a picture with which the Son of man sayings are said to be incompatible. But the case for regarding at least some of the Son of man sayings as genuine is far too strong to be overturned by considerations of this kind. [11] A theory which compels us to jettison such a major element in the tradition as the Son of man sayings *en bloc* is self-evidently based on false premises. In other words, the criterion of dissimilarity leads to a distorted view of what Jesus may otherwise have said.

A fourth point is that the criterion of dissimilarity turns out to be self-refuting. As I have argued in greater detail elsewhere, the strict application of the principle by E. Käsemann leads him to the conclusion that Jesus held messianic ideas in the broad sense about himself; if this is the case, it becomes extremely improbable that Jesus himself never commented on this self-understanding to his disciples, and the picture of him as a person who never made such claims arises in fact out of the presupposition that he did not do so. Hence in this case the use of the criterion in question demands that we accept as historical sayings which would be excluded by the criterion itself; in other words, the criterion breaks down in practice. [12]

For these four reasons the sort of minimal picture of Jesus given by Perrin and scholars of his outlook proves to be inadequate and misleading. The picture of Jesus thus provided is not historical; it is a false picture because it has left much important evidence out of account.

THE CHARACTER OF JESUS

In attempting to sketch a better founded historical picture of Jesus we are provided with an important starting point by C. H. Dodd. After his discussion of preliminary matters Dodd's first main topic in his study of Jesus is headed 'Personal Traits', and it begins thus:

> I have said that the reported sayings of Jesus bear the stamp of an individual mind. It may serve as a test of that

statement if we now ask, How far is it possible to describe the characteristics of the mind that they reveal?

'The style is the man,' they say. What, then, of the style of the teaching of Jesus as it has come down to us in the Gospels? A large proportion of it comes in the form of short, crisp utterances, pungent, often allusive, even cryptic, laden with irony and paradox. This whole body of sayings, handed down through different channels of tradition, has an unmistakable stamp. It is impossible to suppose that they are merely the product of skilful condensation by early Christian teachers. They have the ring of originality. They betray a mind whose processes were swift and direct, hitting the nail on the head without waste of words. [13]

In the rest of the chapter evidence is provided in support of this thesis, and the discussion spills over into the stories about Jesus which reveal something of his character. The significance of this is threefold.

First, it is being claimed that various traits emerge in the Gospels which provide a picture of one person, and which can hardly have arisen in a collection of sayings from a group of early Christian prophets and others. The Gospels reveal the picture of an individual man. By our criterion of coherence this picture is one that deserves respect as a representation of a historical individual — not merely because it is coherent, but because the cohering details are drawn from a variety of sources and form-critical categories.

Second, this picture is an example of unintentional information being provided by the tradition, and is therefore all the more worthy of credence. If the tradition was basically concerned with the theological significance of Jesus, then it is striking that it has preserved these non-theological motifs. To be sure, we have already questioned whether the tradition was so exclusively orientated to the theological interests of the church and did not have a broader historical interest in Jesus. Even so, however, the fact is that material preserved because of its 'content' as teaching of Jesus nevertheless preserves incidentally something of the 'form' of the teacher who gave it.

This leads to the third, and most important point: if the tradition has accurately preserved these incidental features about the character of Jesus, it follows that the tradition itself must also report what Jesus actually said in its theological significance with comparable faithfulness. The sayings which give us a coherent picture of the teacher must at the same time be reliable representations of his teaching.

If this point is accepted, we are able to say that one of the historical features preserved in the Gospels is an impression of the character of Jesus, as evidenced both by the character of his sayings and also by the nature of his actions. [14]

THE KINGDOM OF GOD

From the character of Jesus we turn to his message. Here there is virtually general agreement among scholars that the kernel of Jesus' message was the proclamation of the kingdom of God. [15] It has been particularly emphasised by J. Jeremias that the language used by Jesus in speaking about the kingdom of God has remarkably few analogies in the Judaism of his day, [16] and this point has been followed up by L. Goppelt who observes that the formula 'The kingdom of God has drawn near' is without parallel in Judaism or early Christianity. [17] By the criterion of dissimilarity, therefore, this teaching is distinctive of Jesus. Not only so, but it is significant that in both of our major sources, Mark and Q, this concept is identified as being central in the teaching of Jesus and of his disciples during his lifetime (Mark 1:15; Matt. 10:7). In other words, it would seem that our earliest sources correctly identified what modern scholars have recognised — on other grounds — as the distinctive message of Jesus. Here again, the criterion of dissimilarity does not stand on its own, but its use is confirmed by multiple attestation in different sources.

A full-scale treatment of the historical Jesus would have to go on from this point and explore the tradition of the teaching of Jesus more generally in order to see whether it forms a coherent whole around this concept of the kingdom. This task has in effect been performed by several scholars, and while there are naturally some differences in detail among their presentations, their researches tend to confirm one another. [18] It is not too much to say that the picture of Jesus' central teaching about the kingdom is historically well-founded. Jesus announced that the kingdom of God had arrived, and he looked forward to an act of God which would bring it to its consummation. In the light of this announcement he called men to repentance and offered them a share in the blessings associated with the reign of God.

THE DEEDS OF JESUS

We must now take up in turn a number of issues related to Jesus' proclamation of the kingdom in order to see whether various other aspects of his ministry can be regarded as having a historical basis. First of all, there is the question of his behaviour. Did Jesus bring his message in any other ways than by means of the spoken word? To ask the question in this form, however, is to imply a distinction between word and action which breaks down at certain crucial points. Thus words derive their full significance from their context, not merely in relation to other words, but also in relation to the situations in which they are spoken. Jesus' proclamation of the blessings of God's reign takes a large part of its significance from the fact that it was made to the poor and needy, to the people despised by Jewish society on account of their evil reputations. There is perhaps no better attested fact about the life of Jesus than that he was a friend of 'tax-collectors and sinners'. It is in this historical context that he offered the salvation of God to people. The words and the actions belong together, and either is lacking in significance without the other. [19] But, granted this historical fact, we examine the tradition more closely, and it is obvious that various actions of Jesus, through which he extended friendship to the outcasts of society, fit into place historically; sharing in meals with such people ranked as a sign of accepting them and having fellowship with them, and this fits cogently into the general picture of Jesus.

In this same context we have the mighty deeds ascribed to Jesus. Early Christian tradition is supported by Jewish testimony at this point, and today it is universally acknowledged by New Testament scholars that Jesus claimed to cast out demons, and that he saw the presence of God's saving power in such actions. There is no reason to doubt that Jesus did perform exorcisms. But can we go beyond this and claim a historical basis for other actions of Jesus that involved the miraculous? Here the tradition must certainly be examined with great care. There would be a natural tendency for the early church to exaggerate or even create accounts of miracles. The question is whether this activity wholly accounts for the reports of the miracles. But we must here remember that things which may have seemed miraculous to the contemporaries of Jesus may not seem miraculous to modern people; healing of psycho-somatic ailments can be explained in natural terms, but to ancient people it would have seemed supernatural. There is no good reason for doubting that Jesus performed acts of this kind. Whatever the means involved, such actions certainly brought blessing to suffering people, and could be seen as signs of the saving power of God. Whether we can go further than this in historical explanation is doubtful. The evidence for the miracles of Jesus is not the kind which must infallibly persuade any sceptic that they must have happened. He can always withhold judgment on even the best attested story of the miraculous. Two questions have to be asked. One is whether the stories are likely to be true in their general context, that is to say in the light of the general historical impression made by Jesus and in the light of the historian's total world view. Here opinions will differ, but the present author, writing as a Christian believer, has no doubt that miraculous events were associated with the ministry of Jesus. The other question which must be asked is whether the historical evidence for any particular story of the miraculous is free from difficulty. The evidence may be unsatisfying when it is examined critically, or it may be free from difficulty — other than the difficulty inherent in the miraculous. In the latter case, there is no impropriety in accepting the story. It must, however, be admitted that cases where miracles must be regarded as historical (granted the possibility of the miraculous) in the sense that they are strongly attested (and not merely historically possible) are few. One such fact, is the resurrection of Jesus, for which the evidence is so strong as scarcely to allow of a natural explanation. (In other words, the historical evidence in favour of the resurrection of Jesus should certainly make a person who believes that in principle miracles cannot happen think again). [20]

Whether the early church could have come to believe that Jesus was the Son of God purely on the grounds of his teaching and resurrection and apart from a belief in his miraculous powers is hard to tell; our sources shed little light on the development of this aspect of Christian belief, so that it is a moot point whether the stories of the miracles contributed to the belief in Jesus as the Son of God or vice-versa; probably the two beliefs reinforced each other. Consequently, it is doubtful whether we can argue here from the faith of the early church back to an adequate historical cause for it.

JESUS AND THE FUTURE

The second issue which arises from Jesus' teaching about the kingdom is that of his expectations regarding the future. We said above that Jesus looked forward to an act of God which would bring the kingdom to its consummation. In the view of many scholars it is clear from certain statements ascribed to Jesus that he expected this consummation to take place in the immediate future. The most famous form of this interpretation is that of A. Schweitzer who held that when Jesus sent out his disciples on mission he did not expect them to return before the coming of the Son of man (Matt. 10:23). [21] More recent scholars, while rejecting this interpretation, based on one single text which may be out of context, nevertheless often argue that Jesus' expectation of the kingdom in the imminent future controlled his message. If this is the case, then all that Jesus said was directed to encouraging men to repent and prepare themselves for the inescapable judgment that was just round the corner. [22]

If this is a correct interpretation of Jesus' message, two things follow. First, since Jesus' prophecy proved to be mistaken, the teaching and exhortation which he based on it, is also mistaken. A message whose validity depends on the coming of the kingdom in the near future loses its validity if the basic premise is false. Advocates of this understanding of Jesus' message must, therefore, either regard it as having lost its significance — unless certain parts of it can survive the collapse of the whole — or they must reinterpret it in some new way. The latter path has been chosen by R. Bultmann and many of his followers who argue that Jesus' message about the temporal nearness of the kingdom was a way of emphasising the existential significance of the present time as a time of decision. [23]

The second thing is that the early church too must have been conscious of this problem. Much of the teaching ascribed to Jesus in the Gospels in fact assumes that the consummation of the kingdom will not take place all at once: normal life will go on for some time, the church will exercise its ministry, there will be various premonitory signs, and only then will the end come. Since this kind of teaching is contrary to the texts which expect the kingdom to come immediately, it must follow that it stems from the early church, wrestling with the 'delay of the parousia', and not from Jesus. The way is then open to a reconstruction of the history of the Gospel tradition in terms of the influence of this motif of delay. [24]

The consequences of this view for the historicity of the Gospel tradition are fairly devastating. It implies a very thorough reworking of the tradition by the early church. There are few texts which are not affected by this attempt to come to terms with the non-fulfilment of Jesus' prophecy. But does this theory fit the facts?

At the outset it must be noted that it is surprising that so much of the tradition has had to be modified by the early church in order to credit Jesus with a prophetic outlook which is attested in comparatively few texts. (To defenders of the view, this is of course a sign of the thoroughness with which the early church did the task). We may well wonder whether a view which requires such a wholesale reinterpretation of the major part of the evidence does not rather suggest that perhaps it is the small number of texts which appear to speak of an immediate consummation which have been misunderstood by modern scholars.

Next, it may be significant that none of the texts which

belong to Perrin's assured minimum (by the criterion of dissimilarity) prophesies the imminence of the end. Perrin in fact ascribes texts which prophesy the imminent coming of the Son of man to the early church: the early church created its own difficulty regarding the delay of the parousia on this view! But Perrin's view at this point would not be generally accepted, and we cannot use it as an easy way out from the problem. It is more important to examine the texts in question to see whether they demand the view that Jesus did prophesy the end as taking place in the immediate future. Such an examination reveals that he did not do so. He certainly talked of certain events as taking place within the lifetime of his hearers, but this is not the same thing as saying that they would take place next week. He also qualified his statements by the explicit admission of ignorance regarding the time of the end which we find in Mark 13:32. Part of the difficulty is due to the association of prophecies regarding the destruction of the temple (which happened in AD 70 — *i.e.* within the lifetime of some of Jesus' contemporaries) with prophecies regarding the end. Nevertheless, it is hard to avoid the impression that Jesus spoke as if the end might come within the lifetime of his hearers; warnings to them to be ready lest the Son of man comes and finds people unready for his coming are pointless if there is not a real possibility of his coming within their lifetime. Even the writer who apologises for the apparent delay in the parousia by telling his readers that a thousand years are like a day to the Lord (2 Pet. 3:8) hardly expected that the end would be as much as two millennia (or more) distant. Granted all this, however, there is no apparent reason why the church should have proceeded to re-interpret the tradition at the early date required by this theory; it can only have been after some years that people began to feel that the interval was becoming unduly long. In short, it is doubtful whether the feeling of delay arose sufficiently soon or in a sufficiently acute form to lead to a radical rewriting of the Gospel tradition. The suspicion which many critics feel towards any saying attributed to Jesus which presupposes the continuation of human life for any appreciable time is unjustified. [25]

THE PERSON OF JESUS

The third question which arises in connection with Jesus' message about the kingdom of God is whether he made any attempt to define his own position in relation to it and in relation to the God who had sent him as his messenger. A prophet can foretell what God is going to do without being any more than a herald of the divine action which takes place independently of him. Was this true of Jesus? The early church certainly regarded Jesus as the agent or instrument of God's action. It spoke of him as the Messiah, a term which referred to a ruler on behalf of God, and it attributed to him a status second only to that of God the Father. But did this estimate of his task and person fit in with his own ideas? Such an estimate would appear to be contained in the use of various titles, 'Son of man', 'the Son (of God)' and the 'Messiah' which either were used by Jesus himself or were attributed to him by others. These, however, were titles that were used by the early church, and by the criterion of dissimilarity many critics would claim that all such titles have been read back into the lifetime of Jesus, whereas in fact they were not used until after his death and resurrection. [26] Jesus, it is argued, made no overt claims for himself, and was little more than the herald of the kingdom, at least so far as his conscious claims went. If so, it again follows that a good deal of the Gospel tradition must be unhistorical.

Even Bultmann seems to realise that he has gone too far in adopting a position of this kind, for he admits that 'Jesus' call to decision implies a christology'. [27] This appears to mean that the ministry of Jesus as a whole leads men to the point where they must ask the question, 'Who is Jesus?' It is not so clear that it means that the people confronted by Jesus during his ministry were compelled to ask the same question, and it does not mean that Jesus himself expressed any opinions on the subject. But this view of the matter fails to do justice to the evidence and is historically unsatisfying, for the following reasons.

First, the ministry of Jesus shows that who he was and what he did were closely related to his message of the kingdom. B. Gärtner has drawn attention to five features of Jesus' ministry: he acted in the place of God in forgiving sins; he considered himself to be greater than Moses in separating the rule of God from acceptance of the Old Testament law; he claimed divine authority to exorcise demons; he spoke authoritatively of God's judgment on sinners; and in his activity he manifested the actual presence of the kingdom. From these features Gärtner concludes: 'Jesus represented the Kingdom in his person, and, therefore, one may say that the person of Jesus, his words and deeds, are all aspects of one thing, the Kingdom'. [28] This conclusion is based on reliable evidence and shows that Jesus' person and status were closely related to his message in a way that went beyond the relation of a prophet to his message.

But, second, if Jesus himself was so closely related to his message, it is hard to see how he could have been unconscious of the fact. Admittedly there are scholars who would deny this conclusion. Thus E. Käsemann appears to concede the fact just stated, when he says: 'The only category which does justice to his claim (quite independently of whether he used it himself and required it of others) is that in which his disciples themselves placed him — namely, that of the Messiah'. [29] But then he goes on to assert that there can be no possible grounds for believing that Jesus understood himself to be the Messiah. It is more than difficult to see how this denial can be defended. Käsemann himself has offered evidence that Jesus performed the functions of the Messiah, especially in his assertion of a claim to authority greater than that of Moses. [30] But if Jesus made such a claim, could he have been ignorant of the messianic claim which was inherent in it? What could have led Jesus to act and speak as he did, if he was not conscious of a 'messianic' calling? Jesus' call to decision must surely have implied a christology *in his own mind.*

Then, third, if Jesus was conscious of a 'messianic' status, we must ask the question whether he expressed this in his teaching in any way. For Käsemann and many others, he did so only in indirect ways, not making use of any christological titles; all occurrences of such titles in the Gospels stand under suspicion of being anachronistic expressions of the church's belief about Jesus. But this reasoning has now become implausible. For if Jesus acted and spoke in 'messianic' fashion, and if the early church used various titles to refer to him, the possibility opens up that Jesus himself guided the church's thinking. The use of titles in the Gospels may be *both* an expression of Jesus' own self-consciousness *and* the means of the church's confession of his status. Our historical task would then be to examine the use of the titles to see where attribution of them to Jesus' own teaching is historically compelling. Here there can be little doubt that Jesus' use of the term 'Son' in reference to himself (Matt. 11:27; Luke 10:22) appears perfectly natural in the context of his personal relationship with God as his Father, especially since the term 'son' is here close to its origins in a metaphorical expression about the relation of fathers and sons in general. Again, there is little doubt that Jesus used the term 'Son of man'; attempts to explain the use of this phrase which appears almost without exception on the lips of Jesus and of nobody else as a Christian creation fly in the face of all probability. Neither of these titles appears to have been especially current among the Jews at the time, and hence one aspect of the criterion of dissimilarity can rightly be invoked here in confirmation of our conclusion. Without some such lead from Jesus himself it is difficult to account for the particular form which the development of christology took in the early church. Negatively, it is significant that Jesus made little use of the term 'Messiah' which became of cardinal importance in the early church, and this suggests that he avoided overt attachment to the more 'orthodox' type of Jewish expectation.

Again, we cannot go into the details of this particular topic. [31] But enough has perhaps been said to show that the historical Jesus did act in a broadly 'messianic' way, and that his self-consciousness in this respect found expression in the use of 'messianic' titles. Whether this fact is of theological significance for the reader of the Gospels is a matter that lies beyond the province of the historian. He can at least demonstrate that there are historical facts about the ministry of Jesus which demand some kind of theological evaluation.

THE DEATH OF JESUS

A fourth question remains to be tackled in connection with

Jesus' message of the kingdom. What exactly did he expect to happen as regards the future establishment of the kingdom of God and his own rôle in relation to it? His preaching ministry did not lead to a successful mass movement among the Jews, but rather to his arrest and execution. Was this what Jesus expected to happen? Or did he die in the realisation that his mission had been a failure?

The Gospels do not suggest that events took Jesus by surprise. On the contrary, they contain a number of sayings in which Jesus spoke of the divinely destined path of the Son of man through rejection and suffering to resurrection. Critics regularly discount these as 'prophecies after the event', the evidence of attempts by the early church to show that Jesus foresaw his death and resurrection. It can be argued that the sayings reflect a knowledge of what actually happened, that they used terminology characteristic of the early church's theology, and that an ordinary man (such as the 'historical' Jesus was, on one definition of 'historical') could not have foreseen the future in detail. A further difficulty is that there does not seem to be any organic connection between Jesus' message of the kingdom and his own death. Indeed, to generalise the point, Jesus' prophecies about his death refer to him as the 'Son of man', and it has been argued that 'kingdom of God' and 'Son of man' are two distinct and independent motifs which are never brought into real union in the teaching ascribed to Jesus.

Here, then, is yet another case where the picture of Jesus in the Gospels and one view of the 'historical' Jesus differ considerably from each other. Once again there is good reason to ask whether the cleavage postulated between Jesus and the Gospels at this point is justified by historical investigation. Closer inspection suggests that this is not the case.

In the first place, the volume of evidence that Jesus must have reckoned with the possibility of his own violent death is quite considerable. Any man who ran up against the Jewish authorities so frequently and so decisively as Jesus, must certainly have reckoned with the likelihood of a sticky end, and anybody who was aware that his mission was in danger of being misunderstood as a nationalistic movement directed against some Romans would have realised that there was probably a price on his head. Since, moreover, it was the Romans who possessed the power of life and death over criminals rather than the Jews themselves, and their method of dealing with insurgents was crucifixion, it would not require much imagination to guess at the probable nature of an alleged rebel's fate.

In the second place, a person brought up on the Jewish Scriptures and inheriting the traditions of Israel's history since the time of the Maccabees would have realised that the path of faithfulness to God carried the risk of persecution and even death as part of the divinely ordained way for the righteous in an evil world. Simply on a human level Jesus must have reckoned with the possibility of his own death.

In particular, thirdly, there is good evidence that the sayings attributed to Jesus understand his suffering and death in terms of the Son of man and the suffering Servant portrayed in Dan. 7 and Isa. 53 respectively. But neither of these motifs appears to have been conspicuous in the theology of the early church, and this strongly suggests that we must look to Jesus as the source of this unique combination.

Fourth, in Dan. 7 the figure of the Son of man is connected with the motif of rule, dominion, glory and judgment, and it can be argued that from here an organic unity between the two motifs of kingdom and Son of man can be developed. It remains true that the actual terms 'Son of man' and 'kingdom of God' are not brought together in the teaching of Jesus in any significant way. It is also probable that the predictions of Jesus' death would have been 'written up' in the light of the events — it would be surprising if early Christians could have resisted the unconscious temptation [32] — but this does not prevent us from isolating a core of probably authentic material. On balance, it remains historically probable that Jesus did anticipate his own death and vindication by God, and that he saw in this event the crisis by means of which the kingdom of God would be established. The early church was in no doubt that the death and resurrection of Jesus did constitute this decisive event. [33]

THE HISTORICAL JESUS

In the above pages we have been able to do no more than outline the reasons which can be given for believing that at certain cardinal points we possess a considerable body of reliable historical information about Jesus, and that, for all the development which the tradition may have undergone, the picture presented by the Gospels is substantially based on what actually happened. What conclusions can now be drawn from this discussion?

First, we have seen that the nature of the sources and the character of the methods of study open to us are such as to enable us to know something about the historical Jesus. It is possible to work back from the Gospels to an underlying historical event. However much the Gospels may contain the reflection of the early church, they are closely based on the ministry of the historical Jesus.

It has also been argued that the amount of material which can be traced back to the historical Jesus is far from meagre. The question of the existence of Jesus is not in any real doubt. [34] The question is how much can be known about him, and with what degree of probability it can be known. While one substantial group of scholars regards what can be known about Jesus as being quite small in amount, we have argued that their conclusions rest on a misjudgment of the nature of the sources and on the application of a faulty historical method. Without wishing to adopt a historical method any the less exacting and critical, we have argued that a study of the evidence by the appropriate methods leads to the conclusion that we can have a clear idea of the main features in the ministry of Jesus.

In so brief a discussion as the present one, it has really not been possible to do more than present an agenda for future research. In other words, the argument enunciated here can do little more than serve as an encouragement to study of the Gospels by assuring the student that he has strong reason to expect positive results from his study. We have surveyed the sources, and found that they rest on a historical basis; we have outlined a method of approach which is free from the drawbacks of alternative proposed methods; and we have indicated what happens when this method is applied at certain key points in the investigation of the historical Jesus. We have produced results for which a high degree of probability can be claimed, and this fact suggests that similar investigations carried out in other parts of the field will also produce reliable results.

Second, we can now ask the question: in what sense can we speak of knowledge of the historical Jesus? At the outset of our enquiry we tried to catalogue the possible meanings of 'historical', and it is now time to compare our findings with this initial agenda. Accordingly, we may say that we have gathered evidence which indicates that the person called Jesus actually existed. 'Jesus' is not a character in fiction but the name of a person who really lived. The fact that we have been able to compile a set of historical facts about him is adequate proof that he existed.

We have also been able to gather evidence which enables us to distinguish between the historical Jesus and the later portraits of him presented in the Gospels and to see whether the portraits correspond to historical reality.

Although we have not been able to accomplish the task in the limits set by this book, we have gathered enough evidence to suggest that Jesus is a historical person in a way that Asyncritus is not. We know sufficient about Jesus by historical methods in order to produce a recognisable figure with his own 'history'. We know sufficient of his character, his teaching and his actions to feel that he is a real person, even if it is not possible to give a detailed sketch of the main course of his career. So long as we do not insist on the need for the latter, we can legitimately claim to have a historical picture of Jesus.

Throughout the closing stages of the enquiry, we have tried to indicate the relative probability of the various historical facts which we have established concerning Jesus. Some of these facts lie beyond all reasonable doubt, while others can be regarded as very highly probable. In the case of other facts, there is no good reason to doubt them, even though they might be wrong. We would submit that in any area of historical study, particularly in study of the ancient world, the situation is going to be very similar. To restrict the term 'historical' to the facts which stand beyond all dispute is to make unreasonable demands on the historian in any area.

In our enquiry we have not arbitrarily defined the term 'historical' in terms of 'non-supernatural' facts. We believe that historical method is capable of dealing with supernatural facts. Although the facts about Jesus which we have discussed have been largely non-supernatural, we noted that he was credited with deeds which appeared miraculous to his contemporaries, and we argued that in at least some cases a supernatural explanation is probable, granted that the historian is willing to admit the possibility of the supernatural.

The 'historical Jesus' is Jesus as he really was. The full range of that event lies beyond the historian. What can be claimed is that there is good reason to believe that the 'historical Jesus' in this sense is accurately represented in the 'historian's Jesus', the Jesus of critical reconstruction.

Although the Gospels were not written by scientific historians, we have found good reason to believe that they incorporate reliable information about Jesus, so that the ordinary reader, who has neither the time nor the scholarly skills to carry out historical research, may rest confident that the portraits of Jesus in the Gospels are based on historical fact. To be sure, the Gospels and their sources give 'interpreted' pictures of Jesus, but these interpretations represent an understanding of Jesus based on the historical facts. Our final question must be concerned with the validity of their understanding of Jesus.

NOTES

1   I have given a very brief summary of the facts as I see them in my article, 'Jesus in the Gospels', in F. Gaebelein (ed.), *The Expositor's Bible Commentary*, Grand Rapids, forthcoming.

2   N. Perrin, *The New Testament. An Introduction*, New York, 1974, 287-301.

3   R. H. Fuller, *A Critical Introduction to the New Testament*, London, 1966, 99-103.

4   R. Bultmann, in C. E. Braaten and R. A. Harrisville, *The Historical Jesus and the Kerygmatic Christ*, New York, 1964, 15-42, especially 41f.

5   It must be admitted, however, that Perrin's own position here is far from clear. Although he says that 'we may safely assume that while on

the road to Damascus Paul did have a vision of a figure who identified himself as Jesus of Nazareth' (*op. cit.,* 94), he also attempts to understand the resurrection in terms of myth and endorses Bultmann's statement cited in the text (*op. cit.,* 24).

6   This result is by no means surprising, since the criterion of dissimilarity used by Perrin automatically rules out any evidence which testifies to continuity between Jesus and the early church.

7   V. Taylor, *The Formation of the Gospel Tradition,* London, 1935, 41.

8   D. E. Nineham, 'Eye Witness Testimony and the Gospel Tradition', *Journal of Theological Studies* 9, 1958, 13-25, 243-252; 11, 1960, 253-264.

9   It may be noted that little stress has been placed in our earlier discussion on the existence of eye-witnesses of the ministry of Jesus. This has been done deliberately in order to show that even without recourse to this point a strong case for a historical basis to the Gospel tradition can be erected. The inclusion of this point renders the case all the stronger.

10   N. Perrin, *A Modern Pilgrimage in New Testament Christology,* Philadelphia, 1974. *Cf.* E. Käsemann, *Essays on New Testament Themes,* London, 1964, 38.

11   I. H. Marshall, *The Origins of New Testament Christology,* London, 1977, ch. 4.

12   *Ibid.,* ch. 2.

13   C. H. Dodd, *The Founder of Christianity,* London, 1971, ch. 3, citation from 49.

14   For detailed backing for this section see G. N. Stanton, *Jesus of Nazareth in New Testament Preaching,* Cambridge, 1974, ch. 6.

15   The only significant exception known to me is E. Bammel, 'Erwägungen zur Eschatologie Jesu', in F. L. Cross (ed.), *Studia Evangelica* III, 1964, 3-32. Bammel's objections are insufficient to overturn the consensus.

16   J. Jeremias, *New Testament Theology* I, London, 1971, 31-35.

17   L. Goppelt, *Theologie des Neuen Testaments* I, Göttingen, 1975, 106.

18   R. Schnackenburg, *God's Rule and Kingdom,* Freiburg/London, 1963; G. E. Ladd, *Jesus and the Kingdom,* London, 1966. Scholars differ as to whether Jesus regarded the rule of God as having already arrived or as being close at hand; in both cases the thought of Jesus is controlled by the nearness of the rule of God, and the time of his ministry is seen as one of fulfilment.

19   Thus without some knowledge of what Jesus said about sinners we might be tempted to concur with the verdict that he was merely 'a glutton and a drunkard, a friend of tax-collectors and sinners' (Luke 7:34).

20   See G. E. Ladd, *I believe in the Resurrection of Jesus,* London, 1975.

21   A. Schweitzer, *The Quest of the Historical Jesus,* 357.

22   R. Bultmann, *Theology of the New Testament* I, 9.

23   For a review of modern interpretations see G. Lundström, *The Kingdom of God in the Teaching of Jesus,* Edinburgh, 1963.

24   The most thorough-going such reconstruction is that of E. Grässer, *Das*

Problem der Parusieverzögerung in den synoptischen Evangelien und in der Apostelgeschichte, Berlin, 1957.

25   See A. L. Moore, *The Parousia in the New Testament*, Leiden, 1966; D. E. Aune, 'The Significance of the Delay of the Parousia for Early Christianity', in G. F. Hawthorne (ed.), *Current Issues in Biblical and Patristic Interpretation*, Grand Rapids, 1975, 87-109.

26   For a convenient summary of this approach see E. Schweizer, *Jesus*, London, 1971, 13-22; the author allows that Jesus used the term 'Son of man', but without making any exalted claims for himself by means of it.

27   R. Bultmann, *op. cit.*, 43.

28   B. Gärtner, 'The Person of Jesus and the Kingdom of God', *Theology Today* 27, 1970, 32-43, citation from 38.

29   E. Käsemann, *Essays on New Testament Themes*, London, 1964, 38.

30   *Ibid.*, 37-45. For a more positive study of the evidence see O. Betz, *What do we know about Jesus?* London, 1968.

31   For details see my book *The Origins of New Testament Christology*, London, 1977.

32   The most probable reason for the changes from 'kill' and 'after three days' in Mark 10:34 to 'crucify' and 'on the third day' in Matt. 20:19 is reformulation of the saying in the light of the event.

33   See J. Jeremias, *New Testament Theology* I, 276-299; H. Schürmann, 'Wie hat Jesus seinen Tod bestanden und verstanden? Eine methoden-kritische Besinnung', in P. Hoffmann (ed.), *Orientierung an Jesus*, Freiburg, 1973, 325-363.

34   We may now return to the denial of the existence of Jesus by G. A. Wells discussed earlier, and can claim to have substantiated our view that the existence of the Gospel tradition cannot be explained without postulating the existence of Jesus.

CHAPTER 11

The 'Historic' Jesus

WHAT IS THE significance of the historical Jesus, the Jesus to whom we have tried to open up the means of historical access in this book? By any account Jesus ranks as a historic figure, *i.e.* a figure of importance in history, simply because of the impact made by his life on the world since his time. For this reason alone it is of importance to the historian to study Jesus in order to understand the relation between him and his subsequent effects in human history. Such an enquiry might lead to the conclusion that Jesus had been over-rated — that what he said and did was not as significant as later people thought it to be, or even that his immediate followers misjudged him and founded the church on a mistake. To undertake such an enquiry is not easy, perhaps indeed impossible, without the historian himself being involved in the enquiry. What does he himself think about the significance of Jesus? It may be that as a historian he feels that it is his duty simply to present the facts and leave others to determine their significance. Whether, however, he can completely avoid dealing with the significance of the historical character whom he is studying is debatable. Certainly as an ordinary man he has to face up to the question of the significance of historical facts. In what sense is Jesus a historic person for me?

HISTORY IN RELATION TO FAITH

One way towards an answer to this question will be by means

of an enquiry into the relation between the historical facts
about Jesus and the estimate which the early church formed
of him. How far do the historical facts support the Christian
understanding of Jesus? Is the Christian belief in Jesus
justified by the historical facts?

We may note first that the historical facts of the earthly
ministry of Jesus were not by themselves sufficient to lead to
Christian faith. After the death of Jesus the two disciples who
had met an unknown stranger on the road from Jerusalem to
Emmaus described the dead man as 'Jesus of Nazareth, who
was a prophet mighty in deed and word before God and all
the people...our chief priests and rulers delivered him up to
be condemned to death, and crucified him. But we had
hoped that he was the one to redeem Israel' (Luke 24:19-21).
Whether or not this is an exact transcript of what they
actually said, it represents perfectly the significance of the life
of Jesus as seen from the vantage point of men who knew only
of his death. His life had been that of a distinguished prophet,
and it had awakened hopes of his delivering Israel. Admittedly, whether as a prophet he was 'mighty before God' lies
beyond historical enquiry. But the picture of a man who raised
the question of whether he was the deliverer of Israel is a
correct interpretation of the facts. But this question cannot be
answered apart from the resurrection; it was the appearance
of the risen Jesus which confirmed the belief that he was in
fact the deliverer of Israel and led to a deeper understanding
of his significance. Moreover, the followers of Jesus believed
that it was the sending of the Spirit by the risen Jesus which
enabled them to share his spiritual power and which opened
their eyes to recognise his significance. In short, the historical
facts alone — short of the resurrection — were inadequate to
arouse a sure and lasting faith. It is true that the Gospels
report that some of the disciples recognised Jesus as the
Messiah during his lifetime; but this faith, we may be quite
certain, would have proved to be groundless and would have
been utterly shattered if they had not believed in his
resurrection. It may be a moot point whether the resurrection
should be accounted among the historical facts of the life of
Jesus; it is quite clear that apart from it those facts lack the

power to produce ultimate conviction. Without the reality of the risen Lord there can be no lasting, well-grounded faith.

Second, we may note that belief in Jesus as the Lord is corroborated by historical investigation. There could be no Christian faith in Jesus if it could be shown that he never existed or that he never rose from the dead or that his career was substantially different from that recorded in the Gospels. Historical study can, therefore, justify faith in a negative manner by showing that objections to the historicity of Jesus are unfounded. This is true even of an event like the resurrection; the historian can at least discuss whether there are any historical grounds for denying that the resurrection of Jesus took place, or whether any alternative explanation can account for the rise of the Christian church.

At the same time, the effect of our discussion has been to show that the historian can move beyond the negative task of showing that there is nothing impossible about the historicity of Jesus, to advancing a critical discussion of the evidence which allows us to conclude for the positive probability (to varying degrees) of various facts about Jesus. In this way a basis is provided for faith.

But we need to remind ourselves what is going on here. It has become clear that for any one historian the relative probability of the various facts about Jesus varies very considerably, and that the historical estimates made by different historians also vary considerably. In our discussion we have given reasons for rejecting the radical approach to the Gospels which finds a very scanty residue of historical fact in them, and we have argued for the acceptance of a much more positive attitude to the material. Even within the general circle of those who share this attitude, there are considerable differences as regards the historicity of the various items in the tradition and the detailed reconstruction of the facts into a portrait of Jesus. There is, therefore, a fair amount of uncertainty regarding various aspects of the basis for faith. In the case of many facts scholars must remain uncertain of their historicity and significance. To this extent the basis for Christian faith is uncertain and changing.

Nevertheless, in our discussion we deliberately probed the evidence about the ministry of Jesus at certain key points concerned with what the Evangelists evidently regarded as central aspects in it, and we were able to conclude that on these basic issues there was good reason to accept the reliability of the tradition. Instead of the tradition resembling a cloud of shifting composition and uncertain size, it is better to think of it as a reasonably solid mass with fuzzy edges. Despite the uncertainty concerning many of the facts there is a sufficient basis of historically reliable material for faith.

Now it might be argued that there was an element of circularity in our argument. One of the criteria which guided our discussion was whether the historical facts about Jesus were such as to have led to the rise of the church's faith. We argued from the historical fact of the church's faith in Jesus to the necessary causes of that faith, by claiming that a Jesus who was a perfectly ordinary man would hardly have triggered off the church's faith in him. It could be objected that working with this criterion we have found precisely what we might have expected: we have been historically sympathetic to elements in the tradition which account for the church's faith instead of assessing them critically. Our historical basis, it may be argued, is purely what the church felt it had to postulate in order to justify its own faith.

But this objection is palpably mistaken. It ignores the fact that we used other criteria in addition to this particular one, and that we felt on safest ground when the results of applying the various criteria coincided. Further, our question was not concerned with what the church believed to be necessary to establish its own faith, but rather with what historical causes needed to be postulated by a historian to account for the rise and development of that faith. The objection, accordingly, does not hold.

The results of our discussion thus show that historical study both clears away the objection that faith is impossible because the basis for it is non-existent, and also establishes the basis for faith by confirming the historicity of the facts which faith is required to accept. What, then, do we do with these facts? What is the relation of faith to them?

THE SIGNIFICANCE OF THE HISTORY

We have already seen how faith may to some extent be involved in the establishment of the historical facts themselves. The historian has to exercise faith in the validity of the historical method and in his own powers of deduction. He has to have faith in the possibility of deriving historical information from the evidence at his disposal. But in a deeper way the faith of the historian may affect his judgment of the historicity of the facts surrounding Jesus. This is obviously true of the resurrection, the miracles, and the various sayings which imply that Jesus was more than a mere man. Here questions of fact and significance are so closely tied together that it is hard to separate them.

Some four possibilities open up at this point. In the first place, the historian may claim that all the historical facts may be given a convincing 'natural' explanation, so that the 'historical' Jesus turns out to be a 'natural' Jesus. In this case, the historian may conclude that the question of religious belief does not arise.

Second, the historian may claim that all the historical facts can be given a 'natural' explanation, but he allows that what has happened 'naturally' may have a deeper significance — 'transcendent' is perhaps the word. For example, the Israelites may have been able to cross the Jordan dryshod (Joshua 3-4) because of a perfectly natural damming of the waters upstream from Jericho by an earth slide, but the timing of the event disposed them to see in it an act of God. Similarly, the 'star of Bethlehem' may have been a perfectly natural stellar phenomenon (such as a 'nova' or a planetary conjunction), but it could have been regarded as having a deeper significance. In both these examples the event in question could be interpreted in relation to the activity of a transcendent God who did not disturb the processes of nature. In the case of Jesus, the category of the transcendent may be used in the same way, or even without implying the existence of a personal God; Jesus may be seen as 'pointing beyond himself' to some ultimate values, challenging men to existential decision about their inmost being.

Third, the historian may come across elements in the story which defy natural explanation, and he may say, 'These elements appear to lie beyond ordinary historical explanation in natural terms. As a historian I cannot tell whether they happened or pronounce on their significance'. In this case he may adopt an attitude of disbelief or of agnosticism. He does not feel that the facts compel him to believe.

Fourthly, the historian may act as in the previous case, but say that as a private individual he is prepared to accept the possibility of the supernatural and to believe in the Christian estimate of Jesus. Alternatively, he may be prepared to allow for the category of the supernatural within the historian's field, and therefore to avoid the dichotomy between what he believes as a historian and what he believes as a private individual. In either case, he accepts the reality of the supernatural and the consequent Christian estimate of Jesus.

So far as these two alternatives are concerned, it seems to me that it is valid and proper for a historian to allow for supernatural events in historical study. W. Pannenberg has argued convincingly that a historian can cope with abnormal, unique events provided that the witnesses were acting normally and their reports cannot be explained away as due to their imagination. He then says:

> As long as historiography does not begin dogmatically with a narrow concept of reality according to which 'dead men do not rise', it is not clear why historiography should not in principle be able to speak about Jesus' resurrection as the explanation that is best established of such events as the disciples' experience of the appearances and the discovery of the empty tomb. [1]

If this argument is valid, it follows that the supernatural

features in the story of Jesus are not beyond the scope of the historian, although it may not be his province as a historian to discuss their theological implications, and although they are not entirely accounted for within history.

But the crucial factor is to be found in the qualification: 'As long as historiography does not begin dogmatically with a narrow concept of reality according to which "dead men do not rise"'. On what basis does the historian begin with or without such an assumption? The suggestion that he should at least have 'an open mind' may be thought to involve a pre-judgment from a Christian point of view. The Christian assumption at this point may be thought to be dependent on a prior belief in the resurrection of Jesus, and this is what determines the Christian's world view in which resurrection is possible. It may well be that the Christian is involved in a circle: his attitude to the evidence for the resurrection is based upon a world view in which resurrection is possible, and this world view in turn is based upon acceptance of the resurrection of Jesus. In other words, there is a hermeneutical circle here: the nature of the presuppositions is governed by the nature of the historical facts, and vice versa. The historian may plead that he needs better evidence than what may be merely a circular argument to justify his having an open mind towards the resurrection, but we may legitimately respond by saying that possibly he himself operates with a similar circular argument: no possibility exists of resurrection in general, therefore Jesus cannot have been resurrected, therefore... The choice between the two hermeneutical circles must be made in the light of the historical evidence. The historian must be open to the evidence, or rather open to the significance of Jesus which is suggested to him by the evidence. And that significance may be expressed in terms of the supernatural without the historian feeling that he has sacrificed his intellect to faith.

It is becoming increasingly popular, however, to interpret the ministry of Jesus as having a transcendent significance. On this view, the supernatural elements are interpreted not as accounts of the miraculous but as attempts to indicate the significance of Jesus as a pointer to another dimension of reality. The New Testament writers are regarded as having clothed Jesus in the trappings of myth in order to bring out this significance, but it is no longer possible for us to take this myth literally.

Despite its popularity, this suggestion is surrounded by considerable difficulty. It is doubtful whether it offers less difficulty to the historian who thinks in terms of natural causes and effects than the use of the category of the supernatural, since the recognition of a transcendent dimension is an admission of the inadequacy of the purely natural as a category of explanation of reality. It must be admitted, however, that a historian who is dissatisfied with the adequacy of natural explanations may be drawn to this category as one which avoids the problems associated with the supernatural.

A further problem is that this approach is clearly subjective: how does one recognise the presence of the 'transcendent' when one sees it? Is it a category to be invoked only when difficulties arise?

From the Christian point of view some serious objections are raised by R. A. S. Barbour who looks at the possibility that 'Jesus himself, that remarkable figure with his passionate awareness of God, is only significant for us as some sort of parable of the fact that man is a spiritual being always capable of being open to the transcendent.'[2] But this formulation immediately raises the question as to the right by which we are entitled to take Jesus' awareness of a personal God and transform it into the capability of being open to the transcendent. What inner necessity in the teaching of Jesus allows or compels this step? Barbour himself draws attention to a fundamental flaw in the approach: this view 'cannot really hold together the figure of long ago — be he historical Jesus or Christ of faith — and the contemporary reality. They are no more than successive manifestations of the transcendent which share the same name or the same characteristics. The historical or human existence of Christ has come to an end on the Cross, in this view, and the myth finally reigns supreme'.[3] In other words, this view destroys the uniqueness of Jesus, and above all his position as mediator between God and man, and man and God. Despite its attractions, the idea of a Jesus with merely 'transcendent' significance ultimately fails to do justice to the incarnation and cannot be regarded as an expression of the Christian significance of Jesus. Nor is it satisfactory from a historical point of view. By what right can it be claimed that the stories of the miracles of Jesus and his resurrection are 'really' mythical expressions of his significance? This approach persists in treating as myths stories which have a historical basis and which cannot be explained away as non-events or as ordinary events falsely interpreted as miraculous events.

So the reader of the Gospels is brought face to face with the biblical Jesus as the Son of the living God. The accounts, seen in the light of the resurrection, call out for his decision and invite him to faith. And the object of his faith is then the Jesus whose existence and ministry have been confirmed and illuminated by historical research, but whose significance is only fully seen in the light of that experience of the risen Lord which has coloured the interpretation of Jesus offered in the Gospels and the rest of the New Testament and which continues to illuminate the mind of the believer. For as we have seen, ultimately the earthly Jesus is inadequate. Christian faith joyfully embraces the Jesus of the Bible, assured that the biblical accounts have a firm basis in history, but knowing that 'the Jesus of the historians' is not enough; only the biblical Jesus Christ, the earthly and the heavenly Lord, is adequate as the object of faith.

I believe in the historical Jesus. I believe that historical study confirms that he lived and ministered and taught in a way that is substantially reproduced in the Gospels. I believe that this Jesus gave his life as a ransom for sinful mankind, and that he rose from the dead and is the living Lord. And in view of these facts I trust in him and commit my life to him.

NOTES

1 W. Pannenberg, *Jesus — God and Man*, London, 1968, 109. *Cf.* D. F. Fuller, *Easter Faith and History*, Grand Rapids, 1964.

2 R. A. S. Barbour, 'Jesus of Nazareth — History and Myth', *Aberdeen University Review* 45 (no. 149), Spring, 1973, 19-31, citation from 30.

3 *Ibid.*, 31.

Bibliography

Bibliography

1. Works on the Problem of the Historical Jesus

P. Althaus, *The So-called Kerygma and the Historical Jesus*, Edinburgh, 1959.

H. Anderson, *Jesus and Christian Origins*, Oxford, 1964.

D. M. Baillie, *God was in Christ*, London, 1948.

C. E. Braaten and R. A. Harrisville (ed.), *The Historical Jesus and the Kerygmatic Christ*, New York, 1964.

C. Brown (ed.), *History, Criticism and Faith*, London, 1977.

F. F. Bruce, *Jesus and Christian Origins Outside the New Testament*, London, 1974.

R. Bultmann, *The History of the Synoptic Tradition*, Oxford, 1968.[2] *Theology of the New Testament*, London, 1952, 1955.

F. Clark, *The Rise of Christianity*, Milton Keynes, 1974.

J. Denney, *Jesus and the Gospel*, London, 1909.

M. Dibelius, *From Tradition to Gospel*, Cambridge, 1971[2].

C. H. Dodd, *History and the Gospel*, Cambridge, 1938. *Historical Tradition in the Fourth Gospel*, Cambridge, 1963.

F. G. Downing, *The Church and Jesus*, London, 1968.

G. Ebeling, *The Nature of Faith*, London, 1961.

E. Fuchs, *Studies of the Historical Jesus*, London, 1964.

B. Gerhardsson, *Memory and Manuscript*, Uppsala, 1961.

E. Grässer, *Das Problem der Parusieverzögerung in den synoptischen Evangelien und in der Apostelgeschichte*, Berlin, 1957.

E. Güttgemanns, *Offene Fragen zur Formgeschichte des Evangeliums*, München, 1971[2].

F. Hahn (*et al.*), *What can we know about Jesus?* Edinburgh, 1969.

V. A. Harvey, *The Historian and the Believer*, London, 1967.

C. F. H. Henry, *Jesus of Nazareth: Saviour and Lord*, Grand Rapids, 1966.

M. Kähler, *The So-Called Historical Jesus and the Historic, Biblical Christ*, Philadelphia, 1964.

E. Käsemann, *Essays on New Testament Themes*, London, 1964.

L. E. Keck, *A Future for the Historical Jesus*, London, 1972.

E. and M.-L. Keller, *Miracles in Dispute*, London, 1969.

K. Kertelge (ed.), *Rückfrage nach Jesus*, Freiburg, 1974.

W. G. Kümmel, *The New Testament: The History of the Investigation of its Problems*, London, 1973.

X. Léon-Dufour, *The Gospels and the Jesus of History*, London, 1968.

H. K. McArthur, *In Search of the Historical Jesus*, New York, 1969.

T. W. Manson, *Studies in the Gospels and Epistles*, Manchester, 1962.

W. Manson, *Jesus the Messiah*, London, 1943.

I. H. Marshall (ed.), *New Testament Interpretation*, Exeter, 1977.
The Origins of New Testament Christology, London, 1977.

C. L. Mitton, *Jesus: The Fact behind the Faith*, London, 1975.

C. F. D. Moule, *The Phenomenon of the New Testament*, London, 1967.

S. Neill, *The Interpretation of the New Testament 1861-1961*, Oxford, 1964.

D. E. Nineham (ed.), *Historicity and Chronology in the New Testament*, London, 1965.

H. Palmer, *The Logic of Gospel Criticism*, London, 1968.

N. Perrin, *Rediscovering the Teaching of Jesus*, London, 1967.

J. Peter, *Finding the Historical Jesus*, London, 1965.

A. Richardson, *History Sacred and Profane*, London, 1964.

H. Riesenfeld, *The Gospel Tradition and its Beginnings*, London, 1957.

H. Ristow and K. Matthiae (ed.), *Der historische Jesus und der kerygmatische Christus*, Berlin, 1960.

J. M. Robinson, *A New Quest of the Historical Jesus*, London, 1959.

J. Roloff, *Das Kerygma und der irdische Jesus*, Göttingen, 1970.

K. L. Schmidt, *Der Rahmen der Geschichte Jesu*, Darmstadt, 1969[2].

H. Schürmann, *Traditionsgeschichtliche Untersuchungen*, Düsseldorf, 1968.

A. Schweitzer, *The Quest of the Historical Jesus*, London, 1954[3].

G. N. Stanton, *Jesus of Nazareth in New Testament Preaching*, Cambridge, 1974.

V. Taylor, *The Formation of the Gospel Tradition*, London, 1935.

H. E. W. Turner, *Historicity and the Gospels*, London, 1963.

G. A. Wells, *The Jesus of the Early Christians*, London, 1971. *Did Jesus Exist?* London, 1975.

H. Zahrnt, *The Historical Jesus*, London, 1963.

2. Historical Studies of Jesus

C. K. Barrett, *Jesus and the Gospel Tradition*, London, 1967.

O. Betz, *What do we know about Jesus?* London, 1968.

G. Bornkamm, *Jesus of Nazareth*, London, 1960.

H. Braun, *Jesus*, Stuttgart, 1969.

R. Bultmann, *Jesus and the Word*, London, 1934.

H. Conzelmann, *Jesus*, Philadelphia, 1973.

M. Dibelius, *Jesus*, London, 1963.

C. H. Dodd, *The Founder of Christianity*, London, 1971.

D. Flusser, *Jesus*, New York, 1969.

R. T. France, *The Man They Crucified*, London, 1975.

T. R. Glover, *The Jesus of History*, London, 1917.

L. Goppelt, *Theologie des Neuen Testaments* I, Göttingen, 1975.

D. Guthrie, *Jesus the Messiah*, London, 1972.

A. M. Hunter, *The Work and Words of Jesus*, London, 1973[2].

J. Jeremias, *New Testament Theology* I, London, 1971.

W. G. Kümmel, *Promise and Fulfilment*, London, 1957. *The Theology of the New Testament*, London, 1974.

W. Lillie, *Jesus — then and now*, London, 1964.

T. W. Manson, *The Servant-Messiah*, Cambridge, 1953.

P. de Rosa, *Jesus who became Christ*, London, 1975.

E. Schweizer, *Jesus*, London, 1971.

E. Stauffer, *Jesus and his Story*, London, 1960.

V. Taylor, *The Life and Ministry of Jesus*, London, 1954.

E. Trocmé, *Jesus and his Contemporaries*, London, 1973.

H. E. W. Turner, *Jesus: Master and Lord*, London, 1953.

G. Vermes, *Jesus the Jew*, London, 1973.